The Lure of Faraway Places

Front cover: Herb Pohl had a very distinctive look and style in everything that he did, and his choices of canoe and paddle were no exception. Because he travelled alone so much of the time, there are not a lot of photographs of the man paddling the canoe. But two of his paddling cronies, both of whom have since died, adopted the identical look—a 15′ 8″ Femat CDR-C2 with double-bladed paddle. This lovely shot, taken by Herb on the Petawawa River on Thanksgiving weekend, 1983, is of his friend Dave Berthelet who, except for the natty fedora, could be a stunt double for the singing solo Austrian himself.

The Lure of Faraway Places

REFLECTIONS ON WILDERNESS AND SOLITUDE

Herb Pohl

Edited by James Raffan

NATURAL HERITAGE BOOKS

A MEMBER OF THE DUNDURN GROUP

TORONTO

Published by Natural Heritage Books
A Member of The Dundurn Group
3 Church Street, Suite 500
Toronto, Ontario, M5E 1M2, Canada
www.dundurn.com

Library and Archives Canada Cataloguing in Publication

Pohl, Herb, 1930–2006
    The lure of faraway places : reflections on wilderness and
solitude / Herb Pohl ; edited by James Raffan.

Includes bibliographical references and index.
ISBN 978-1-897045-24-4

    1. Pohl, Herb, 1930-2006. 2. Canoes and canoeing—Canada.
3. Canoeists—Canada—Biography. I. Raffan, James II. Title.

GV782.42.P64A3 2007   797.122092   C2007-901726-6

1   2   3   4   5   11   10   09   08   07

All photographs are by Herb Pohl, unless otherwise credited.
Cover design by Neil Thorne
Book design by Norton Hamill Design
Copy editing by Jane Gibson
Printed and bound in Canada by Marquis Book Printing

Care has been taken to trace the ownership of copyright material used in this book. The author and the publisher welcome any information enabling them to rectify any references or credits in subsequent editions. — *J. Kirk Howard, President*

We acknowledge the support of the Canada Council for the Arts and the Ontario Arts Council for our publishing program. We also acknowledge the financial support of the Government of Canada through the Book Publishing Industry Development Program and The Association for the Export of Canadian Books and the Government of Canada through the Ontario Book Publishers Tax Credit Program and the Ontario Media Development Corporation.

To Maura and Wilderness, the two loves of Herb Pohl's life

Contents

Acknowledgements

The surprise of working on the posthumous publication of a self-described cur-mudgeon's writing is the number of people who came out of the woodwork, after his death, with genuine affection for the man and heartfelt offers to assist in projects to honour his achievements. Many members of the Toronto-based Wilderness Canoe Association, particularly George Luste and the delegates at the annual Wilderness Canoeing Symposium held in Toronto in February 2007, came forward with donations to The Canadian Canoe Museum in Herb's hon-our as well as with suggestions about how he might be remembered in that context. Deb Williams and attendees at the Snow Walkers' and Paddler's gath-erings at the Hulbert Outdoor Centre in Fairlee, Vermont, did the same, all expressing interest in the publication of his book. Without this broad base of support and affection for Herb Pohl, this unusual publishing venture and plans to donate his canoe and his books, maps and journals to The Canadian Canoe Museum would never have been launched.

Although Herb was an intensely private person, there were friends and col-leagues in whom he confided about his route making and writing and whose editorial advice he sought (and occasionally heeded). Among those were his ping-pong partner and fellow traveller, Dr. Bob Henderson; Aurelia Shaw of the Hamilton Association for the Advancement of Literature, Science and Art (of which Herb was a much valued member), who gave Herb detailed editorial feed-back on the early drafts of this book; veteran paddlers and correspondents Pat Lewtas and John McInnes, whose wilderness knowledge and pluck Herb truly admired. The person we have perhaps most to thank for Herb's canon of wilder-ness writing, besides Pohl himself, is Toni Harting, who for twenty years

(1985–2005) was the editor of *Nastawgan,* the newsletter of the Wilderness Canoe Association. Toni edited most if not all of Herb's accounts and published them for the first time, taking care always to make the best possible black-and-white renderings of his photographs; but he was also the one who poked and prodded the occasionally reluctant scribe to draft another fine trip account when Herb might rather have been rambling instead of writing.

   As editor and principal shepherd of this project, I am indebted to Maura Pohl for her always warm welcome in Burlington as well to her for the offer to donate the royalties of this project to The Canadian Canoe Museum; to George Luste who extracted files from the dim recesses of Herb's antique hard drive and to my daughter Molly who re-transcribed a goodly portion of this book when corrupted electronic versions went astray in translation between PC and Mac platforms; to Rob Butler for his patience and tireless effort on his good friend Herb's behalf; to Larry Ricker (a.k.a. Nibi Mocs), Toni Harting, and Bill Ness for permission to use their photographs of Herb; kudos as well to Bill Ness for his information about Herb's canoe; to Bob Henderson for looking after Herb's canoe and helping to make the book happen; to Janice Griffith and the gang at The Canadian Canoe Museum for their help in bringing Herb's boat to the 2007 Wilderness Canoeing Symposium in Toronto; to WCA stalwarts Bill King and George Drought for their comments on the prologue to the book as well as their general advice as the project proceeded; and finally, to Barry Penhale, Jane Gibson, Shannon MacMillan and the production team at Natural Heritage Books who, from the very beginning (a scant six! months ago), believed in this project and worked magic to make it happen. My thanks to all of you.

JAMES RAFFAN

Foreword

The Remarkable Life and Legacy of Herb Pohl

In the summer of 1987, I had the good fortune to paddle the Clearwater River in Nouveau Québec on an assignment for the National Geographic Society.[1] Good work it was, that began with a quest to find *kasagea*, the illusive freshwater seal described in Arthur C. Twomey's 1942 classic, *Needle to the North*.[2] Along the way, I had the opportunity (and the means, for at that time National Geographic story budgets knew no bounds) to talk via Inuit and Cree translators to a number of people in the area who knew the old travel routes from tidewater to Lac à l'Eau Claire and beyond.

In a presentation about this grand adventure, given some time that fall or winter, I mentioned that one of these informants had drawn a detailed line on my map showing the old paddle and portage route that the Cree in the Whapmagoostui[3]/Richmond Gulf area would use to get to the Eastmain height of land. Mention of the line was a small point in an otherwise rambling travelogue that focused on our journey down the Rivière à l'Eau Claire, but it was a point not missed by one member of the audience. And that's how I met Herb Pohl.

A few days following the presentation, the phone rang and it was Herb calling to ask if he might have a look at the line that Cree elder Matthew George had drawn on my map. "If you're like me," he said in his clipped Austrian accent, "you'll be hesitant to mail off your maps to someone you hardly know so, when it is convenient for you, I would like to come down to hear about the conversation and to transcribe the line from your maps to mine." And that's exactly what he did.

It merits explaining that, as members of the wilderness paddling community, such as it was at that time, Herb and I had crossed paths here and there, on the trail and off. We had been introduced or introduced ourselves—me very much the novice and Herb very much the master whose reputation preceded him—but, beyond that, we had exchanged very little in the way of small talk or pleasantries. Herb just wasn't that kind of person. My supposition was that in Herb's eyes I was very much a member of the unwashed, unadventuresome crowd who paddled *known* or, as Herb characterized them, pejoratively *popular* canoe routes that were of little or no interest to him. Herb Pohl never said much to me because there wasn't much to say.

But here he was on my doorstep, with a snootful of questions about the back route to Ungava Bay. And this time, I had answers. Or at least my audio tape of the conversation with Matthew George (translated, to Herb's absolute delight, by Elijah Petagumskum, grandson of Daniel who was Twomey's guide for the Carnegie Museum of Pittsburgh's expedition in 1938) and my trail-worn map, with the elder's shaky pencilled line on it—these had answers.

I also had a bottomless pot of tea and birch logs crackling on the hearth, both of which revealed sides to Herb Pohl that I'd never seen or imagined. He was gentle. He was curious. He was funny. He was respectful. And he seemed to have in his bones a fire for finding his way on untravelled land, or on routes that had been travelled only by moccasined feet, a passion for wilderness travel that I'd never encountered anywhere else, or in anyone else. I was sad when he packed up and headed home. And now he's gone.

Herbert Karl Joseph Pohl was born, the second of two sons for Oskar and Leopol-dine (Tripp) Pohl, surrounded by the snow-capped Alps and the stacks of iron foundries and steel mills in the Mürz River valley, near Kapfenberg, Austria, on March 26, 1930—under the zodiac constellation Aries the Ram, the initiator. Herb's father, an accountant, fell ill soon after Herb was born and died when he was about three years old. Although Herb was born during the Great Depression, family circumstances for the Pohls, which included a house with maid and all of the material comforts of the middle class while his father was alive, declined sharply as Herb's mother tried to make her way as single parent. To try to create a better circumstance for Herb and his older brother Oskar, their mother sold the matrimonial home and bought a small peach farm, up the valley of the Mür River, a tributary of the Mürz, about 25 kilometres south of the City of Graz in the Carpathian Mountains not far from Slovenia. It was here, as Herb would later write, in rolling hills amid the ruins of an old Roman city, that a lifetime of seeking new horizons began.

Of his early years, we know little. He attended school in Graz and, as a boy, may have stayed with maternal grandparents in town. As he got older, perhaps of high school age, he may have commuted in and out of town by train. Raised in a devout Catholic family, mass was an integral part of Herb's daily round. The legacy of this churchgoing had less to do with the catechism than it did with the half penny the parish priest used to give him as reward for attending mass, which he used to purchase a steady diet of adventure stories that included German translations of classics like *Treasure Island* and *Robinson Crusoe*. Although he later married a strong Irish-Catholic woman, Herb never took the Eucharist as an adult, but the bookish legacy of his early churchgoing was a trait that followed him to the end of his days.

School was a necessity. Herb loved sports—any sport he could play—individual or team, ball or racquet, winter or summer, he was a keen and able competitor. He swam, when he could, in the river and, for the rest of his life, never really

For Herb, growing up in the Mür River valley in Austria, shown here, meant that the wilderness, in mountain form, was always within sight.

liked salt water. When he was not outside playing sports, he was inside listening to music—at home on the radio or, on special occasions, at concert halls in Graz or Kapfenberg where the music of Austrian composers like Franz Schubert, Leopold Hofmann, the Mozarts and, the Viennese waltz kings, Johann Strauss and Johann Sebastian Strauss, became a central and organizing passion in his life.

Surprisingly, perhaps for those who knew Herb as a canoeist, after his death his wife, Maura, said that *music* was number one in his life. He told that her would never be lonely as long as he had music. His only regret in life, she said, was that he never played a musical instrument. As his journals would later testify, however, the lack of instrument or technical ability to play never stopped Herb from singing the songs or hymns of his childhood at the top of his lungs when he was happy, or from remembering the great music of his youth, or from enthusiastically conducting the home or car stereo when he thought no one was looking.[4]

Throughout his school years, Herb's attachment to his mother and to the farm was strong. As a business the farm struggled, but the boys and their mother did their best. They kept a cow, and pigs occasionally, and grew as much of their own produce as they could. Life was full but often difficult. Some mornings, after he arose at 4:30 a.m. to do his chores before boarding the train into town, all he would have to eat was porridge or yellow meal—plenty to keep him going, but very simple fare for which he never lost an appetite. Food was fuel. Herb lived to ramble with his dog through the wild country beyond the farm, down toward the river or up into the hills. It was here that his deep love of nature and the freedom to explore it was born.

Throughout his teenage years, of course, the Second World War raged on. The extent to which he was aware of the Nazi activities during his coming of age is unclear, but it is known that he got a crash course in wartime politics when he was drafted at fifteen or sixteen years old into the Hitler Youth, and shipped south for service in the Balkans. Although the Jugend corps was not involved in front-line fighting, Herb was close enough to the full face of war, digging trenches and mass graves, to have experienced things about which he had very little to say in later life. And he was close enough to the action to be accidentally wounded by a hand grenade that put him in an English hospital for five months, and left him with a large and nasty scar on his left thigh.

One story from this time in his life that Herb did tell involved his mother coming to see him for the first time after the accident. As he lay there, his thigh swathed in bandages, she gingerly lifted the sheet for a quick peek to see if he was "still a man." Barely, but yes, thanks to luck and a pair of good thick German army woollen underpants.

Herb finished high school after the war and, like so many of his classmates, went to work as a blacksmith in one of the Mür valley ironworks. His recollections of this time in his life were less about his time hammering hot metal than they were about the way in which his peregrinations through the mountains and valleys expanded his world. Even at this time, when there were walking and climbing clubs for a young man to join, Herb explored those group options, but he also loved to wander on his own. That way he stayed in control. So much the better if these rambles employed routes that no one else used.

But all of that came to an abrupt halt in 1950 when, at the urging of a chum who was emigrating to work in the gold mines at Rouyn-Noranda, Herb decided to leave Austria and sail across the Atlantic to Canada.

At twenty-years old, with an Austrian high school education, speaking almost no English, Herb made his way into Canada with three or four other Austrians. After a stint underground in the gold mines of northwestern Quebec, the group scattered and Herb worked his way west—washing windows, sleeping in used cars, hitchhiking on trains, doing maintenance for the CNR at Peterbell, working construction amongst the Ukrainians in Winnipeg, taking advantage of hostel services offered by the Salvation Army (that made him a lifelong supporter of this charity), and finishing up as a feller in a British Columbia logging camp. There he ate like a horse (six eggs and a pound of bacon for breakfast, followed by toast and porridge with lashings of canned fruit if a man was still hungry), learned bush skills and learned to speak English from the radio and from a friend and co-worker he called Frenchie.

Frenchie and Herb got wheels after a couple of years in BC and lived out in the open for a couple of years, camping, fishing, travelling about and taking work when the money ran out. Quite a couple they made: Frenchie liked to drink and to gamble whereas Herb was more interested in keeping his savings in his pocket, drawn more to rambling on beaches or trails in the backcountry than to the bright lights of Vancouver. Eventually, they tired of the vagabond life and drifted east, Frenchie back to Quebec where he married and had six children with his high-school sweetheart, Herb to Thunder Bay where, in the mid-1950s, he met and married a young Irish émigré, Maura Mullan, a hardworking nurse who became the love of his life and the mother of his only son, Oscar.

With the arrival of a child, Herb realized that if he was to provide for his family in the way he had always dreamt, then he would have to get a post-secondary education. Working as a shipper and receiver in the winter and in the summer as a crewman for the Canadian Pacific Railway around Thunder Bay would never give him the life or the lifestyle to which he aspired. The only problem with that was that Canadian universities would not accept an Austrian high-school diploma as proof of academic readiness. Knowing that more education at the high-school level would bring his English up to par, and being an extremely pragmatic man, Herb enrolled at Lakeview High School in Port Arthur. His teenage classmates wondered about the old guy, until they saw his enthusiasm for sports and the contribution he made to Lakeview school teams. He finished his Grade 12 requirements going part-time but took on Grade 13 as a full-time occupation, graduating as an Ontario Scholar (meaning he achieved 80% or higher in his final exams) about the time son Oscar turned five.[5]

Herb applied to universities, and, to take the next step in his plan, Maura got a nursing job at Joseph Brant Memorial Hospital in Burlington and the three of them moved into a two bedroom apartment on Maple Avenue, just up the road from Lake Ontario. Herb studied biology at McMaster University, working summers in various jobs either back in Thunder Bay or other places where he could breathe the clean air of the boreal woods. In 1968, he graduated with a Bachelor of Science. Having done so well during his undergraduate years, Herb, upon graduation, was offered a job as a laboratory demonstrator in the McMaster Department of Biology. In due course, he was promoted to senior demonstrator and, after taking courses in conjunction with his work in the labs, in 1975 graduated with a Master of Science.

In the Maple Street apartment, they raised Oscar who eventually graduated from high school and moved to the west. Maura continued to nurse. And, for a full 25 years, until he retired in 1994, Herb continued as senior demonstrator in the Biology Department, setting up labs, teaching and marking papers. Playing sports wherever and whenever he could, Herb kept himself actively involved in the university community through the Hamilton Association for the Advancement of Literature, Science and Art.[6] And it was from this modest two-bedroom ground-floor apartment, with a very supportive spouse, a set of shelves for his books, a drawer for his maps, two storage lockers for his gear and a little garden outside where he could store his canoe, that Herb Pohl mounted what became perhaps *the* most remarkable solo canoeing career of our time.

When asked in later life, Herb pointed to a summer job during his undergraduate years, working for the Petawawa Forest Experimental Station near Chalk River, Ontario, as the place where he was bitten by the whitewater/wilderness canoeing bug. With access to Department of Lands and Forests canoes, Herb and a co-worker would load up a government truck and rattle their dusty way back through the Petawawa Forest (now part of Canadian Forces Base Petawawa) to rapids on the Petawawa River between McManus Lake and the town of Petawawa. Through trial and error, and more than a few near misses, Herb honed his paddling techniques and developed a love for the rhythm of the paddle that left him hungering for longer, more remote trips.

Herb returned to Austria regularly to visit with his mother and with his brother and his wife. Here he is with his mother in the summer of 1986.

How and where he might satisfy that hunger sent Herb back to the books, but instead of reading in biology, he moved over to the history section of the McMaster library, and he found his way to the map library as well. Pouring through the journals and routes of the fur trade, checking more recent canoe-trip reports when he could find them, and weighing the risks of remoteness against the sureties of developing skills and certain access to road or rail or help of some kind, Herb made a plan. As he had done before, on the farm in Austria, when he came to Canada and countless other times, he eventually bought a canoe and acquiesced to the lure of the faraway. In the summer of 1969, his thirty-ninth year, he packed up his things, said goodbye to Maura and Oscar, and drove north. He pulled off the TransCanada Highway at Iroquois Falls and, with the Ontario Northland Railway as his handrail, paddled the Abitibi River to Moosonee, his *first* big canoe trip—totally on his own.

This trip represented a departure from the type of holidaying Herb had been doing with Maura and Oscar. Together they car camped and hiked, extending west and often south to explore the National Parks of the United States. However, as he researched ways to scratch the canoeing itch, he found other paddling enthusiasts who, during the early '70s, were coalescing into the Wilderness Canoe Association. Affiliation with kindred paddling spirits meant that he could canoe on weekends in the spring and fall. These episodic junkets helped hone his skills and allowed him to meet the family holiday agenda without compromise or negotiation.

But the lure was in his bones. In 1976, Herb returned to Peterbell, where he had worked as a railwayman and paddled again to Moosonee, this time via the Missinaibi River, which didn't have a railway paralleling it for most of the way to the James Bay coast. He had upped the risk and adventure ante and thoroughly enjoyed himself.

After the Missinabi, Herb moved next to the Moisie and on, during his thirty-eight-year paddling career, to twenty-two other major wilderness journeys, most of them by canoe and about three-quarters of them solo. This book is a portrait of that life.

How the book came to be is another story. In September 2006, the phone rang again—same house, different phone. This time, just weeks after Herb's untimely death at the mouth of the Michipicoten River, it was his friend Rob Butler calling to see if I might lend a hand turning Herb's wilderness writings into a book. Tall order that, but one I felt I must engage out of respect for such a distinguished member of the wilderness paddling community.

Like many people, I'd read Herb's frequent accounts of his journeys in *The Wilderness Canoeist* and *Nastawgan*, the newsletters of the Wilderness Canoe Association.[7] I'd attended a number of his presentations at the annual Wilderness Canoeing Symposium in Toronto and, over the years, had been beguiled by his stories. He described going places that made me often just laugh or shake my head—places that I'd never contemplate going in a *rental* canoe, with a brush-clearing bulldozer and a bus load of sherpas on board. In his quiet and singularly engaging way, Herb talked, showed slides, and audiences hung on his every word. With humour and incisive observation, clear-eyed mishap reporting and a powerful sense of reverence for the weather and the wilderness, especially in backcountry Labrador, Herb blossomed into a superb storyteller. About this his friend and long-time WCA member, Bill King, wrote: "If there could be said anything negative about Herb's [storytelling], it would be the pangs of jealousy which [it] induced in lesser mortals, unable to believe that anyone could be so literate in a second language."[8]

What not many people knew was that in retirement, Herb had rounded up his lecture notes and all of the pieces he had written about his trips over the years. He had sorted out the ones he thought would work best in a collection. He had written some new material and he had massaged the whole lot, seeking editorial advice from friends and colleagues, into what he hoped would be a book he would call *The Lure of Faraway Places*. After his death, there the manuscript sat, in hard copy on his desk and in electronic format on the hard drive of an aged computer in the second bedroom of the Burlington apartment, awaiting his return from Superior. But, as Maura's and Oscar's long hours of waiting revealed, he would never come home.

In agreeing to becoming shepherd of this project, I didn't know if we'd be heading down to the local copy shop for a bit of desktop publishing, or if we'd gang together a series of friends and supporters who would raise some funds and get the book out through the new on-demand publishing process. Either way, before delving into the manuscript, I assumed that Herb's work, as a collection, would be too specialized or possibly esoteric for a general readership.

How wrong was that assumption. Here were stories of places no Canadian will ever see, tales of close calls, of near-biblical suffering, of animal encounters—first descents, first *ascents* (which, in practice, no self-respecting canoeist should try to emulate until and/or unless being diagnosed as slightly mad). He writes of river trips, coastal trips, linear trips, circle routes, chaffed skin, burning boats, bugs beyond belief. In these tales are echoes of John Hornby, George Douglas, Grey Owl, Albert Faille and probably Tom Thomson—all thoughtful, eccentric and, each in his own way, passionate souls. I don't know if Bill Mason ever met Herb Pohl but, if he did, I think he would have been captivated by a man—Pohl—who had done in practice, going from tidewater to height of land and back to tidewater on a journey of completion, what Mason could only *try* to recreate cinematically in his final feature, *Waterwalker*.

If Herb Pohl is anything, he is authentic. He's been there, under his own steam, up mountains, through swamps and down the other sides. He has lived life to the lees and been a part of all that he has met, like the old sailor Ulysses, himself.[9] He has taken pictures, kept a journal and chosen *not* to buy the T-shirt, opting instead to show by example that exploration is more about heart and reverence for the great beyond than it is about fancy gear and conquest.

To be sure, Herb Pohl was a bit snobbish about the road not taken. It is not accidental that, in choosing the stories for this collection, he did not include accounts of his journeys in Nahanni or Auyuittuq National Parks—two examples of his travels on *taken* roads. On these trips, which happened to be with groups, he found what he sought when he was travelling alone on less popular routes, just with less uniqueness, less intensity.

Persnickety doesn't begin to describe how he could be when it came to how things should be done on the trail—or anywhere, for that matter. Just ask anyone of the lucky few who travelled with him. Just ask any of the students whose labs he graded at McMaster. Herb Pohl had his ways and he had exacting standards, none higher than those he held for himself. Confident? Absolutely, in his own abilities, having gotten himself into and out of—save one... perhaps—a host of life-threatening circumstances. Arrogant? He certainly could project that air, but what people saw might be better described as a man self-contained and self-assured, for in close company no one would laugh sooner or harder about his over-particular ways than Herb himself. What the self-described misanthrope has left behind, however, is a treasure.

The beauty of this work is not so much in the master traveller's disciplined and often understated reporting on his Herculean trips—although these are surely precious commodities. *The Lure of Faraway Places* glistens when we are invited into the private world of a man alone, often in physical places that are as close to the proverbial "middle of nowhere" as a person might get, with only the simple material assets he has brought with him and his own considerable wit to see him through. Here is the opportunity to dwell in these pages with a true ascetic, an anchorite, in the cerebral space—the "landscape of his imagination" that was his frame of mind on these solo journeys—and to be with him as he attends and responds to the often ambiguous exigencies of deep wilderness. To these he came, again and again, with unfettered joy and a winsome sense of his own mortality and insignificance in the greater scheme of things. In the end, what makes this collection unique in the literature of adventure, is that it's not really a canoeing book at all. It's a love story. It's a story about intentional exploration of wilderness without and wilderness within—with the unspoken message that we absolutely must preserve one to access the other—and why we *must* do both.

JAMES RAFFAN
SEELEY'S BAY, 2007

The Lure of Faraway Places

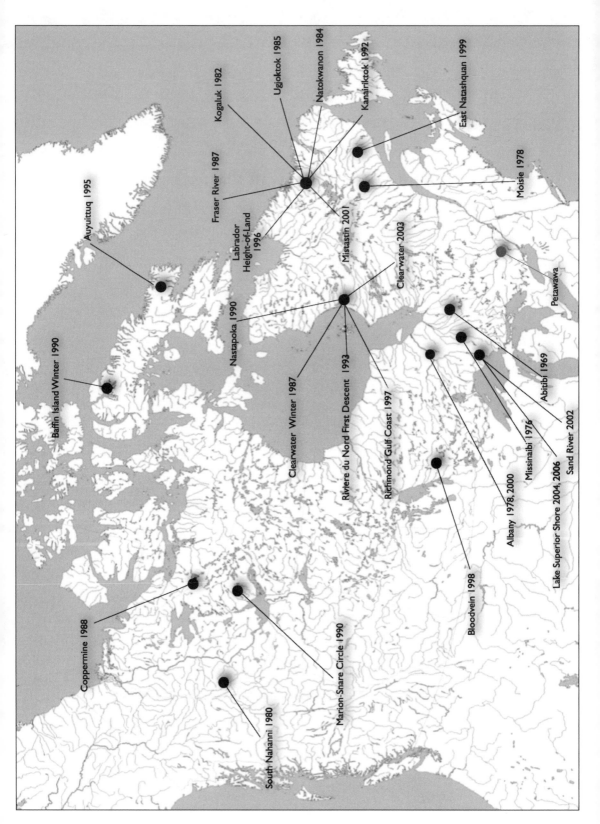

Map showing Herb Pohl's canoe travels from 1969 to 2006. *Courtesy of James Raffin.*

ONE

The Lure of Faraway Places

I don't think it was ever a conscious thought, but as far back as I can remember there was always a fascination with the unknown world beyond home. When I was three years old, home was a small farm in Austria and the world beyond was a treasure trove of fields and streams and forest. Perhaps most fascinating of all was a huge limestone cave which the Romans had excavated from beneath our fields nearly two thousand years earlier to supply the stones to build *Flavia Solva*,[1] a Roman garrison town. The cave contained a large lagoon, miniature stalagmites and stalactites, and a population of bats numbering in the hundreds.

For adults it was a time of worry and hardship—the Great Depression—but for me a period of unfettered freedom. Mother was much too busy, trying to run the farm by herself, to keep a close watch on my brother and myself. We were often left to fend for ourselves. This allowed me to disappear into the unknown and mysterious universe that beckoned just beyond the house. Many times my explorations would occupy me from early morning to dusk. Sustenance in the summer was readily available—grapes, apples, plums, tomatoes, hazelnuts—and so there was no need to take along provisions. The homeward journey was always tinged with hesitation because invariably mother would try to persuade me to stop my wandering by the liberal application of the bamboo handle of the feather duster to the nether regions. It never worked. It wasn't that I was rebellious. On the contrary, I understood even at that early age that my disappearances caused Mother a great deal of worry. The real problem was memory loss; the next morning it would be all forgotten and I'd be off again.

As the years went by, the journeys became longer and took on a slightly different flavour. Exploration became a group enterprise and the targets were most often heretofore "unknown" areas in the mountains. As is often the case when males travel together, competition was an ever-present albeit unspoken element of adventure. It put the emphasis at times on speed and stamina rather than the natural world around us. While I liked the competition, I preferred unhurried wanderings to high ground by myself. Alone, the focus could be on the sights and sounds around me—the murmuring of a distant brook, the sighing of the wind in the trees or the busy life of an ant colony.

The very first book I ever bought was an unabridged translation of *Robinson Crusoe* by Daniel Defoe, a version that included the many adventures after the return from his island, a part of the story missing from modern editions of the book. Defoe introduced me to a new world—slave traders, plantation owners and ship's captains who sailed to exotic places, and to a whole new vocabulary of nautical terms and the language of commerce of the times. Here was drama of the highest order that raised the horizon of adventure to a new level. It was the start of a long period of sleep deprivation as I became immersed in books on exploration and adventure travel, and afternoons were often spent on a park bench reading rather than attending classes.

Despite the preoccupation with the mysterious world *beyond*, I never had the urge to leave home, for I had barely begun to examine my own backyard. My departure for North America therefore came as much of a surprise to me as to friends and family. One evening, over a beverage or two, a friend confided that he was thinking of emigrating to Canada but didn't like the idea of going to a strange place by himself. Would I join him? Three weeks later we came ashore in Halifax and since then I have only seen him once in the last fifty-odd years. I had entered into the adventure with the vaguest idea of making my way west, spending some time in the Rocky Mountains and, at the end of two years, returning home. But life very rarely evolves as planned. Within days of my arrival I felt caught up in a magnificent adventure and any thought of ever turning back vanished.

Because I arrived in Canada without job and money, I was detained by the immigration department in Quebec City for some time. I have vivid memories from inside a detention room in the city on those late September evenings in 1950, listening to the haunting whistle of the daily transcontinental train as it pulled out from Lévis, across the St. Lawrence River, before vanishing into the dark void. I knew that these trains continued for another five days to reach Vancouver. For someone whose idea of a long train ride was measured in hours, this was almost beyond my comprehension.

I eventually got my working papers, crossed the river and, for the first time, heard the whistle close up and felt the rhythm of a Canadian train. The foremost concern at this time, of course, was to get a job and with the search came adventure.

Some time after Herb and his friend Frenchie bought a panel truck and tried the vagabond life on the west coast for a couple of years in the early 1950s, Herb bought a good little German car and made his way back east to Port Arthur, where he met and married his wife Maura. *Courtesy of Maura Pohl.*

Most often it involved some on-the-job training and occasionally a written examination, but I quickly learned from my Canadian peers to claim whatever competency was required for the job at hand and, somewhat to my surprise, it often worked. For several years I slowly worked my way west and back, and in the process became acquainted with a wide variety of survival modes, largely because employment was often hard to get and social assistance programs were still in the planning stages. Somewhere along the way I became the proud owner of an ancient panel truck (one that burned nearly as much oil as gasoline) and all the necessary accoutrements for outdoor living. It allowed me to take full advantage of the tremendous freedom the country offered to the itinerant traveller—thousands of kilometres of backcountry roads where one could pull off to the side and spend the evening roasting a bit of bologna or an unfortunate grouse at a comforting fire, or perhaps just to *think* how good the next meal was going to taste. It was altogether a most intense educational experience, one that left me with the conviction that I could cope with whatever came my way.

Canoeing and travel beyond the end of the road did not enter the picture until several years later when I spent a summer working at the Department of Lands and Forests Research Station at Chalk River, Ontario. A part of the station's domain extended to the Petawawa River, which was readily accessible by dirt road (since that time the area has been taken over by the military and is now closed to the public); the station also had several canoes, which we had permission to use, and so much of our spare time was spent on the water. Despite a reminder from an old station staffer that "rapids are for portaging," we had to try "the easier" way, which often meant swimming the lower part of a riffle. On one

Ontario Northland Railway caboose. For his first trip, Herb chose the Abitibi River, which has, as a safety feature, the Ontario Northland Railway running beside it for much of the way between the TransCanada Highway and Moosonee. *Courtesy of James Raffan.*

occasion my paddling partner nearly drowned and we wrecked the canoe. It put an end to the summer's adventures, but it could not quench the enthusiasm that these escapades had sparked. A new door had opened.

All of a sudden, the stories I had read years earlier, books by Jack London, stories about the '98 gold rush, the travels of Hudson's Bay people, which had in the first instance been stories about events in a faraway land, were now seen in a different light. After a few trips to the map library I realized for the first time that the canoe made it possible to reach even the far corners of this land—all one had to do is paddle and portage. When I mentioned the idea of going on canoe trips to some acquaintances, it was endorsed with great enthusiasm, and several of them expressed interest in participating. To my surprise the number of people on these modest excursions always decreased as the starting date drew near, and more often than not I would be the only person left. And so, more by accident than design, I started tripping alone.

The selection of my first trip in '69, down the Abitibi and Moose rivers, was heavily influenced by the fact that the Ontario Northland Railway parallels the route. It offered an escape route should I get into trouble. The only information about the river route that I had, was what one sees on the road map of Ontario. I prepared for the trip by paddling over seven hundred kilometres and felt very fit, but all other aspects of my preparations had the hallmarks of the rank novice. I had no idea about waterproofing, in fact, I had not even a rain jacket. My canvas tent and poles weighed fifteen kilograms and I slept on the bare ground. My food was bacon and beans every day, an experience that permanently banished beans from the menu. It was a most intense learning time. When I reached Moosonee it was with a sense of considerable accomplishment. That feeling was somewhat diminished later on when I phoned my wife Maura. My opening line, "I have arrived in Moosonee," intoned with suitable self-importance, was countered with "Yes…, so why are you calling?" Despite this sobering reply I was permanently hooked on backcountry travel.

Not long thereafter I discovered the Wilderness Canoe Association (WCA). Its members were an eclectic group of people whose common bond was a love of the outdoors and a sense of adventure. Most, like myself, were relative newcomers to canoeing and club outings always had an element of discovery on routes few of the participants had ever travelled before. It was also a time before

Almost from the outset of his canoeing career, Herb chose a decked canoe made by Femat in Shelburne, Ontario. He went through at least three of these in his paddling career, but throughout all of his trips he stuck with the same design and paddled with his trademark double-bladed paddle. *Courtesy of Toni Harting.*

large corporate outdoor equipment manufacturers prescribed the fashion of gear and clothing. Without this proper guidance, members of the association congregated with a most varied collection of tents, boats and assorted homemade paraphernalia. Nonconformity was rampant and I felt very much at ease in this congregation. Among the members of the WCA was a small group of people with experience on long northern trips; they became the role models for the rest of us greenhorns and pointed the way to a wider horizon.

During this collegial association I retained my preference for paddling solo and going on long journeys alone, but fiscal realities sometimes forced a compromise, particularly on journeys that required charter flights. On these occasions it was always easy to find partners from among the large pool of competent members of the WCA. On all my trips over the next thirty-odd years I have always kept a trip journal, and accounts of many of the journeys described below have appeared previously in *Nastawgan*, the quarterly journal of the Wilderness Canoe Association. I should point out that after an early period of following popular canoe routes, I found the greatest satisfaction in visiting areas off the beaten track. Even now this leaves an enormous number of choices and to this day I often look at maps with a feeling of regret. If only I had started twenty years earlier!

TWO

Moisie River, 1978

Even a casual glance at the map reveals an astoundingly large number of rivers entering the Gulf of St. Lawrence between Tadoussac and the Strait of Belle Isle. Many of these rise in the Quebec and Labrador highlands and fall approximately 550 metres within a distance of 300 to 600 kilometres. The relative isolation of the region and the steep gradient of the rivers promise exciting white water in a true wilderness setting. Deeply carved riverbeds offer the traveller ever changing mountain vistas, which are frequently shrouded in mist, and turbulent rivers often punctuated by spectacular waterfalls. Shorelines are a wasteland of boulders and tangled black spruce forest through which portaging is slow and arduous.

At least this was the picture that emerged after a winter of reading and many hours in the map library, doing river profiles in an effort to decide which river to choose as the next destination. There was little doubt in the end that the Moisie had the most to offer: the headwaters are readily accessible both in terms of cost and time; the start and finish are near the terminus of the Quebec North Shore and Labrador Railway in Sept-Îles; the river gradient is remarkably uniform, and the rugged beauty of the river valley has been praised by many paddlers over the years.

The route I chose is one of at least four by which one can reach the headwaters of the Moisie. The most direct way is to start on the Pekans River, which crosses the highway connecting Baie-Comeau and Labrador City, and follow it to its confluence with the Moisie. The other three options involve crossing the height of land that represents the Quebec-Labrador border. John Rugge and James W. Davidson[1] travelled from Lake Ashuanipi in a westerly direction to reach the

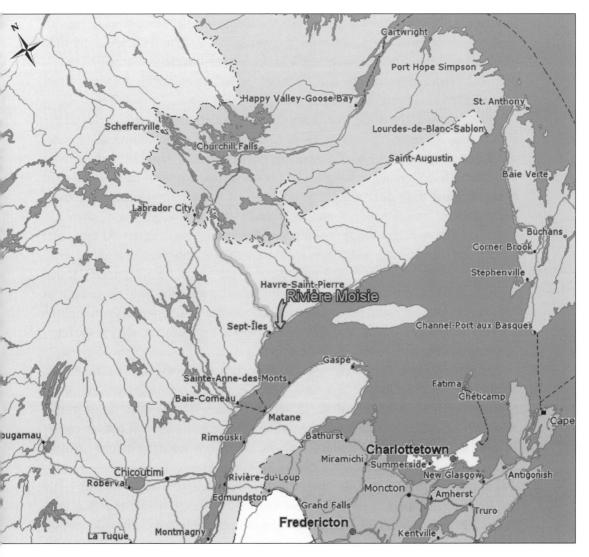

The Moisie River area, taken from Toporama, Atlas of Canada Web site.

Moisie watershed. Others crossed the height of land directly from Wabush to reach the Carheil River, a tributary of the Pekans. My choice, and by all indications a popular one, was to start from Lac De Mille and travel south over the height of land to Lac Ménistouc, the headwater lake of the Moisie.

On arrival in Sept-Îles, I was surprised to find a busy, modern town of 35,000 inhabitants and had some unexpected difficulty in finding the railway station without asking for directions. Part of the difficulty was that the structure in question didn't look like a railway station but more like a warehouse—which it was. The business of the Quebec North Shore and Labrador Railway is to bring iron ore from Labrador to the St. Lawrence. As an incidental sideline it also serves as the main supply line of consumer goods to the interior. I had arrived in the middle of the hubbub that surrounds the loading of the twice-weekly passenger train, which was due to leave the following morning, and it took some time to have my canoe and gear deposited in the proper boxcar and a bill of lading prepared. There were already three canoes in the car belonging to a party that also planned to descend the Moisie along the same route.

After spending the night like many other travellers in the parking lot of the station, I woke early the next morning filled with the apprehension and excitement that the beginning of a canoe trip always evokes. By 7:00 a.m. a large crowd was lined up and waiting for the ticket office to open—miners and their families going back after a holiday, busloads of Indians carrying an incredible assortment of bundles, boxes and bags and last, but not least, fishermen and canoeists like myself, already looking suitably grubby and excited. At this point I met Dave Winch and Luc Farmer, two Montrealers, who were also going down the Moisie and with whom, as it turned out, I would paddle many miles. It had been overcast during the early morning, but shortly after the train moved out of the station, the low cloud cover lifted and revealed a countryside of rolling hills covered with birch, poplar and spruce interspersed with moist, dark rock faces glistening in the sun.

The first glimpse of the river at the Skatchewan (swift water) Rapids was impressive. In pre-railway days, this was the site of a dreaded six-mile-long "Grand Portage," over very difficult terrain, which bypassed the river gorge. From my elevated vantage point the rapids seemed tame enough but, as events would prove, observations made from a height of one hundred metres or more are not the best way to assess the difficulty of rapids.

The railway follows the Moisie upriver to the entrance of the Nipissis (little water) River, formerly called the East Branch (of the Moisie), and then runs alongside the latter through increasingly mountainous territory, with glacier-polished cliffs rising up almost perpendicularly a hundred metres or more. As the slope of the river valley increases, the river alternately foams and cascades over bedrock or rests in quiet pools as it narrows and finally disappears altogether.

As we approached the tablelands near the top of the river, periods of sunshine gave way to rain squalls; black spruce became stunted and more scattered amongst low hills. Here, reindeer moss (*Cladonia*) is more prevalent as ground cover. In this region the railway follows the shoreline of Lake Ashuanipi for many kilometres, and the whole territory seems to be drowning in immense bodies of water, fed by streams that seemingly spring up full-blown and rush off in one direction or another in direct contradiction to the apparent flatness of the land. By the time the train reached Lac De Mille in late afternoon, a steady rain was falling. Disembarking and unloading gear in the wet was not a high point of the trip. The people belonging to the three canoes mentioned earlier seemed to be inexperienced trippers, judging by their outfit. The cheapest fibreglass

Herb wanted to enter a river on its terms, if possible, by crossing a height of land. On this trip, during which he fell in love with the landscape of northern Quebec, he made a point of climbing to a point of prospect soon after crossing the divide to see the valley of the mighty Moisie starting to take shape.

canoes, which could crumble in the first heavy swell, a mountain of gear including bows and arrows and, the *coup de grâce*, a pet duckling in a cardboard box.

I worked very fast to exit this scene and within five minutes started to paddle in a southerly direction across the lake. With only about an hour of daylight left, I was anxious to find a campsite. A diligent search of the far shore turned up nothing until, with twilight approaching, I discovered a cabin. The two Montrealers had by this time caught up with me and we lost no time heading for shore. The cabin, perhaps a trapper's abode in season, was well insulated, a feature I would gladly have done without. Luc and Dave decided to cook their supper on the wood stove and soon had a roaring fire going, which quickly transformed the cabin into a sauna. Squadrons of ravenous mosquitoes, made opening the door to dissipate the heat totally out of the question. It took hours for the heat to subside to the point where I could get to sleep and yet I was grateful to be inside as a heavy rain continued well into the night.

By daybreak the rain had ended. I crept out leaving the others fast asleep, and continued to the southernmost end of Lac De Mille. The few clouds that greeted the morning soon disappeared as I approached the height of land. The lake runs out to a narrow spur and disappears in string bog, dotted with skinny black spruce lying between widely scattered trees on low hills in the distance. The height of land here is only a thin sliver of swamp, no more than two hundred metres wide, yet I was quite impressed by the feat of crossing over since this was a first for me.

I had planned to celebrate the occasion with a hearty breakfast, but the blackflies quickly convinced me that this was no place for lingering meals.

I followed a tiny creek into Lac Ménistouc, a large and shallow expanse of water, and quickly became aware of a strong westerly breeze, which would have made things very dicey without a spray cover. Wind, waves, sunshine and solitude make for a marvellous frame of mind and the potentially tedious lake travel seemed much shorter then the hours it actually took. Going into the mouth of the stream, which connects Lac Ménistouc with Lake Opocopa, gave me a few anxious moments as metre-high waves carried me into the shallow, boulder-strewn narrows. While it is not so identified on the map, I consider this to be the start of the Moisie and even here the volume of flow was substantial. The river enters Lake Opocopa with a flourish in a short but taxing rapid.

Once out on the lake, progress against the wind was slow and tiring and I quit after only four more kilometres even though there was no decent campsite to be seen. The process of clearing underbrush to set up the tent seemed to fascinate the blackflies, but I had a few minutes of near panic when I escaped into the tent, to find that the door zipper had failed. The thought of having no bug-free refuge for the rest of the journey was disconcerting, but luckily I managed to solve the problem with gentle manipulation of the slider with my pliers.

About 4:00 a.m. a southerly breeze sprang up and I quickly got underway lest the wind set me back another day. By noon I had covered twenty-five kilometres against a stiff headwind and decided to put to shore. The land immediately adjacent to the route is quite featureless, just black spruce with a smattering of tamarack and the occasional birch tree. The shores are lined with alder and there is considerable evidence of past forest fires, which have exposed the rocks below. By mid-afternoon, now well-fed and rested, I noticed a pitching craft approaching from the north and gaining ever so slowly against the wind and waves. When Luc and Dave pulled up alongside, we proceeded to the south end of the lake and made camp together amid the debris of an Indian hunting camp.

It rained hard for most of the night and as I set out with the big lakes now behind me, clouds were scurrying along at incredible speed, almost at treetop level, and now and then giving up small promise of a positive change in the weather. But on Lac Felix, the sky turned darker still and brought forth a torrential downpour that quickly revealed the lie to my 100% waterproof rainsuit. Gusts of wind that nearly overturned the canoe had me hurrying for shore to wait out this onslaught. But when that had come and gone, I left this last lake on the river in glorious sunshine to begin the descent to the St. Lawrence in earnest.

Within the next thirty-five kilometres the river drops two hundred metres, which made me more than a little apprehensive. At the outflow from Lac Felix the river splits into two arms and I followed the southern, smaller channel. The first rapids were a challenging rock garden about one kilometre in length, with a fifteen-metre drop in elevation terminating in a waterfall. Catching my breath on a short portage around that falls, the river follows a delightful two-kilometre-long run that ends at the brink of a truly awesome and much higher waterfall. This cataract marks the transition from tableland to recessed river valley. Unlike the majority of portages that followed, the trail from the brink of this falls to the put-in near the base was well-defined. It leads to the summit of a hill overlooking the gorge and the river below, offering one of those views that elevates the spirit and makes one feel glad to be alive.

The two Montrealers had by this time caught up with me and we decided to make camp at the foot of the portage, amid a staggering abundance of blackflies. The latter were pressing their attack with such vigour that Dave retreated into the tent that evening at the first opportunity and reappeared only for breakfast—with a face so puffed up that he could scarcely see. As if some small compensation from the gods for this discomfort, while getting a pot of water that evening, we found a bottle of wine—Prince Philippe from the house of Rothchild—sitting right at the water's edge. It helped to stabilize Dave's mental state.

The next three days proved to be the most strenuous of the trip. The river drops in a series of ledges, most of which are not negotiable. The remainder tax one's skill to the limit. More than once, one or the other of our boats barely escaped disaster. Abnormally high water that year meant portages were longer. Approaches and put-in points around obstructions were the source of much

The valley of the Moisie takes on a much more imposing "Nahanni of the East" character as the river progresses down toward the Gulf of St. Lawrence.

anxiety, and many of the campsites, which Luc had used on a previous trip, were now under water. I was often intimidated by the force and sheer volume of the river but couldn't help admiring the grand setting—the valley of the Moisie is as good as it gets.

As one proceeds downstream, the valley, which has been called "the Nahanni of the East," becomes deeper and both large and small tributaries enter the river in quick succession. The largest of these is the Pekans, which makes a spectacular entrance from the west as it foams and cascades down the hillside, dropping eighty metres in less than a kilometre.

On the evening of the sixth day on the river, we camped at the mouth of the Taoti River. It had been another long day that ended in the semi-darkness with clouds of hungry flies, so I settled for a pot of tea instead of supper. The weather had improved during the afternoon and now a full moon cast its silvery light on the rippling river. Through the netting on my tent door, I could see that the rapidly dropping temperature had brought about the condensation of water vapour over the river, which showed up in the moonlight as a ribbon of fog stretching down the valley as far as the eye could see. By morning the valley was filled with dense fog that was soon dispelled by sunshine.

Luc and Dave soon set off down the river, but I decided it was time for a serious attempt at cleaning up and drying out. It was nearly noon before I got under way; this was the halfway point of the journey, from here on portages are much less frequent and the current uniformly strong. Within the next fifteen kilometres the scenery changes substantially. Mountains rise up two to four hundred metres above the narrowing valley floor. Fingers of lighter green vegetation run up indentations in the mountainside where poplar and birch have invaded the black spruce forest. The river here runs deep and dark, reflecting the steel-grey rock faces that crop up more and more prominently.

After three hours of paddling, I came to the top of a rapid and proceeded cautiously along the shore until the turbulence became so great that I decided to put to shore and scout. My first reaction upon looking at the boiling waves was to look for the portage, but there was no evidence of a trail along the steep and bouldery shoreline. Then I noticed my companions sitting in their canoe at the bottom of the first half of the cauldron. I assumed from their presence at that location on the river that the section was negotiable and decided, despite serious misgivings, to make the run, influenced in good part by the conviction that if other people can do it, so can I.

It was by far the scariest run I have ever made.[2] Several times my upstream gunwale was forced down by the brutal force of surging waves, and I just barely recovered each time. Halfway down I had to traverse the river to avoid some particularly wild rollers, and fear provided the additional impetus to get me across. From then on it was luck and a high brace that kept me from capsizing.

When I joined Dave and Luc, I learned that they had dumped and had only just clambered back into their canoe when I arrived on the scene. Luckily their spray cover prevented anything from falling out and, other than a waterlogged camera, the only other detrimental effect was a severe loss of confidence.

At this point we were still only halfway down the rapids. Luc and I scrambled down the boulders along the shore to look at the rest of the problem. Compared to what was behind us, it looked less demanding and we were further encouraged to try running it by the great difficulty any attempt at portaging would have presented.

I set out first and was only about halfway when trouble visited. A surge occurred just as I was passing a critical spot and a small hole suddenly became a big hole. The current took over and carried me straight towards a house-sized boulder in midstream, which was girded by a wall of water. Moments later, I was floating with the canoe beside me, riding upside down in the water. Fortunately, I managed with the help of a strong eddy to get up on a flat rock and empty the canoe, but I was trapped in a bad spot.

It took two hours to clamber up a near-vertical rock face and shimmy back down to an eddy a mere hundred metres downstream, where I joined my companions who had made a clean run. The most serious loss was my double-bladed paddle. I really dreaded the thought of having to negotiate the next two hundred kilometres on this unruly river with the unfamiliar single blade replacement, but that was what it was going to have to be. Fortunately, for the next fifteen kilometres, the river was not too turbulent thus giving me a chance to regain some confidence.

We made camp opposite the mouth of the Caopacho River in semi-darkness and soon retired to the tent to escape the bugs and the inevitable period of rain. I slept poorly that night. My fingers were very tender from nicks and bruises during my rock-climbing excursion, but most of all I was disturbed about the lack of judgment I had shown. The next day dawned with mist and rain alternating. We quickly broke camp and shipped out on the fast-flowing river at the urging of Luc, who must have had a hormonal surge because he suddenly remembered that his girlfriend would be flying in from Paris the following Sunday, and he wanted to be there to meet her. That left only three days to finish the trip; it seemed a good challenge.

For the next fifty kilometres, the Moisie valley is deeply recessed with cliffs on either side that intimidate paddlers at water level by their sheer height. A forest fire four years earlier had blackened the mountain sides, giving the whole region an aura of incredible desolation, which was emphasized by low cloud and rain. Land and rock slides had left their scars. Sometimes, I felt as if I were paddling on the River Styx bound for Hell.

Noon a day or so later found us at the most formidable portage on this river, one that bypasses a narrow gap in the rock through which the river tumbles. It is the site of a fish ladder with two employees of the local salmon club stationed here to monitor the number of salmon going upstream. Our encounter with these two lads provided a welcome excuse for an extended lunch—the steep portage had left me rather fatigued and sopping wet with perspiration. It took another four hours to lift, line around and drag the canoes over huge boulders, and finally run the navigable part of the rapids below the chute before we stopped for the night at the first of several fishing lodges along the lower Moisie. For a mere $1,500 fishermen are flown in here for five days of fishing. The total catch for this season had been two salmon, which, said the biologists, was due to water levels that were more than two metres above normal. With no guests at the lodge, the lads were glad of our company. They put us up in one of the walled canvas guide tents and fed us more than adequately.

The next morning saw us on the water by 7:30 a.m. and, after a few customary showers, the weather improved to mostly blue skies and strong winds. The river from here to Grand Rapids is a canoeist's dream, a nice mixture of challenge and relaxation. Kilometre after kilometre of class II and III rapids are separated by stretches of fast water with hardly a wave. With the exception of one class IV rapid,

Friends on the trail, Dave Winch (bow) and Luc Farmer await Herb's verdict on another segment of the Up-and-Down Portage on the Moisie.

which Dave and Luc ran in style, I never had to portage and was beginning to feel a little more at ease with my new single-bladed paddling style. At 2:00 p.m. we reached the mouth of the Rivière à l'Eau Doré. This is where the old travel route to the Labrador highlands leaves the Moisie, leading through a series of lakes almost due north to the upper Nipissis River. But by this time we had covered nearly sixty kilometres, and my aching back muscles demanded rest, so there was no compulsion to explore even a little up that old canoe route.

We reached the last falls on the Moisie by five o'clock and carried our gear over the aptly named "Up-and-Down" portage. The shore below the falls offered a marvellous campsite, clean sand, lots of dry driftwood and, most appreciated of all, sunshine. Since this was going to be our last night on the river, we laid

The last rapids on the Moisie, below the QNS&L Railway bridge. Herb chose to end his trip at the bridge but not before having a good look at what lay below. In the end, he decided that portaging into town was the safer of two options. "Not for the faint-hearted," he wrote on the slide.

on a great supper of odds and ends, which lasted two hours. The smell from this culinary exercise must also have reached the nostrils of the local small mammals; when morning dawned there was very little left of my companion's food pack.

Our last day on the river began with beautiful sunshine and a feeling of regret for having rushed through the last half of the trip in such inordinate haste. There are no difficult sections between the last falls and Grand Rapids (or Railroad Rapids as they are now more commonly known). The scenery is varied as the mountains alternately constrict the river to a narrow channel of bare rock and retreat to allow it to stretch out over a wide valley. Soon the railway appeared on our left and, within another two hours, we came to the first of several constrictions that mark the beginning of the Grand Portage.

The boils and whirlpools associated with this section have all the caprice and power of the surges upriver. The way our canoes were translocated willy-nilly in one direction or another was a scary experience, to say the least. A little way down, I decided that enough was enough, pulled in and made the difficult ascent to the railway tracks that parallel the river at this point. Portaging two-and-a-half kilometres along the roadbed and across the bridge seemed infinitely safer than continuing on down the river. At first I wasn't sure whether I had made the right decision as I watched the other boat make its way slowly along the shoreline, but the roar of the river below the bridge made me feel very happy to be where I was in spite of the long carry.

A dirt road ends at the bridge; all I needed now was a ride into town with the section crew who were at work on track repairs nearby, then return with my car to collect my belongings. A profound language barrier derailed my attempts to communicate my desire, but Luc came to the rescue. He had crawled up the almost vertical cliff when it became obvious to them, as it had been to me, only earlier, that they could proceed no further on the river. In short order we were bouncing along in the back of a pickup truck on our way to Sept-Îles.[3]

THREE

To Labrador—from Schefferville to Nain
—Kogaluk River, 1982[1]

After a gestation period of nearly three years, the big moment had finally arrived—Ken Ellison[2] and I were standing on the shore of Lake Attikamagen, ready to begin a journey that would see us cross the height of land to the headwaters of Rivière de Pas, follow it to its confluence with the George River and continue to Indian House Lake. From here we planned to strike out in an easterly direction to the height of land that defines the Quebec-Labrador boundary. Once back in Labrador we intended to follow the Kogaluk River to the Atlantic and make our way along the coast to the town of Nain, the most northerly settlement in Labrador.

It all started when I came across *The Lure of The Labrador Wild*,[3] by Dillon Wallace, the story of Leonidas Hubbard's ill-fated expedition into the Labrador interior in 1903. I was instantly fascinated. More trips to the library followed. By the time I had finished William Brooks Cabot's *In Northern Labrador*[4] and Hesketh Prichard's *Through Trackless Labrador*,[5] a firm, albeit unfocused, resolve to visit the region had emerged. All accounts painted a picture of isolation, difficult terrain, cold, windy and wet weather, rivers that were mostly unnavigable cataracts and, worst of all, clouds of frenzied mosquitoes and other instruments of winged torture. Inquiries with the RCMP in Nain and the people at the Geological Survey of Canada familiar with the region, strongly advised against the proposed journey. Of course, that just heightened the spirit of adventure.

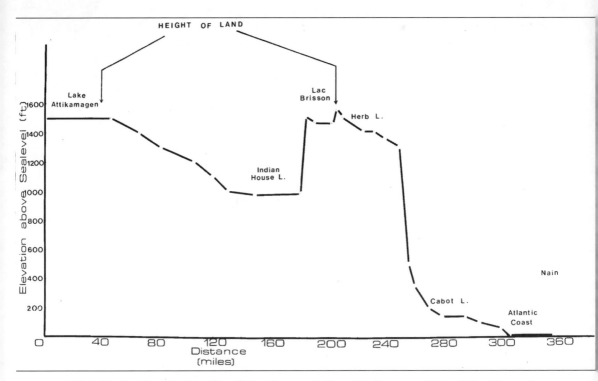

Herb loved to do vertical profiles of his epic watershed-crossing journeys. Although there is a serious exaggeration of the changes in elevation (because the units on the y-axis are much smaller than the units on the x-axis) this profile shows a monumental climb to get to the headwaters of the Kogaluk and a very steep descent on the other side.

The usual process followed—careful perusal of maps and air photos, selection of gear, working out dates, personnel and budgets. The route decided upon included, so far as I could determine, about one hundred and fifty kilometres of untraversed territory that, for me, gave this trip an added dimension. Through the planning process, I hooked up with fellow solo paddler, Ken Ellison, who wanted to paddle the same route. There would be safety and economy in pairing up, but we decided to paddle alone and to stay in separate tents to maintain at least a vestige of the solo paddling experience. While this increased the total weight we had to carry across portages significantly, we felt that it was a reasonable price to pay for the potential of independent movement and privacy; lastly, it provided some insurance in case of a mishap. By starting as early as conditions permitted, we hoped to have a few relatively bug-free days and avoid meeting people, while still enjoying the benefits of high-water levels at the headwaters of streams along the heights of land. So on June 26, 1982, we left Toronto for the two-day drive to Sept-Îles to catch the QNSL[6] train to Schefferville.

Fourteen clattering hours after leaving Sept-Îles, we reached our destination in darkness. The train disgorged a surprisingly large number of passengers, luggage and assorted freight in a scene of animated confusion, while Ken and I stood around like little orphans hoping someone might offer us transportation and shelter. Half an hour later the station was deserted and the only sound was the barking of a tethered husky who objected to our continued presence. Eventually, we decided to pitch the tent on a tiny patch of moss in a sea of muck behind the station. Halfway through the night it started to rain and morning dawned wet and foggy—welcome to northern Quebec!

With the help of the station master, we managed to secure transportation to Lake Attikamagen the next morning. As we descended the last hill, which constitutes the Quebec-Labrador border, a vast expanse of water lay before us, enveloped by a convoluted shoreline and dotted with many islands large and small. Somewhere near the horizon to the northeast was the place where we would recross the height of land to reach the river, which would transport us into territory that for me held an almost mystical quality. Columbus could not have felt a greater sense of excitement when he set out for India.

We pushed off into a gentle breeze under a canopy of towering clouds. With the passing kilometres the magical quality of the enterprise seemed to evaporate. By mid-afternoon the temperature had dropped to near freezing, towering cumulous clouds had become amorphous and grey and a strong headwind whipped periodic showers across the whitecaps. It was late in the day before Ken spied a break in the shoreline vegetation, which led to an Indian campsite. Without fuss or ceremony we finished a cheerless supper and sought refuge in our sleeping bags. By now, rain and wet snow cloaked the sky, as gusts of wind tugged at the tents—my kind of place!

The next day the wind continued apace. Snow squalls raced across the landscape and we pursued our task with vigour driven, if for no other reason, by the urge to stay warm. It was a day of misadventure as we sloshed and stumbled along to find the best route across several portages. By the end of the day I had come to the conclusion that carrying gear solely by means of a tumpline is a pain in the neck. Nevertheless, after eating a substantial supper, and being warmed and dried by a comfortable fire, we went to bed satisfied in the knowledge that for the next hundred and fifty kilometres everything would be downhill.

Freezing rain, driven by a strong headwind, made for very uncomfortable paddling the next day and I was grateful for my pogies. We were now officially on Rivière de Pas, but except for minor constrictions it continued to be lake travel with both topography and vegetation akin to the James Bay lowlands. Finding the outflow of the various lakes at times seemed to be a game of hide and seek. An annoying side wind bothered us throughout, but the cloud cover lifted as we approached the first real rapids at the end of the fourth day, and shortly thereafter the sun came out. Halfway down the white water, a lovely campsite appeared. In twenty minutes the landscape was dotted with odds and ends hung out to dry, the tents were up, the fire going and for a few minutes we felt like kings. Lest we got complacent with the dryness and warmth, a sudden shower had us scrambling to rescue our clothes, the bugs came out and normalcy was restored.

Day five brought us to our first and only portage on the Rivière de Pas. The sun had reappeared and reflected off dancing waves. In the distance, snow patches gleamed brilliantly on the green, treeless hills, which gained prominence during our progress downstream. For days thereafter we found the river rushing along in a recessed gravel bed, cascading around boulders and intermittently, as if tired of the game, slowing to a nearly imperceptible pace. Many of the rapids could be run on sight but, as we progressed, their number and difficulty increased. At the bottom of a particularly nasty stretch of water with several ledges, I spent what seemed like an eternity waiting for Ken. I was about mount an upstream hunt for flotsam when my companion appeared on the scene. He had been forced to shore twice to empty a nearly full canoe but was otherwise unscathed.

The last night we spent on Rivière de Pas it rained yet again. The following day a fine drizzle and low cloud cover shrouded the country and one could not escape a feeling of isolation. When we reached the confluence with the George River, and soon thereafter the south end of Indian House Lake, the sense of remoteness was nearly overpowering. The grey shadows of the surrounding hills lost their form and reappeared as showers passed; snow patches all around us emphasized the damp cold, and we huddled close to the fire that evening.

Noon the following day, ominous black clouds appeared. Wind began to ripple the surface of the calm lake. Powerful gusts brought whitecaps and finally a torrent of rain. By that point in the trip, however, for some inexplicable reason neither Ken nor I felt threatened by yet another storm. We just sat in our boats and smiled at each other. When the system passed, it was as if someone had drawn a giant curtain aside to reveal a dazzling mosaic of intense greens, blues and white—all bathed in glorious sunshine.

Because the wind remained bothersome we put to shore and set off for high ground. From the top of the nearest hill, the eye could follow northward to a distant horizon showing the thin sliver of water that is Indian House Lake, its western shore defined by discontinuous remnants of snow piled up by the prevailing westerly winds during winter. Just below us was the little spit of land that held the lodges of the Naskaupi when Cabot came calling in 1910. In my own mind I had been to no place more remote, more utterly detached from western civilization. To my chagrin, however, this perception was quickly challenged when I discovered a rusty tin can at the base of the rock we were sitting on.

With the wind down, we set off in predawn darkness the next morning and paddled north towards a prominent rise on the eastern shore of the lake some twenty-five kilometres away. At the base of this hill was the start of our route eastward. A little creek, which starts at a small lake a short distance up the gentle incline, had carved a circuitous course through glacial till and created a small bank of sand and gravel at the lakeshore where we landed. A careful examination of the map convinced me that the best route to the height of land was to ascend the steep hill near the shore and then follow a level course across the barren high ground eastward. This would avoid the obstruction posed by alders, willows and bog along the shore of the creek. And so we huffed and puffed our way up the abrupt incline with our first load, only to find that our progress was blocked by an impassable gorge not shown on the map. The lesson learned from this experience—that it pays to scout before committing to a course of action— has never really sunk in, because I've made the same mistake repeatedly.

Two days later we stood atop a rise in the undulating barrens of northeastern Quebec, looking back toward Indian House Lake for the last time. Our longest portage was almost behind us and we were bone-weary. We had walked about 75 kilometres[7] since leaving the lake and now we were straining to keep our balance in the breeze. Before we started paddling again, this incessant wind would have us often reeling in a strange dance with our loads, and twice Ken would have his canoe blown off his shoulders before we reached the shore of Lac Brisson.

"There are caribou over on the left shore!"

Ken always saw everything first. Up to now we had seen only tracks, but this was quite a gathering. The hills were alive with them, some of them bedded down on the snowbanks that lined the lake, but the majority were on the move southward, across the lake and over the hills, thousands of them. Totally oblivious of us, they plunged into the frigid waters in a wide swath and continued to the opposite shore. Their churning hooves created a sound that mimicked that of a high wind in the treetops. They gave us barely enough room to pass through on our way to the eastern end of Lac Brisson and beyond. By evening we were camped on the last height of land, a cheerless pile of glacial rubble; by then, our world was reduced to a tiny circle as dense fog swallowed the surroundings. We were cold, wet and tired, yet well pleased to have found this path.

The caribou swimming across the frigid waters near the height of land at Lac Brisson.

Travelling with repair kit and even minimal food for weeks, Herb did not travel light and had to make three trips on portages. With that back and forth, he reckoned they walked 75 kilometres between Indian House Lake, in the George River valley, and the Kogaluk height of land. All that portaging took its wear and tear on the body, no part of which was more important for continued movement than the feet.

After traversing a series of small interconnected lakes the next morning, we climbed a low hill. Before us yawned a gravelly plain dotted with patches of bog and tiny ponds that stretched to the dreary horizon. Just below us, a shallow trickle of water moved uncertainly in minuscule channels between scores of large and small rocks, but this was the way forward through no man's land. But this was the start of the Kogaluk River. Standing there, we had no doubt that no one had canoed these waters before, which, at the time, however good it felt seemed an almost irrelevant distinction. For 10–15 kilometres we dragged and lifted, until finally the trickle had increased to navigable volume. In the evening, a cold front moved through and a frigid sun set the tents aglow. That night, having come through the bog country to a place where larger plants could grow, we found a tiny clump of misshapen trees to provide fuel and, for the first time in four days, we luxuriated by the fire. I felt deeply moved and immensely grateful to be able to see the sights and feel the silence of this remote and lonely land.

Paddling remained hazardous for several more days as time and again an unseen boulder just below the surface of the shallow waters would bring us to a sudden stop. For four days we traversed a land of lakes and eskers in beautiful sunshine with no sign of human intrusion. Scattered stands of tamarack and black spruce reappeared and hills loomed larger as the river descended in a succession of rapids. Now we were faced with our first portage since crossing the height of land. The river drops over three hundred metres in just three kilometres as it cascades off the Labrador plateau into a deep glacier-worn valley. In this age of overused superlatives, it is impossible to adequately describe the harsh beauty of the place, but we spent the first of two days at this place madly running around taking pictures.

The river below the foot of the steep portage rushes due east toward the Atlantic in the confines of a narrow, boulder-infested stream bed. It was here that I had my closest brush with disaster when I was tossed around by two-metre waves, which gave me a thorough wash. And just below there, the Mistastin River entered from the south. We paddled up the Mistastin for a short distance, because Cabot rhapsodizes in his book about the beauty of the valley, but the strong current quickly forced us to shore. In our rambles across a gravelly plain we came across a campsite, which subsequent investigation proved to be one Cabot used in 1904. He had stuck an empty coffee tin on a tree next to his tent, an action he recorded in his notes. It was still there eighty years later.

After a such dreary start to this trip, the weather finally turned sunny. The breeze kept all but the horseflies in check and we spent several hours roaming to high ground, which gave us an excellent view of Cabot Lake a short distance downstream and the valley of the Mistastin River to the southwest. After nearly three weeks of frequently hard toil we recognized the need for a thorough wash, spent the afternoon on a sandbar on the western shore of Cabot Lake and tried in vain to restore our clothes to their original appearance. It was nevertheless a satisfying evening. To cap off a perfect campsite experience, the wind banished the flies and allowed us to luxuriate in the buff, and we put on a special dinner to celebrate the occasion.

We were now about to enter Cabot's Wind Lake, a slight widening of the Kogaluk where the river is confined between near vertical walls of rock rising more than two hundred metres above water level. Like all the glacier-carved valleys of northern Labrador, Wind Lake gets its name honestly since these U-shaped glacial troughs are natural wind tunnels. Because there are few landing places along its entire length, the traveller has to exercise caution as capricious winds often spring up without warning. We were lucky, because not a breath of wind wrinkled the water the whole time we paddled this section of river. The cloudless sky, grey rock walls and verdure of trees and shrubs along the shore were mirrored in the water and we paddled silently. Near the far end of the lake we stopped for lunch on a little gravelly point where Ken found a well-worn arrowhead, which led to an extended and fruitless examination of the place.

These concurrent hours of sunshine had made the place quite hot, and mosquitoes and blackflies appeared in determined numbers. At our campsite that evening, which was set in among the vegetation, we decided to forego supper and flee into the tents rather than face the onslaught. Before entering my refuge, I crashed wildly through the underbrush in an attempt to reduce the number of blackflies, which were covering me from head to foot. Killing the remainder once inside was fuelled by a desire for revenge. There was no reduction in their numbers the next morning and we didn't bother to eat until we reached a windswept gravel bar. Cabot described similarly tough conditions when he travelled in this area in 1904 with Robert Walcott: "If Walcott had known how he looked the first three days on the river, he would have needed good courage to keep on. He was swelled up nearly to blindness; his nearest friend would hardly have known him."[8]

The river below Cabot Lake is a placid stream with one or two riffles along the way. The shore is defined by the remnants of eskers that gradually merge with the deposits of a gravelly plain, which stretches away toward the northeast. Imposing hills of bedrock continue to parallel the river's south shore to within a few kilometres of the coast. The last obstruction along the way is a magnificent two-step waterfall, potentially a wonderful campsite, but the flies quickly convinced us to carry on. Instead, we filled our containers with water, intent on camping along the shore of Voisey's Bay. A short distance below the falls we were hailed by a man in front of a fishing lodge, and paddled in.

Horace Goudie was one of the last surviving "height-of-landers" in Labrador, a group of men who travelled every fall up the Grand River to the highlands above Churchill Falls to their traplines. Horace was a wonderful storyteller and a welcoming host who obviously liked the old ways. The lodge was a modern building with all conveniences, but Horace preferred the old tin stove, the same one he would use in the tilt on the trapline. In short order, he produced a meal of bannock and a rich broth of peameal and fried salt pork. Stories kept us entertained until well after midnight, when Horace's vodka finally gave out. The evening wasn't all idle talk however; our host had cast a covetous eye on Ken's Old Town canoe as soon as we came ashore and, by the end of the evening, the change of ownership was official. We would continue to Nain where Horace would meet us to take possession.

Our good luck with the weather continued. In the sunshine, Voisey's Bay was alive with hundreds of guillemots. Rising darkly against a calm and shimmering sea were several large islands, which we ticked off on the map as we headed north toward Nain.

On the open ocean, Ken was in his element. Throughout the trip he had been picking away at the countryside and patiently instructed me in the rudiments of geology. Now he kept staring at every passing rock and frequently stopped to fondle a bit of debris; it soon became obvious that his canoe was settling deeper into the brine. My own attention must not have been sufficiently focused on the map because after two hours we ended up at the end of a deep bay and had to retrace our route.

We were no sooner on the right track when a freighter canoe containing Bill Ritchie and Stephen Loring approached. By an extraordinary coincidence, Stephen, who is an archaeologist with the Smithsonian Institution in Washington, is also the archivist of Cabot's writings and photographs. Even more remarkable, he had a large number of Cabot's pictures with him. We got along so well that when we finally parted under a deteriorating sky nearly two hours later, Bill had become the new owner of *my* boat, to be picked up in Nain at the end of our journey.

But we had distance yet to travel. A sudden downpour found us far from shore with the rain suits securely packed away and not accessible in the developing slop. We spent the night on Tabor Island—the site of an abandoned Labradorite mine, Ken told me—and, for the first time in almost two weeks, had to prepare supper in the rain. Ken lost himself in the mine tailings and just barely had time to watch a crimson sunset.

The next morning, after a dense fog lifted, we set off for Nain. We expected to cover the 18 kilometres by noon, but a strong wind and adverse tidal current made for a hard day's work before we finally rounded the last point and landed rather anticlimactically at low tide in the mud flats, next to the settlement's sewage outfall. The 600-kilometre journey had taken twenty-three days. After a wet start, the weather had been uncommonly good, in fact, the whole journey had been blessed with good fortune. It didn't seem so, but it must have been physically demanding because we nearly finished our five-week supply of food and I still lost six kilograms. Two days later we were aboard the coastal steamer *Taverner*, bound for Goose Bay and home.

FOUR

Notakwanon River, 1984[1]

The old truck creaked and groaned as it followed two fingers of light reaching over gravel toward Lake Attikamagen. The road was in terrible condition and it required some adroit manoeuvring to avoid getting stuck. Conditions inside the cab were scarcely better, the mixture of exhaust fumes and gasoline vapour left me hanging out the window for most of the way. It took one-and-a-half hours to traverse the 25 kilometres from Schefferville to Iron Arm, a bay in this lake in Labrador, the starting point of the trip. By one o'clock the tent was set up and I crawled into my sleeping bag well pleased with the way everything had worked out so far.

With the closing of mining operations in Schefferville, train service was now reduced to one train a week, which leaves Sept-Îles on Thursday morning, arrives 12–14 tedious hours later in Schefferville and returns south the following day. I had phoned the Schefferville station the previous day from the Moisie River campground and arranged for someone to drive me immediately upon my arrival to Iron Arm.

According to the records of the weather station at Schefferville there was to be measurable precipitation on twenty-one days of the month during June and July and, true to form, a gentle rain was falling when I woke in the morning. I had been here on exactly the same date two years earlier with Ken Ellison, when we began our Kogaluk trip, but somehow the place looked different. Besides the cottages I remembered, there were now a number of canvas tents set up, complete with stove and firewood, the floors lined with spruce boughs and blankets, but there wasn't a soul around.

As always at the beginning of a trip nothing seemed to be in the right place and it took several hours before everything was finally stored away satisfactorily. Crossing Lake Attikamagen requires careful navigation; besides the many islands and peninsulas that are shown on the map, there are others that are not and it's not difficult to get confused. Once across, a short portage leads into Mole Lake. Reputedly, there is a portage from the eastern shore of Mole Lake into Fox Lake, a distance of half a kilometre, but once again I failed to find it and ended up crashing through the underbrush. I had planned to stop at Fox Lake for the day, and so it was only fitting that a torrential downpour would catch me on the last portage. The rain stopped an hour later, but a cold wind made sure that the comfort level was low until I managed to get a fire going.

The following morning the second portage brought me over the height of land into Quebec. As so often happens in these parts, "height of land" is really a misnomer, as the Quebec and Labrador watersheds often meet in a large expanse of boggy lowland and portaging across simply means sloshing over a quaking substratum that is interspersed with miniature ponds and rock outcroppings.

The weather, as I sloshed and slogged for the next two days, was typical for the region—cool and cloudy with frequent showers. In contrast to the last trip, there was very little wind. Spring had also arrived a little earlier than usual, and these two factors combined to ensure the presence of a multitude of blackflies and mosquitoes. At Lac Jamin, the last of a number of lakes on the upper Rivière de Pas, I came across a fly-in fishing camp where I stopped briefly to talk to one of the guides. When I explained that I was going to cross over to the Labrador coast, he recalled an older fellow passing by the previous year in the company of a young lad who was planning to go upstream all the way to the headwaters of the George River and from there to the Labrador coast. He was obviously impressed—who ever heard of anyone going upstream in a canoe?

Personally I was more impressed with the fact that the old fellow turned down the invitation to stay for supper (with the excuse that they were behind schedule and had to hurry on). The two people were my old friend Karl Schimeck[2] and his son Peter. They had a more than adventurous trip up the George and down the Kanairiktok River. Along the way they had two upsets and lost much of their food and all their maps. Without the latter they did not dare paddle out to the river-mouth and along the coast through a maze of islands to the community of Hopedale. Instead they stopped at Snegamook Lake and eventually managed to attract the attention of a passing float plane, which took them to Goose Bay in a much reduced condition.

Well, nobody asked *me* to stay for supper even though it was about five p.m., and so I carried on, past the only portage on Rivière de Pas, past several kilometres of boisterous rapids at the outflow of Lac Jamin. After spending some time looking, I settled for a campsite on an exposed point of shore opposite the entrance of a substantial tributary. Lots of dry firewood from an old Indian campsite, golden evening sun streaming obliquely through the treetops on the far shore, enough wind to keep the bugs in check—what more could anyone ask for? Oh yes, solitude, blessed solitude! From here on to the end of the trip I never met anyone, never heard or saw a plane, just revelled in primeval wilderness and solitude.

It turned cold during the night and the steaming river generated a dense fog that limited visibility in the morning, but one could feel it was going to be a great day. The section of river I had to cover today was fast flowing. Benign rapids alternated with quiet stretches. The bouldery shoreline was scoured free of vegetation for a considerable distance up the riverbank, testimony to the force and magnitude of spring breakup. By late afternoon and fifty-five kilometres later I had reached the point where I had to leave the river and portage to the height of land which separates Rivière de Pas from the George River. I knew that Stewart Coffin[3] had used this route in 1982, as had Karl Schimeck the following year, and therefore had some idea of what lay ahead. Nevertheless, the prospect of the long haul evoked mixed feelings.

Early the next morning, in the rain, I hefted the first load onto my shoulders and slowly picked my way beside the little stream, the course of which I was to follow for the next two days. At first the going was easy, following game trails through an old burn, but that degenerated into an oozing, gurgling bog, even on the hillsides. With two packs, two duffle bags and the boat, I routinely triple-portaged and thus traversed the same terrain five times. One would think that this provides ample opportunity to find the best route, but in this case even the best route was miserable indeed. The first night found me just a little past the halfway mark, pretty well done in and very aware of an exceptionally attentive insect population. The only respite from the little beasts occurred during the frequent showers. One really learns to appreciate waterproof tents, mosquito netting and a change of dry clothes. By mid-afternoon of the second day I reached the first of several small lakes I had to traverse. Two years earlier Coffin's party had camped here and even left some firewood. Much to my astonishment I also discovered the remains of tent poles and signs of a trapline. I had to wonder how would anyone come here, nearly two hundred kilometres from the nearest settlement and so far from the river?

During the afternoon it had become sunny and oppressively hot, so I decided to relax a little while with the fishing rod before going back for the last load. The lake was full of eager brook trout and home to a very large beaver who was not at all happy about my presence. When I finally set out to retrieve the last load the shadows were getting long; of course I knew exactly where I had left it— about halfway up a hill covered with dwarf birch and right next to a spruce with a twin top. One learns to observe carefully when travelling alone in wild country. I spent nearly an hour looking for my twin-topped reference point among the dozens of twin-topped spruce scattered everywhere.

The following afternoon found me tussock-hopping across the last soggy portage at the height of land. A momentary loss of balance or misjudgment would see me periodically disappear up to my crotch in the morass. The first time this happened the feeling of acute displeasure gave rise to an outpouring of invective, but after several such baptisms I saved energy and just stayed quiet. But with the umpteenth dunking, I could see the stream that would carry me swiftly down to the George River; the long traverse was nearly behind me.

The unnamed tributary I was now travelling descended in a series of ledges, boulder gardens and fantails in a broad stream bed. As I rounded a bend, I could see a large, dark form drop down behind the curtain of willows lining the shore. A noisy flapping of flightless wings by a flock of Canada Geese followed as they scurried for safety and, then, out of the thicket with powerful strokes flew an impressively large Golden Eagle, leaving behind the goose it had just killed. I stopped shortly thereafter as I recognized the signs that unfailingly tell that you are getting tired—the rocks keep getting in your way. At the bottom of another rock garden I spied a narrow bit of scoured shoreline between the river and the willow thickets—home for the evening, and what an evening! The warm and steady breeze had banished all tormentors; the sun, low over the horizon, was reflected by every little ripple of water. Scraggly spruce and tamarack swayed darkly in the wind and the river played an endless symphony as it cascaded over a thousand rocks. Alas, there were chores to do, for this was goose country. Since I am a fastidious man, I spent a considerable amount of time first carefully clearing a tent site and then covering each little deposit in the immediate area with a small rock. By the time I was finished the place looked like a gravel pit, a wordless testimonial to what geese do best.

The following day, two hours of careful dodging and a short portage around two ledges brought me to the confluence with the George River by mid-morning. From there, my plan was to go upstream, first on the George itself and then on a tributary flowing out of White Gull Lake. My new boat[4] had quite a bit of rocker and I was concerned that it might not track too well in the strong current, but I needn't have worried. By evening I had covered nearly fifteen kilometres, and after portaging around a strong rapid, decided to make camp and go for a wander.

It took nearly an hour to reach the unobstructed view of a bald crown of rock two kilometres to the south of my camp. From there, the roar of the rapids was reduced to a gentle murmur. Immediately to the west, the George River glistened in the evening sun and disappeared from view to the northwest. To the south, immense bodies of water dotted with islands nearly filled the vast plain. My route lay to the northeast through a maze of islands and I carefully compared the features before me with the map; as always it never a perfect match. "Good Lord," I thought, "you wouldn't want to be lost in this place."

Satisfied with the orienting view, I headed back to camp to rest the aching body. The next day, three kilometres of tracking proved to be tough going. With the shoreline covered with alder and willow and the river deep and strong, I eventually decided to try my luck portaging. Even after I reached flat water the situation didn't improve, for a strong headwind sprung up and persisted for the rest of the day. Incredible though it seemed, there was a noticeable current and even rapids in this wide island-studded body of water. After several short carries to escape windswept sections I finally reached White Gull Lake. The nearest campsite was still two kilometres away, and when I finally staggered ashore after two more hours of battling wind and waves, I was pretty well fed up with paddling. I spent the evening roaming over the gravelly plain behind the campsite, taking in the view of spidery eskers reaching far out into White Gull Lake before disappearing below its surface. Under the grey threatening sky, the scene looked utterly desolate. The remains of an old Indian grave somehow added to the feeling of total isolation.

I woke at four a.m. to the sounds of rain. Here was an excuse to stay for a day of rest, I thought. But two hours later the rain had stopped and the lake was calm and I couldn't pass up the opportunity to move. It turned out to be a most memorable day. The sun emerged and transformed desolation into dazzling beauty, the lake mirrored the sky and it was time to sing (I always sing when the spirit moves me, not well, but with great fervour). At noon I stopped at the tip of the large peninsula that juts into the lake from the north to stretch my legs. About this time thunderheads started to billow up in the southwest. As I watched, they coalesced into dark centres and deposited their moisture in long trailers on their way across the lake.

When one of these clouds took dead aim at my position, I quickly rigged up a shelter by stringing a tarpaulin over some tree limbs and waited with a feeling of quiet satisfaction for the impending deluge. It always seems to start the same way: a few faint gusts of wind, a brief patter of raindrops, followed by stronger gusts and then—a torrent of good, clean northern Quebec water. This one was no exception, but for once I was prepared and watched it with self-satisfaction. Unbeknownst to me, however, disaster was brewing overhead. A pocket of water had formed in the tarp and had quickly grown to the point where its weight overpowered the ingenuity of my design and presently a wall of water descended upon me, quenching the singing, and everything else.

There was more to come. When I returned after a brief reconnaissance to the nearest hill, waves were breaking on the shore. Getting off proved to be dicey— the first breaker half filled the boat. Eventually I managed to clear a sheltering point of land, returned the unwanted water to the lake and headed off downwind, but my troubles weren't quite over. Looking back over my shoulder I could see another shower approaching. A few minutes later, the sky turned quite dark and the wind picked up to forty or more kilometres per hour. The waves by now were running at more than a metre in height and I was petrified lest I get turned sideways and blown over. About every third wave picked me up and carried me along like a surfboard. And then the rains came.

What a macabre sight!

The inky black water was overlain with a pale grey haze created by the spray from the falling sheets of rain. The sky was completely obliterated and across the grey-black surface rolled the ghostly white combers of the wind-whipped breakers. Despite my precarious position I couldn't help thinking what a photograph this would make. Ever so gradually conditions became less severe, and now my concern was how was I going to land among the pounding waves on the fast approaching shore. Luckily, a little sheltered bay presented itself and with a great sense of relief I landed in the lee of a large east-west running esker on the north shore of White Gull Lake. A spit of sand overgrown with alders at the tip of the esker, poking perpendicularly out into the lake, formed a natural and very welcome breakwater. While the waves continued to rush the shore on the far side, the little lagoon was a tranquil haven. It turned out that I wasn't the first one to discover this place—the tent frames of a fly-in fishing camp occupied one corner of the bay.

My first order of business was to repair the boat. The constant flexing in the waves had caused a leak. A sheet of plywood came in handy as the roof of my makeshift workshop during the periodic showers, and I quickly set to work by starting a fire in front of the shelter to dry out the boat before putting on a patch. Two hours later the job was done except for the curing of the resin, and I rushed eagerly to the crest of the esker to have a look beyond. What I saw was not encouraging. Except for a bit of open water some distance to the north, it was miserable black spruce bog. Far to the northwest loomed a range of barren hills, my target for tomorrow. The 1:50,000 map showed a creek just beyond the esker making its way northward towards Leif Lake, but I could see no sign of it from my vantage point.

Back in the tent, the sound of breaking waves and the wind made for a poor night's sleep, but the morning was glorious. As I attended to my bacon and pancakes I listened to live entertainment—a solitary bird sitting on a weather-beaten tree nearby kept repeating its plaintive call over and over again. I saw no reason to join it in song because for me it was a day of sloshing through the thickets. The little creek (it was there after all) was far too rocky and shallow and so, except for two small lakes, it was a full day of portaging. By mid-afternoon it was back to upstream work on a large river draining out of Lac Machault. Despite all the hard effort I was elated. The worst of the portaging was behind, the sun was shining and the harsh beauty of the surroundings overwhelming.

By evening I was camped at a miserable bug-infested site at the bottom of the last rapid below Lac Machault, and dead tired. Still, I dragged myself to the top of the nearest hill to get some pictures in the evening light. It was well worth the effort. Far away on the southwestern horizon shimmered White Gull Lake; to the north and immediately below was the kilometre-long rapid, whitecaps glowing in the slanted sunlight; to the east Lac Machault, dotted with green islands, was sitting like a jewel amidst the bare hills. Alas, the angry clouds of blackflies, which hovered in the air, soon dispelled the meditative mood.

Another sun-drenched morning followed with not a breath of wind stirring. Lac Machault was like polished glass except for a peculiar haze on the surface that turned out to be a carpet of dead blackflies, millions of them, and legions more very much alive. On the far side of the lake I had lunch at the foot of the stream, which represented the outflow of a series of small lakes that would take me to the height of land. After a short portage I put in above a falls into what was shown on the map as a small lake. Instead, this, and the next two "lakes," were broad boulder-choked stream beds and the only way to get past was by lifting and wading. The current was sufficiently strong to have washed away all the small rocks between large rounded boulders and the water in the intervening spaces was a metre or more in depth. It made for slow going. After another portage I had had enough. I was too tired to bother with a campfire. All I wanted was to boil enough water on the stove for a freeze-dried dinner and a pot of tea. I was badly overheated and longed to strip down in the safety of the tent but, before I got that far, the blackflies descended on me in clouds that neither head net nor fly dope could deter. In near panic I made a little smudge fire with lichen to try to get at least some of the pests off me before retreating into the tent. To hell with supper!

A few minutes later I heard a faint crackling sound outside.

Fire!

I rushed out, quite naked at this stage. The first thing I saw was thick black smoke billowing up and flames enveloping the bow of the boat. I rushed over to my ever-present pail of water and poured it on the flames—to no avail. Then I tried to smother the fire with an empty canoe pack and at last succeeded. What a mess! The bow of the boat was reduced to the blackened skeleton of roving and matting and, in a strangely dispassionate way, I wondered whether this was my last canoe trip. I was within sight of the height of land that demarcates the Quebec-Labrador boundary and almost exactly at the halfway point of my trip. Behind me lay an immensity of bog and large lakes, a hopeless endeavour on foot; ahead a tortuous hike of hundreds of kilometres to the coast with the nearest settlement, Davis Inlet, located on an island in the Labrador Sea. These thoughts were quickly put aside by a more pressing problem of blackflies feasting extravagantly on acres of exposed skin.

How the fire started, I could only guess. The boat was at least five metres upwind from my smudge fire and the latter had not spread across the intervening space. Presumably a burning cinder had been propelled across, landed on the coiled polypropylene bow rope and set it on fire. This would have provided enough fuel to eventually get the fibreglass resin to burn. Whatever the process, it was irrelevant now. The first thirty centimetres of the bow were reduced to a blackened mass and an additional thirty centimetres were partially burned or scorched and of doubtful strength. I had neither enough roving or resin to build a new bow, and so the critical issue was whether I could infiltrate the existing roving with resin and have it adhere.

It turned cloudy and cool overnight, My first task was to build a fire to dry out the damaged section and to speed up the curing. Next I taped up the loose roving to a semblance of its original shape and carefully impregnated a small section of it with resin. A nervous half-hour later it became clear that the operation was successful—resin and sooty roving had bonded well enough and now it was just a question of continuing the repair in small steps as far as the limited resources allowed. It was an all-day job complicated by periodic showers. The final task involved covering the repaired section with duct tape because it was by no means waterproof. For years I had carried a large roll of tape without ever needing more than a few scraps; this time it helped save my bacon. The much weakened bow meant that I had to be very careful launching and landing the boat, but otherwise it performed as well as ever. When the repairs were done, in spite of the late hour, I packed up and paddled away from the scene of the crime as quickly as possible.

I am sure it was as much relief about the outcome of the repairs as anything else, but it seemed an extraordinary evening. I made camp just a few kilometres further along with the last rays of the sun gilding the bare hills. The bugs were as numerous as ever, but seemed less offensive. The nearest little lake had somehow retained a thick covering of ice and snow in one corner that glowed mystically in the fading light, but the real centre of attraction was a range of high hills to the east—Labrador. Soon a cozy fire crackled away beside the stream connecting two lakes, an Idaho potato of generous size was boiling in the pot and I was busy frying bacon and fresh onions to produce my favourite meal,[5] a true thanksgiving dinner.

Travelling alone allows little time for contemplation for there are always chores to do, but this was an exception. Fortified with a quart of tea, I watched the western sky gradually darken to the indigo colour that precedes night, all the features around me gradually lost form and melted into darkness except for the little ring of light around the dancing flames. In time all magic spells are broken, and I set to work building up the fire in order to enlarge the sphere of protection against the humming hordes, heated some water and stripped down for my first good wash since leaving Sept-Îles thirteen days before.

When I woke at three, the morning sky was tempting, but I quickly dismissed photography when I looked at the welcoming committee waiting outside. By seven a breeze was up and I was on my way; three more portages and four more

After slogging his way up to the Quebec-Labrador height of land from Lake Attikamagen, Herb was undaunted by miles of unrunnable rapids on the other side.

small lakes and I'd be in Labrador. As height-of-land lakes tend to be very shallow, their bottoms covered with large boulders that often protrude above the surface, virtually the only way to navigate is to stand up and pole your way through the maze of obstructions. Progress is consequently slow. Just before noon I reached the rocky half-kilometre portage that separates the waters of Quebec and Labrador. On the far side were the headwaters of the Notakwanon River, this year's route to tidewater.

The inspiration for this particular journey had come from a map in Cabot's book *In Northern Labrador,* which bore the notation "Sketched from an Indian Map." The uncertain line starts at Resolution Lake on the George River and ends at the mouth of the Notakwanon. This supposedly was the Montagnais route to and from the HBC trading post at Davis Inlet. In several places the indicated route left the river, only to rejoin it later on, indicating an impassable stretch of water. I was now looking forward to finding signs of this trail. Equally intriguing was the prospect of canoeing stretches of river shunned by the Natives—just how difficult would it be?

Several hours later, I was standing atop a high rocky ridge. Below me and running southwest to northeast lay a long and narrow water-filled trough carved out of bare rock. Other bodies of water could be seen parallel or at right angles to it. Interrupting the mosaic of grey and blue—rock and water—were green patches of spruce and tamarack in all the sheltered places. Clouds were welling up in the

west, periodically hiding the sun. Each time the light changed the transformation was remarkable—brilliant contrasting colours would fade to dismal shades
of grey and with them the impression of warm friendliness would give way to
one of cold hostility.

A short distance beyond I came upon an Indian campsite. The remains of tent
poles, scattered over a large area, seemed to be very old. Decay in these parts is
very slow and I thought it quite possible that this might well have been a hundred-
year-old site. For the next little while I was excitedly looking around for artifacts
but, finding none, I pushed on. In the meantime the weather had deteriorated considerably; strong headwinds had raised whitecaps and between periodic showers
and wind-borne spray I was not only wet but thoroughly chilled. By a stroke of
good fortune a sheltered bay was not too far away. But even there the hastily
started fire gave little heat. All night long the tent shook and flapped as gusts of
wind tore at it, but early in the morning the rain stopped and, with an expectation
of improvement, I packed all but my cooking gear and started to prepare breakfast. Even by the fire, the cold dampness had me shivering and when showers
returned I decided to stay put. Only venturing outside when necessary, I spent the
day cooking meals on the camp stove in the vestibule of the tent and sleeping.

By the second morning the wind had died down, but a dense fog reduced my
world to a small sphere. Navigation would be tricky, but it was time to move on.
Paddling was a bit awkward with warm underwear, heavy sweater, down vest,
windbreaker, life preserver and rain jacket layered one over the other. A ridiculous amount of clothing and more than I would wear at minus thirty in the
winter, but I was barely comfortable for the first two hours.

The feeling of isolation in this uncertain, soundless world of grey was strong.
Several times the silence was broken by the muffled sounds of a riffle up ahead.
This was curiously reassuring because in the absence of a noticeable current for
most of the way, it demonstrated that I was still in the right channel. Once I had
passed the range of hills that dominate the height of land and entered the first of
several large lakes, the weather had improved. This was caribou country and histor-
ically a place where the Naskaupi and Montagnais hunted. At virtually all potential
caribou-crossing places the remains of hunting camps could be seen. With one
exception they were all very old. A stiff east wind had me ashore by mid-afternoon.

I was now in the middle of the Labrador plateau, a vast expanse of barrens
with little pockets of gnarled trees in the more sheltered spots of the gravelly
plain. It's a place of wide horizon and immense sky. I know of no other place
where the monumental insignificance of one's own existence is so decisively
brought into focus than in this windswept isolation.

At a particularly attractive spot I stopped for an early camp. Before long, the
vegetation in the neighbourhood was adorned with articles of clothing to dry and
it was time to scour the countryside in search of photographic subjects. I had

barely set up the tripod on a rocky knoll some distance from the tent when a rousing chorus from a pack of wolves a few hundred metres away began. Somehow my interest in wildflowers diminished. I know all the reassuring statistics, and I know Farley Mowat's stand on the matter, but I couldn't be sure that these vocal creatures were aware of how they were expected to behave. And so I strode purposefully toward the tent and lit a reassuring fire.

I woke to a clear and frosty morning. Judging by the fresh tracks, a large number of caribou must have passed right in front of the tent during the night without my hearing them. Five hours of hard paddling and a short portage later I was nearing the end of the lake region. I had seen small groups of caribou here and there, but now I was looking at a massed herd. Taking no notice of me they continued to strip the bushes at the water's edge of their foliage. Further inland, a sea of antlers stretched to the horizon. Because of the flat terrain I could not get a vantage point to estimate their number, but surely there were thousands.

Somewhere in this region the old Indian route to the coast takes a more northerly route to bypass forty kilometres of rapids. The first half of this stretch of river is of the drop-and-pool variety, which gives way to continuous boulder rapids as the gradient gradually increases from 5–8 m/km. I negotiated about 25 rapids, mostly class II, which could be run on sight, and one very long and lively one that had me well-washed by the time it was finished with me. By late afternoon I had used up the day's ration of adrenaline and it was time to put to shore.

Once the camp chores were done, I hiked to the top of a hill where an enormous and precariously balanced erratic stood like a sentinel. Looking back upstream, it seemed all so tranquil with no evidence of the boisterousness of the river. Downstream the impression of tranquillity was not maintained. Even from this distance it looked like a nasty stretch and the low rumble emanating from it added to my unease. I realized that the early morning sun's reflection off the water would make it difficult to see and so I was on the water by four to negotiate the first rapids, but it was already too late. I went ahead anyway, After a wild ride, I put to shore a short distance above a magnificent waterfall, convinced I had done serious damage to the boat when I crashed on top of a rock hidden by a big roller upstream from it. Much to my surprise, there was no sign of injury.

I spent some time clambering about the falls and the gorge below, a truly extraordinary spectacle, and finally carried on over a very taxing portage to breakfast a kilometre away. I was hardly settled in the boat when the next, much lower, waterfall necessitated another portage. The roar of the river just around a bend beyond the put-in point was a bit unsettling, and so I went to high ground to have a look at the prospect ahead. It was literally *white* water as far as the eye could see. It was too far to portage and not suitable for lining, and so with much nervousness I pursued the third option. For the next seven kilometres the river roared and boiled in a narrow V-shaped valley with no pools to interrupt the

The falls on the Notakwanon, twenty-two metres in height. No matter how long a carry, how wet the weather, how non-existent the portage, Herb always took time to walk and explore to gain perspective on the natural beauty that surrounded him.

action. The force of the water left little room for manoeuvring. It was a question of tucking in behind a boulder near the shore, looking ahead to plan a general course of action to the next boulder and plunging in again. In the gloom of what had become a showery day, the scene looked ever more intimidating. I finally reached a small expansion in the valley and with it quiet water. All though this descent I had been soaked again and again by waves and now, with the release from a state of acute concentration and anxiety, I became aware that I was very cold. Only people familiar with situations like this can appreciate the sensuous pleasure I derived from the roaring fire, which soon warmed body and soul.

The region I had now entered was the most rugged of the whole trip with peaks rising over five hundred metres above the valley floor. I had planned to stop here for a few days and explore the high ground. It should have provided an overview of the whole valley, but the heavy cloud cover and intermittent rain for the next three days hid the peaks. After several attempts at hiking, it became clear that photography here was a lost cause and I moved on. The next day's paddling was a continuation of boulder rapids and included a lift-over and a short portage. And then I got a little careless, or overconfident, because the boat seemed to do such an admirable job. I could see that up ahead the river was gradually narrowing; the current was becoming faster and the waves higher and higher. When I finally realized I should have gone ashore, it was too late—there were no eddies. The haystacks were coming at me at a furious rate in a channel barely ten metres wide.

All of a sudden I was looking at a gaping hole and the wave behind it closed in over me. The first thing that impressed itself upon me was a sense of quietness—gone was the hiss and swish of the waves. There were bubbles all around me and a strange light filtered through from below the boat. And then I decided I better get the hell out because the light wasn't below, I was. Trying to get a canoe to shore in turbulent water can be difficult, but the huge boulder, which was the cause of my upset, also saved me because it created a small pool. It allowed me to get the boat ashore before the river resumed its relentless plunge, but I had to let go of the paddle. Just as I stepped ashore it disappeared downstream never to be seen again.

In this deeply recessed valley, campsites near the river don't exist. The shoreline is chiefly composed of large rounded boulders followed by a dense growth of alders and willows. Farther back and up the steep incline is a tangle of deadfalls among closely spaced trees. Because the sun reaches the valley floor for only a few hours at best and it rains frequently, everything is saturated with moisture. The first order of business was to make a replacement paddle. I had with me a plastic paddle blade, which I carry for just such an emergency, and I fitted it with a green spruce shaft. (To illustrate how slowly trees grow in these parts, I counted forty-two growth rings on the tree, which was barely three centimetres in diameter.) Then it was time to portage, for with the single blade I felt much less confident and there were nearly five kilometres of nasty rapids left. By noon of the second day the worst was behind. The valley had widened considerably with eskers paralleling the river on both sides. I put in opposite a tributary that entered from the west, which I believe to be the point where the Indian route rejoins the river. The latter continued to run along at the same pace as before, but the boulders had given way to gravel, and all one had to do was steer in order to move along at eight to ten kilometres per hour. Just as well too, because my new paddle was so heavy and clumsy, it took the fun out of paddling.

Even with the little I could see of it through the driving rain and low clouds, I was awed by the scenery before me. I couldn't let this go by without an attempt at capturing it on film. Convinced that an improvement in the weather was imminent, I went ashore and clambered up the steep sides of an enormous esker rising nearly a hundred metres above the river. I waited for the rain to stop and the clouds to lift, for this was the most rugged section before the river turns east. An hour later, with the lenses of the camera fogged up, soaked to the bone and shivering with the cold, I gave up. Ten kilometres downstream I landed on a gravel bar, crashed through the barricade of alders and willows to a grove of massive spruce trees, and with the dead branches at their base started a "Labrador" fire (the term as used here means "huge").

In little more than half an hour everything was dried out and I felt like a different man. During this interval the first physical signs of the change in weather I had predicted appeared, and in eager anticipation I made the return journey to the boat left at the water's edge. Of course the vegetation along the way was every bit as sodden as before and, when I emerged at the edge of the river, I was as drenched as ever, but I didn't care. The next six hours were easily the most memorable of the trip. The fog rose and fell, revealing parts of the scenery only to obscure it again. Gradually the revelation became more and more complete. The sun's rays broke through periodically, producing strange patterns of light and shadow in a constant succession of moods. A magnificent double rainbow arched across the valley in brief brilliance and vanished in the fog. Then a shaft of sunlight broke through like a spotlight, found its way to a small grass-covered gravel bar in the middle of the river and illuminated it to an iridescent glow. It wouldn't have surprised me if the fairies had appeared and danced there; it was a magical place.[6]

The following day found me camped on the edge of a cutbank high above the river. Below me the Notakwanon roared past in a giant S-bend. With my first load I had tried to portage along the river's edge but soon saw the error of my ways and took to high ground. Now, with the evening shadows slowly creeping up the far shore, I wondered who had been here before me. For the first time I had stumbled across an outsider's campsite—a piece of shock cord was hanging from a tree near an old fireplace, so it was unlikely a Native party, even though traces of the old portage trail shown on Cabot's map were nearby. I no doubt raised the same question for the next traveller to pass through this unlikely spot, because I left my fork and spoon there. The half-kilometre portage back down to the river the next morning took over three hours to complete, testimony to the density of alders and willows along the way. Ever since leaving the "magic valley," the paddling had been easy with the river flowing swiftly in a gravel bed interrupted by

Herb was captivated by the exceptional scenery along the Notakwanon River.

an occasional riffle. With the exception of a few ice-scoured domes of steel-grey rock, the country was now clothed in densely growing spruce.

Fifteen kilometres upstream from the mouth of the river I came upon the last rapids in brilliant sunshine. I was almost at the far end of the portage with the first load when someone pulled the plug overhead. By the time I returned to my rain suit, it was floating in the back of the boat in five centimetres of water. The mood in the camp that evening was very subdued. It continued to rain and the only spot for the tent was on an overhang poised over the river, which seemed ready to drop into the waves below at any moment. I pondered the question: "How do you get out of a zippered-up tent floating in the river in the dark of night?"

After a peaceful night, the rain stopped about mid-morning and the sharply defined boundary of fog blanketed everything a few metres above the river. The Notakwanon meandered endlessly in shallow channels amid the sandbars. Perhaps it was just the knowledge that this was the last day on the river, but it seemed a very tedious day. I had been told that there are usually several Naskaupi families from Davis Inlet camped at the river mouth at this time of the year. The idea of being surrounded by people had little appeal for me and I stopped well short of the tidal flats. With a good push I knew I would be able to reach Davis Inlet the next day. For a long time that evening, I sat by the fire looking back upstream. Periodically the curtain of clouds rose to reveal a mosaic of snow patches on the distant hills glowing in the sun. It felt like a last goodbye from a tempestuous mistress. It had been quite an affair!

But Labrador hadn't finished with me yet. For two days fierce winds accompanied by rain had me trapped on a bare corner of an island in Merryfield Bay, and I began to wonder whether the tent would withstand the constant battering. On the third day, in the twilight of dawn, I managed to slip away with the outgoing tide. Pushing as hard as I could in a quartering slop among remnants of pack ice, I covered the 31 kilometres to Davis Inlet in four hours.[7] There I had the good fortune to run into Horace Goudie whom I had met two years previously on the Kogaluk River. He promptly escorted me to the Grenfell Mission nursing station where Selina Conn was a model of hospitality. Because of the bad weather, aircraft had been grounded for several days and I was fortunate to get a seat on the first plane out the next morning. Left behind was my boat, the burned bow now augmented by several cracks and a belly worn thin with abuse.

FIVE

Ugjoktok River, 1985

The pilot banked the plane steeply as he circled several times to find a safe landing spot on rock-strewn, island-studded Bonaventure Lake. Minutes later boats and gear were unloaded on a tiny island; a last wave from the cockpit and the plane roared off and disappeared over the western horizon. So far everything had gone exceedingly well. Jim Greenacre[1] and I had left Toronto three days earlier, driven to Sept-Îles in Quebec and boarded the weekly train to Schefferville. We had made prior arrangements with Air Schefferville for accommodation for the night and transportation to their air base at Squaw Lake. Our plan was to start paddling down the George River to Resolution Lake, then head off in an easterly direction toward Labrador and the Ugjoktok River. For maximum independence we paddled solo and used separate tents.

The morning of the flight dawned in cloudless glory and our spirits further brightened when we discovered that my boat would fit inside the Single Otter, which was to fly us one hundred thirty kilometres to the nearest lake on the headwaters of the west branch of the upper George River. That saved us a tidy sum of money. Unlike many other carriers, Air Schefferville refuses to strap more than one boat on the pontoons. Had we not managed to squeeze the second boat inside, it would have required two flights to our put-in point. Still, with very little change from seven hundred dollars, it could hardly be called cheap transportation.

For me, the start of a long wilderness trip is always accompanied by a flood of emotions. At first, apprehension and joyful exhilaration are curiously intermingled, but with a little time on the land, this eventually gives way to a feeling of restfulness, a sense of belonging. And here this wash of feelings was again, amplified by the gentle breeze and the soporific lapping of the waves on the shore, the warm June sun biting into the remnants of last winter's snow and bird song floating down from scraggly tamaracks.

Bonaventure Lake is not a large body of water but is extremely fragmented, full of little islands and shallow bays. Even the large-scale map is at substantial variance with reality, and it took some two hours to find the well-masked out-flow. The rocky stream, which descended in benign rapids, was populated by large numbers of trout, their backs frequently exposed above the surface. For some distance the course of the upper George River is very close to and paral-lels the height of land, which, in a few places, rises a modest ten or twenty metres above am immense waterlogged plain. Stunted black spruce and tama-rack are the dominant vegetative cover in this part of the world, their individual forms melting into an dark-green carpet near the horizon. Not a single promi-nent feature interrupts the seemingly limitless expanse.

By late afternoon the George had grown substantially. When we reached a tiny island, scraped flat and clean by spring ice and barely projecting above the water, we stopped for the day. Neither the resident beaver nor Jim seemed very enthu-siastic about this decision, but with the importation of a canoe load of firewood, a homey atmosphere was quickly established and reinforced by the smells of our first supper cooking on the fire. Early the following day we reached Elson Lake, where the east and west branches of the upper George River combine. The event was highlighted by our first exposure to jets of the German air force screaming past at treetop level. Because they travel at supersonic speed, there is no advance warning of their approach and the sudden eardrum-shattering explosion of noise in this tranquil setting splits more than just the air.

After the confluence of the east and west branches, the upper George is less like a river and more like one continuous lake, compartmentalized by a few con-strictions, which are the sites of shallow, wide boulder rapids that are easily negotiated. The most serious obstacle to travel is wind. The morning of our third day, a northwesterly breeze sprang up, which gradually increased to bothersome intensity. By noon we had reached a spot where the river narrows as it breaks through a large esker.

A brief reconnaissance revealed the presence of a large tent of a fly-in fishing camp in the bay beyond. A short discussion ensued—heads was for putting up our own tents, tails for using the existing structure. I lost the toss and soon a warming fire crackled in the stove and Jim was busy bug-proofing the big tent by closing off the holes in the fabric. We spent a most wonderful sunny after-noon and evening hiking along the esker and the low hills on both sides of the river. The highlight of the day was the discovery of four ancient teepee sites on the crest of the esker on the western side of the river, with the stones of the cen-tral fireplaces still easily recognizable. Throughout the night the large tent flapped noisily and the sound of waves rushing the shore continued. We were anxious to get away in the morning, yet undecided about the prudence of the undertaking. Finally, our minds were made up for us when a plane appeared on the horizon and deposited four fishermen from Schefferville. For the cost of the plane ride plus three hundred dollars per person, they had the use of the tent and a boat for the weekend. All of a sudden the wind wasn't so bad and we got the hell out of there before somebody asked for our contribution.

Progress against the 30–40 kilometre per hour headwind was slow. By the time we stopped for lunch on an island in Lac Lacasse we were wet and cold from the wind-borne spray. A huge fire set us right again, but once out into Resolution Lake the wind picked up even more and metre-high waves marched in columns at an awkward angles across the wide expanse. It was time to call it a day.

Much of the shoreline on this shallow lake is not particularly suited to camping, but with a bit of landscaping we did quite well. The evening was of rare quality and possessed of a paradoxical serenity despite the tumultuous waters and rush of the wind through the long, tortured tamaracks at the shore. The clouds that night were arranged like a thick-stranded fishnet through which the sun, now nearing the horizon, sent shafts of light radiating across the sky.

With conditions slightly improved the next morning, we pushed off, hoping to gain the north shore of the lake where a prominent esker runs eastward toward Lac Raude. By the time we reached the next headland just two kilometres away we were forced to shore once more. Sheer boredom soon had us roaming through the neighbourhood. In the process we climbed a small hill near the shore. It was devoid of trees and the ground cover included a variety of grass not native to the area. Strewn everywhere were caribou antlers. Boredom vanished instantly. There were at least three generations of occupation identifiable, the oldest consisting of several longhouses about three-and-a-half-by-six metres in size, with a fireplace at each end. Superimposed over one of the longhouses was the outline of a large teepee about five metres in diameter. The most recent remains were those of several smaller teepees of which fragments of tent poles were scattered about.

I was instantly reminded of Mina Hubbard's encounter with a group of Montagnais on this lake while on her journey from the Northwest River to the mouth of the George River in 1905. In her book, *A Woman's Way Through Unknown Labrador*,[2] she writes: "I went up for a brief look at the camp on the hill. The situation was beautiful and commanded a view from end to end of Resolution Lake, which extended about four miles both north and south of the point." On the map that accompanies the book she indicates the camp to be approximately midway between the southern shore and the northern extremity of the lake and names it Montagnais Point. Modern mapmakers have shifted the location to the north end of Resolution Lake, but there is little doubt in my mind the actual site is the one we stumbled upon.

Making their way to the height of land, Herb and Jim Greenacre (with his yellow canoe, to the right in the distance) used a prominent esker to traverse the four kilometres between the George River and Lac Raude.

Sometime during the afternoon, the winds moderated and we proceeded to a little bay on the northeastern shore of Resolution Lake. Here we left the George River and struck out toward Lac Raude some four kilometres to the east, using a prominent esker as our portage trail. In the evening we camped at the foot of the esker close to the shore of the lake. While Jim was busy preparing supper— he seemed to get stuck with the task with great regularity—I hiked up a nearby range of hills to survey our kingdom of the day. Below me the esker, like a giant snake, wound its way westward and disappeared in the setting sun. The shimmering waters of Resolution Lake were almost hidden by the many headlands and islands that dot its surface. To the northeast lay a range of high hills, their bare flanks gilded by the magical evening light. Leading to them and barely discernible in the dusky lowland was a string of convoluted lakes—our trail for the next day. Lac Raude, through some interspersed and nameless lakes, drains into White Gull Lake, and this the route we followed.

Unlike the previous year on my journey to the Notakwanon, this time through the lake was dead calm and every cloud was mirrored in its clear waters. Just a few kilometres north of where we entered White Gull Lake, another river enters from the east in a wide and rocky stream bed. Alternately wading and paddling we ascended it until we reached the base of the hills I had observed the previous evening, and then made camp despite Jim's assurances that he wasn't the least bit tired. Nevertheless, the light was right and the hills were beckoning.

Over the years, exploring the surroundings on foot has become an even more important component of wilderness travel to me, such that now I find it quite absurd to rush through terrain, specially selected after months of pouring over maps, without pausing to look at it. With the tents set up I struck out alone at first, but it was plain that Jim, who had stayed behind to cook supper once again, had enough of the unequal division of labour, for shortly he joined me in my meanderings over high ground.

Jim and Herb had travelled before and, although they had their differences (Jim was nine years older), they were both hardy first immigrants who loved making their self-powered way into their chosen land. They had their routines—Jim cooked and Herb hiked.

The next day a lengthy portage into Lac Rochereau was briefly interrupted by a feeble attempt at fishing in the rapids. After losing a lure and getting the attention of clouds of blackflies—the only time on this trip that insects appeared in numbers—we carried on, driven by a strong tailwind, which persisted until we entered Lac Chapiteau several hours later. After waiting out a brief but heavy downpour the tents were set up, the cravings of the belly satisfied and it was time to watch the magic of the evening light. All around us there was a rugged harshness to the surroundings, a feeling of remoteness emphasized by banks of clouds among the hills.

To get to the eastern extremity of Lac Chapiteau took most of the next morning. Up to now we again followed Cabot's sketch of what he believed to be the route which the Montagnais used to travel from Resolution Lake to trade at the Hudson's Bay post in Davis Inlet. From the east end of Lac Chapiteau the Indian route goes in a northeasterly direction through several lakes to the headwaters of the Notakwanon River. To reach the Ugjoktok watershed, we headed off in a southwesterly direction. Two portages brought us into Labrador waters. Our last portage of the day, while not particularly long compared to some that followed, is not fondly remembered. It traversed a high ridge and ended in quaking bog on the edge of a small stream too shallow to navigate. It was getting late, but there wasn't a campsite anywhere, just bog and Precambrian rubble. Finally, with daylight failing, we settled for a nasty sleep on a bit of sloping ground next to the debris of a winter hunting camp.

The region east of the height of land is dominated by a range of hills with an elevation in excess of seven hundred metres. An ancient stream bed demarcated by an esker, follows the glacier-worn breach through the hills. The whole area is a mosaic of ice-scoured bedrock and sand and gravel beds. In the morning sun it seemed all so exquisitely beautiful I felt compelled to announce to my companion that it was my intention to stop paddling and start hiking the moment we reached the base of the highest elevation. There wasn't any discussion about it, but Jim clearly had other priorities, for he kept paddling with great determination past several suggested campsites.

Since I stopped a number of times to capture the visual highlights on film, he was always ahead of me and it took some determined paddling to catch up to him. It was only much later that I understood the reason for his action. Several years earlier Jim had taken a trip down the Thelon River to Baker Lake. After a few days he became alarmed about the slow pace of the trip and repeatedly expressed his concern to the trip leader, who told him not to worry. As it turned out, the party had to be picked up far short of their intended destination.[3] The experience left its mark on Jim and it explained why he asked me every day, "How far are we going today?" to which my stock answer was, "I don't know, we'll find out, but don't worry, we'll finish on time." In light of his experience that wasn't very reassuring.

During this needless acceleration of our pace on the Ugjoktok trip, we passed Border Beacon, once an extensive DEW line[4] installation. Associated with it is a long runway and an automated weather station, which are still maintained. The buildings are extensively vandalized, presumably by the Natives who hunt and trap in the region in the winter, for we came across a campsite that contained not only the usual remains such as pots, pans and clothing but items from the station as well. We stopped for the day at the outflow of the last of the lakes where the south and west branches of the Ugjoktok combine to begin the descent to the coast in earnest. As the day progressed, a strong wind made paddling hard work and I was well-worn when we finished setting up camp.

When a brief shower interrupted proceedings, I retreated into the vestibule of my tent, sat down, and was instantly asleep. I woke with a start a short time later, the skies had cleared and Jim was busy around the campfire. After supper I went for a short stroll to high ground, none too pleased to have missed out on a nice day of hiking earlier on. If only I had been by myself.

Just a kilometre below the campsite the Ugjoktok drops into a narrow gorge in a spectacular 25-metre waterfall. About a third of the way down the tumbling waters are hurtled skyward in a giant rooster tail as they hit a rock ledge. The portage to the bottom of the gorge is short, but precariously steep. While the Labrador highlands, corrugated and largely barren, extend eastward at undiminished altitude, the river drops two hundred and twenty metres in the next thirty-five kilometres in a series of strong cataracts, into a narrow glacial valley. Early on we tried to run a deceptively benign-looking rapid and both nearly came to grief. It was a useful lesson that made the decision to portage later on much easier.

After an uncertain beginning the clouds lifted, and for the next two days the sun glorified the rugged landscape. It would be untrue to say we were constantly enraptured by the scenery, grand though it was, for a considerable amount of time was spent trudging up hill and down dale past impassable sections of river. On the third day, and halfway through yet another long portage, it started to rain. Camp that evening was set up on two huge flat-topped boulders above a little bay, the only half-decent spot around. Immediately to the north and below our campsite the river issued forth in wild confusion through a narrow gap in the rock face, slowed momentarily as it skirted the bay and dropped over a ledge at the start of yet another rapid. The next morning we returned to high ground in mist and drizzle to retrieve our boats and had a view of the other face of Labrador—dreary, desolate and fog-shrouded.

Back at the river we had barely started to paddle when we were faced with the next portage. It was no more than a hundred metres, but well-defended against trespassers. Deadfalls and driftwood were piled high among the boulders and intertwined throughout was a thriving stand of alders and willows. I don't know whether it was the prospect of what lay ahead or just Jim's statistical mind keeping track of everything, but as soon as he came ashore he strode purposefully up to me. With the index finger of his right hand jabbing repeatedly at his watch, he explained that it had taken him exactly three minutes of paddling to get here, "Three minutes!" I've always admired the orderly and reasoned way in which Jim did everything, but I didn't know whether to accept blame for the obstructions the river had presented that day, so I replied, "I think you beat me by a second."

As if to respond to Jim's concern, the river offered no further obstacles past this portage. For several kilometres it raced along over gravel beds, past small islands and then stopped altogether. For thirty-five kilometres the river is transformed into a narrow lake with no perceptible current. Towering to a height of two hundred metres above the valley floor on either side of the river-lake are dark grey, near vertical walls of Precambrian rock. It was a most impressive sight on this drizzly day; mist frequently obscured the higher elevations, softened the contrast and heightened the feeling of isolation. At supper time we were camped at the midpoint of this quiet stretch on a spit of gravel amid the remnants of a much older camp. By now it was clear that Jim thought his partner was much too sanguine about making headway, another Hubbard in the making perhaps, and felt compelled to save this poor fellow from himself by setting the proper example. My assessment was that Jim felt insecure and just wanted to get out, the sooner the better.

The next day the sun reasserted itself and I spent all morning alternately taking pictures and then chasing Jim who kept at the paddling without pause. At
lunchtime we had reached the first rapid, which marked the end of the flat section. From this point onward the valley gradually widened and the vertical rock
walls were replaced by sloping boulder-strewn eskers. For the next twenty kilometres the river rushed through a series of rapids. Periodically the boulder
gardens were interrupted by rock outcroppings that give rise to scenic falls and
ledges. Many of these obstructions were not negotiable and much more time was
spent portaging than paddling.

Early in this stretch, Jim had developed a limp that got progressively worse.
At first he brushed it off as nothing to worry about, but one evening, after a particularly onerous day, he asked me what I thought the cost of a helicopter
evacuation would be. Since we had no way to make contact with the outside
world, the implication was that I would finish the trip alone and arrange for a
pickup, while Jim would remain at the same place. Following this discussion I
retired to my tent and spent a restless night worrying how to divide our food supply. Clearly he would have to retain more than half because of possible delays in
getting him out. However, the next morning Jim felt he was well enough to continue, provided I carried his canoe on portages the rest of the way.

Starting about halfway down this turbulent section of river, and for many kilometres beyond, a forest fire had devastated the countryside. The conflagration had
burned away all organic material save the skinny skeletons of trees. Except for the
scattered invasion of alders and the odd pocket of spruce, which had somehow survived, the countryside was a desolate grey wasteland. On the morning of our third
day of tribulation in this section, Jim took off first and I saw him make a spirited
descent of yet another rapid. I thought he did a fine job of it, but when I joined him
at the bottom he made it plain by mutterings and gesticulation that he was not pleased
with the amount of water in his boat nor the moisture content of his clothing.

Once again Jim's wrath paid off, for just around the next bend the river's pace
slowed and we floated out into a wide valley. In the next three hours we covered
a greater distance than in the preceding three days. The gravelly river bottom
flashed by at ten kilometres an hour, a balmy breeze banished the bugs and for
the first time on the trip I took off my shirt and soaked up the sun. About ten
kilometres above the confluence with the Harp River we left the burned shores
behind. Here the Ugjoktok runs swiftly around islands and gravel bars. The left
shoreline is demarcated by low cutbanks. The flat lichen-covered flood plain
beyond offers ideal campsites. Running parallel to the right shore are massive
boulder eskers that rise to a height of fifty metres or more. The southern horizon
is dominated by the rugged peaks that ring Harp Lake.

For a long time we just floated along and enjoyed the tranquil beauty all
around. It was too good to last. An immense up-welling of dark clouds behind

us looked ever more threatening. Just as we reached the mouth of the Harp River, a cold blast of air blew in from the west and sent the temperature plummeting. The wind increased to gale force and as we scrambled to shore the heavens opened up. There was no time to put on rain gear and so we just stood there getting drenched. Suddenly Jim keeled over and fell flat on his face in a dead faint. He was only out for a few seconds and seemed alright afterwards, but I was gravely worried. He had seemed wobbly for the last few days and fell several times for no apparent reason. I put it down to fatigue because the going was hard and Jim, at sixty-four, was no youngster. It had been my intention to track up the Harp River and spend a few days exploring Harp Lake, but now it seemed best to get out to the coast as quickly as possible.

Below the Harp River the mountains give way to a lowland plain of sand and gravel into which the river has carved a much more tranquil course. In a few places the ancient bedrock protrudes and here the old boisterousness returns. One carries around these obstructions. I was usually in the lead because Jim had shown a remarkable propensity to take off in the wrong direction. However, at the head of the first portage below the entrance of the Harp River, I was detained for a few minutes and, ever anxious to get going, Jim went ahead alone with the first load. When I reached the put-in point downstream, less than a kilometre away, there was no sign of Jim or his pack. When I came back with the second load and there was still no sign of him I started to get very anxious. It was rough country, and I knew full well that one can slip and fall, break a leg or, in Jim's case, get disoriented and wander off to who knows where.

I started to look up and down the shore, then back and forth in a rough grid, all the while hollering and listening. It's amazing what an avalanche of thoughts race through one's mind: if I don't find him soon, what's the best way to proceed? Keep looking for a day or two, hurry to Hopedale and return with a search party? What will I tell his wife or the RCMP?

After a frantic hour of searching I ended up back at the starting point, and there was Jim. From opening invective to my last greeting breath, no one would have suspected that I was glad to see him. Of course, he vigourously denied that he was ever lost. How could he be? he protested, with the river right there!

A day's journey from the sea the Ugjoktok divides into two channels, which reach the ocean in separate deep bays some thirteen kilometres apart. Parks Canada's Wild Rivers Survey[5] recommends the southern arm to the coast as the better option, but since the northern route provides a more sheltered passage to Hopedale, our finishing point, we chose the latter. At breakfast of our last day on the river, it started to rain and never let up for twenty-four hours. With only a minor rapid along the way, it was a dreary paddle. By mid-afternoon we had reached the last obstacle—a steep, narrow gorge and waterfall followed by a long rapid that dissipates its force into Adlatok Bay. Jim's condition had deteriorated to the point that he was now having difficulty just walking unencumbered over rough ground, and so it took quite a while to get all the gear to the put-in point below the falls. With all the gear, except my boat, at the water's edge, I went back to the high ground for a quick assessment of the rapids ahead. My last words to Jim before I went back for my boat were, "When you get to the first bend, stay right, the left looks very nasty. But *wait for me* before you start."

Not unexpectedly, when I returned Jim was gone. This was a bit of rough water and it took me two tries to get out of the eddy. As I cautiously approached the bend in the river and looked at the scene, my first thought was that if Jim had taken my advice there was no way he'd have made it through without upset. Working my way left around the corner, I was totally relieved to see Jim safely ashore bailing large quantities of water from his boat back into the river. He was obviously shaken by the wild ride but keen to continue. Not more than 50 metres from tidewater, Jim became trapped in a hole. I watched helplessly as his canoe was jostled about, convinced that eventually man, gear and conveyance would float out separately into the briny bay, but somehow (with great skill, he would insist) he managed to stay upright, and after an agonizing minute or so, he shot out sideways and thus escaped, but there was little room to differentiate the water-level inside and outside of the boat.

By now it was seven o'clock and we were dripping wet and cold. Swallowing our pride, we knocked at the door of the private fishing camp conveniently located right at the mouth of the river and asked for asylum. The sole occupants of Adlatok Camp, owned by a group of businessmen from the States, were the cook and a fishing guide. They took us in but didn't seem particularly excited about our arrival, asked no questions, and soon returned to their card game. We had brought with us a great amount of moisture that gradually migrated across the floor and under where our stoic hosts sat. The fellows, to their credit, said nothing, but I am sure they were not pleased. We gave them $50 to show our gratitude, which they accepted without a word, and very early the next morning we left with the outgoing tide.

The paddle to Hopedale, an Inuit community of about 500 inhabitants some 50 kilometres away, was the easiest of the whole trip—blue sky and calm sea all the way. Despite Jim's concern about our slow progress, we ended the trip a full week ahead of schedule. All things considered we could easily have accommodated a side trip into Harp Lake. Petty sniping between travelling companions aside, we were instantly the centre of attention of a crowd of children as we pulled up to the town wharf. In the distance I heard someone ask, "Who are these people?" and someone answer, "Just two old men."

The previous year in Davis Inlet, Horace Goudie had suggested that the best place to stay in Hopedale was Garfield Flowers' Bed and Breakfast. Garfield is a descendant of one of the early settler on the Labrador coast and mayor of the

The Labrador coastal supply vessel, *Taverner*, stopped at Hopedale wharf.

little, largely Inuit community. Within half an hour, our host ushered us into the house and settled us into the kitchen where Mrs. Flowers produced a freshly baked loaf of bread and a plate of smoked salmon. I had always considered Jim a very moderate eater, but there was something about the fragrance of the bread and the flavour of the fish that changed the man, because before long the salmon was gone and the bread was begging for mercy.

Later on a large number of people materialized out of the woodwork and so did bottles of beer and rum of exotic origin. Farley Mowat would have loved it. It was rather late when we went to bed and I had the distinct impression Jim was feeling much better already. The evening wasn't all gluttony and the telling of tall tales; there was talk of winter-hunting trips into the interior, about the state of the fisheries and many other topics that gave a man "from away" insight into the local scene. I arranged with Garfield to leave my boat with him, because my next target, the Fraser River north of Nain, was already on my calendar. By a stroke of good luck, the next day the *Taverner* called in on return from her first trip of the season to Nain, and carried us south to Goose Bay.[6]

SIX

Clearwater Winter, 1987

For many canoeists winter is a period of relative dormancy, a time spent planning and organizing the next foray into the unknown. Some wait impatiently for the first chance to launch their boats into the spring freshet, but there are others who look forward with equal fervour to the coming of winter. They see the blanket of snow and ice as access to the most remote places. One of these people is Craig Macdonald. A long-time member of the Wilderness Canoe Association, he is largely responsible for introducing traditional Native ways of winter travel to a wide audience. For the converted, traditional "hot camping" is the way of gospel comfort, because *home* at the end of the travelling day is a heated cotton tent.[1]

Shortly after New Year of '87, I received a call from Craig to ask if I would be interested in joining a trip into northern Quebec. He knew the answer of course; the difficulty was getting away during the academic year. By scheduling the trip to coincide with reading week the problem was solved. For me, the time leading up to our departure was unusually stress free, since preparations were limited to my personal gear. Craig, who supplied all the equipment, transportation, accommodation and arranged the air charter, had a different story to tell. His wife Doris cooked all the dinners and froze them in individual servings, and looked after lunches and breakfasts as well.

Beside myself, Craig had invited Tony Bird and Bill King, both experienced winter travellers, but none of us had ever been this far north in the winter before. As part of our pre-trip assignment Craig suggested we read *Needle to the North* by Arthur Twomey. It is an account of the 1938 Carnegie Museum of Pittsburgh expedition to the Seal Lakes of northern Quebec and the Belcher Islands in Hudson

Bay. Part of the expedition's route into the interior was from Richmond Gulf to Clearwater Lake in the winter of '38, and was made with the assistance of local Natives using traditional methods of travel. I suspect it provided the inspiration for Craig to attempt a trip in the opposite direction, albeit slightly farther north and at the northern limit of trees, an essential resource to provide tent poles and firewood. We didn't know it at the time, but I have since acquired a copy of the map made by George Atkinson II, which shows the Native summer route he used in 1819 to reach the Upper Seal Lakes. It was, with one minor deviation, identical to our winter route of 1987.

The day of our departure from Craig's home in Dorset had a rare quality. Morning mists partially obscured the Haliburton County landscape, the rose-coloured rays of the early sun created long soft shadows and added a mystical element to the scene, but for some it was not a time for contemplation. At Craig's driveway the focus was on loading a mountain of gear into the back of his cavernous Suburban and tying two sleds on the roof. Before long we were on our way. The mild day became even milder as we drove northwards, the sun disappeared, and by the time we stopped for the night in Amos, north of Val-d'Or, it was raining. This unexpected turn was cause for some anxiety because the one thing we were not prepared for was wet weather.

It rained most of the night, but, by the time we reached the bridge over the Rupert River the next day and stopped to take a look at the awesome rapids upstream, the temperature was thirty below. That evening the concern wasn't about rain. A full-blown blizzard was rattling Auberge Radisson, our abode for the night, and the radio airwaves were carrying a mantra of severe weather warnings with wind chills of minus 85 degrees. In the short time it took Craig to go out and plug in the block heater of the van, he froze one of his ears.

When we assembled in the heated airport hangar in Radisson[2] the next morning, sombre faces betrayed an air of apprehension. The sensible thing to do was wait for the storm to subside, but we all had a tight deadline and so the choice was to go now or abandon the trip altogether. David Peace, the pilot, was willing to give it a try and within an hour we were on our way north.

From the air, the dark boreal forest and small frozen lakes stretched endlessly, the latter frequently populated by skeins of caribou. Once past the Great Whale River great domes of wind-scoured bedrock became more prominent and trees were restricted to the sheltered lowlands. After what seemed a very long time, the high hills of the western shore of Clearwater Lake came into view. The surface of the lake was hidden under a cloud of swirling snow. The pilot, worrying about the presence of large sastrugi, or snow ridges, hidden beneath the ground drifts on the open lake, headed for the long, narrow arm of the lake, which we planned to follow on our westerly course to the Hudson Bay coast. Even here the surface had the texture of a giant washboard and the landing was correspondingly rough.

Unloading at Clearwater Lake. Temperatures were so low that the pilot was paranoid about shutting the engine down for fear that the oil would turn to sludge again and he would never get it restarted.

Dave's only concern at this point was to get the hell out of there before the engine cooled too much in –36° F temperatures with 60 kph winds. While we tossed all our gear out of the old Otter, Dave quickly pumped some fuel from a 45-gallon drum into the plane's fuel tank, restarted the plane (to his great relief!) and ten minutes later we were alone.

Meantime, the sun appeared out of the mists and emphasized the brilliant whiteness of the land. Our highway for the next few days was a glacier-carved trough extending more than 35 kilometres from the western shore of Clearwater Lake back toward Richmond Gulf. The shore of bedrock here and there supports a smattering of small trees that stood out darkly against the immense expanse of white but, with luck, these would be sufficient to make a frame each night for our tent and to serve as fuel wood to keep us warm. The bracing gale was all we needed to spur us on to action.

Our means of transportation for our food and gear were two sleds and one toboggan. This meant that one man's job was to break trail and find the best route while the others followed in order of first sled, then the toboggan and finally the second sled. By constantly rotating positions we could recover somewhat from the onerous job of pulling the sleds. None of us had ever been out in conditions as severe as those we were facing on this journey. The main problem was that the low temperature and consequent snow-crystal conditions made pulling the sleds an exhausting enterprise. While they only carried about eighty kilograms, we could get them to start moving only with the utmost exertion and would be unable to continue for more than 50 or at most 100 metres without stopping and changing positions. Every sastrugi along the way was an insurmountable obstruction that required a detour and further slowed forward progress. After four hours of heavy hauling we stopped for the day in a sheltered bay, having covered no more than three kilometres.

Setting up camp in the evening with this travel method takes between two and three hours. Each individual is assigned to specific tasks—the cutting of tent poles, sill logs and brush for the tent floor, procurement of firewood and kindling, setting up the tent and stove, cutting a hole in the ice to get water and finally working to thaw and heat a pre-cooked meal. It's a period of frantic activity at the end of an usually long and tiring day. Once all the chores are done everyone takes refuge inside the comfortable tent, basking in the stove's radiant heat, drinking in the odour of food bubbling in the pots. And the collective feeling of contentment is palpable. At bedtime all the items of clothing and boot liners that need drying are hung up on the ridge lines. Craig insists on keeping the stove going all the time; whoever wakes during the night adds a few sticks to the box as needed and thus ensures everything is dry by morning.

Our first evening wasn't quite as comfortable as described above. The main problem was the lack of good firewood. It took hours for the blocks of frozen suppers to lose their rigid form. (In future we would chop them up into little pieces to speed the thawing process.) The much more serious concern was the storm outside and the slow and sandpapery quality of the snow over which we had to haul our sleds. At the rate of advance we managed the first day, it looked as though we wouldn't get even halfway to our destination before running out of food—a sobering thought.

The morning dawned bitterly cold and the west wind blew with unabated vigour. A pale sun was partly obscured by ice crystals, which continued to fall throughout the day. At lunch time we huddled in the shelter of a tarp held by the wind against a few sticks. The content of Craig's insulated gallon jug, filled that morning, was frozen solid and so were the sandwiches and my camera. Bill was shaking with hypothermia within a few minutes and we wasted no time getting back into harness. I shall always remember this as the coldest lunch break ever.

During the day we were constantly watching each other for signs of frostbite as we continued along our wind tunnel at a pitifully slow pace. Late in the afternoon Craig, who had a wonderful eye for such things, spied a suitable clump of trees in another sheltered cove and here we settled for the night. Despite the fact we had only covered six hard-won kilometres, the mood was upbeat. This time we had the benefit of dry standing deadwood to feed the stove, the chopped up blocks of frozen dinners were piping hot by eight o'clock and we even found time for a short stroll to look at what Craig called the "barbaric" landscape.

By the end of the third day we had left the narrow Clearwater Lake channel behind and were now progressing through a number of small lakes. The wind had moderated somewhat, but the air continued cold and filled with ice crystals. We now had to traverse the low hills that separated these lakes, an exercise that required our combined pulling power to get the sleds to the top of each rise. The last of these traverses brought us to the headwater lake of the small stream that we planned to follow to the Caribou River and thence to Richmond Gulf.

Top: The tent, home sweet home to the crew in a frosty northern Quebec landscape. *Bottom:* The Richmond Gulf winter crew, *left to right:* Craig Macdonald, Bill King, Herb Pohl and Tony Bird.

The panoramic view from the top of the last rise revealed the mere hint of a valley running in an easterly direction. Compared to the austere face of the land farther east the contours were now softer and trees, while still widely separated, were much more prevalent. Most appreciated of all was that for the first time our sleds moved a little easier—at least we didn't have to pull them while going downhill. Obviously we were benefiting from a subtle change in the texture of the snow, which was also reflected in an increase in the daily distance covered.

Because we had to make up distance lost at the start of the trip, our travelling days were long and our camp chores usually finished under a big moon bright enough to create sharp shadows. One evening in particular stands out in my memory. We all went out after supper for a short stroll under a canopy of stars and a full moon that illuminated and transformed the surroundings into a fairyland. It was probably the coldest night of the trip (we had no thermometer with us, but I am sure it was well below –40°). In the absence of exertion, one quickly felt the icy chill creep into the bones and so we soon turned back toward the tent, a warm comfortable refuge.

Our nameless stream started a hesitant descent through a poorly defined valley in discrete steps. Low ledges soon gave way to waterfalls of ever increasing height and steep rapids—all of it totally encased in ice. I always felt a bit uneasy travelling down these rapids, because the sound of turbulence underfoot was at times quite audible. The thought that anyone breaking through the ice would be instantly swept under concentrated the mind and lightened the step.

For the last ten kilometres above the confluence with the Caribou River, high hills dominated the landscape. Several times it required team effort to lower the sleds past falls. At the bottom of one of them, we set up our last camp on the river at an uncharacteristically early hour. A short climb to the nearest lookout revealed an exquisite panorama. The long shadows of the late sun dramatized the wind-carved snow. Remnants of raised beaches could be seen high up on the hillsides to the north. Due west and far below stretched a wide glacier-worn valley through which the Caribou River had carved a deep, meandering course across deposits of sand and gravel.

The snow in the recessed riverbed of the Caribou was deep and soft. The job of the trail breaker, which had been by far the easiest at the beginning of the trip, was now the most onerous. There was not a breath of wind, and concern about frostbite was replaced by complaints about overheating. Our last camp on the river was just a short distance from the shore of Richmond Gulf. Despite the awesome landscape and a breathtaking display of northern lights that evening, the focus of our discussion in the tent was on how to proceed from here on.

Our target was the village of Umiujaq. Just newly established by Inuit expatriates from Great Whale River, it was not yet shown on any map. All we knew was that it was located on the shores of Hudson Bay and immediately west of Richmond Gulf.

The problem was that the western shore of the Gulf is 40 kilometres long and, with the exception of three widely separated gaps, is a near vertical rock face 400 metres high. There are no trees on the western shore of the Gulf large enough to serve as tent poles and the Hudson Bay coast in this region is altogether devoid of trees. The best estimate was that it would take us three days to reach the village. Two nights without shelter isn't a problem in good weather, but the region is known for nasty storms that could make survival an issue.

We were not prepared for this problem because Craig, in conversation with Noah Inukpuk, the mayor of Umiujaq, had been assured that we would meet people camped near the mouth of the Caribou River. All we came across were the old and indistinct traces of a snowmobile track. Later on, and quite by accident, I stumbled on a *tupek*,[3] completely buried under snow, the inside quite cosy and habitable. Presumably it was the abode of the people we expected to meet, but they must have left some time ago. For us, time was now an important element, not just because we were short of food, but we wanted to avoid the cost and ignominy of a search party looking for us if we were unduly delayed. And so Craig decided we should send out a search party of our own based on the assumption that somewhere in the neighbourhood there had to be tracks that could be followed to Umiujaq.

Early the next morning Craig and Tony set off with the toboggan that carried only the most basic outfit—tarp, sleeping bags and foam pads, axe, saw, kettle, thermos and a minimum of food. By travelling fast and light the hope was to cover more than twice the distance per day than we could cover with all our gear and thus reach our destination as quickly as possible. They could then secure someone to collect us by snowmobile. Fortunately, the fine weather of the last week continued. For a short while Bill and I watched our companions make their way towards the mouth of the river and turn north into the wide expanse of Richmond Gulf. They were heading into a long and exhausting day and an uncomfortable night. Bill and I, by contrast, faced a day of leisure and the comfort of a less-crowded tent. Because leisure quickly leads to boredom we soon set off toward the high hills behind our camp. They offered a marvellous view back upriver as well as the cliffs beyond the western shore of Richmond Gulf. Of our travelling companions there was no sign on the vast expanse of ice.

Around noon the following day the sound of motors caught our attention. Soon two snowmobiles came into view. Their Inuit occupants had been on their way to the mouth of the Caribou River when they encountered Craig and Tony. They informed us that they would spend the afternoon fishing and would pick us up later and take us to Umiujaq. When the time came we threw all our gear onto the *komatiq*, I took my seat behind the driver, Bill hopped on the *komatiq* and off we went. It was my first ride on a snowmobile and the experience soon convinced me that this type of locomotion was not for me.

The corrugated hard-packed snow made for a brain-rattling ride that took us to the north end of the Gulf. Here, the remains of glacial deposits have created a more gradual slope towards the west such that snowmobiles can just make it to the top. The descent to Hudson Bay was a bit nerve-wracking for Bill, I suspect. Several times the *komatiq* raced alongside the snowmobile, each time the driver would allow the towing rope to run under the runners of the komatiq to slow it down, all this at the very edge of a steep rock face.

In Umiujaq, Mayor Noah Inukpuk showed the way to our accommodation, a large three-bedroom trailer; it had every conceivable amenity, even fully stocked kitchen cupboards. It was now late afternoon and there was no sign of our companions. We hadn't seen them anywhere along the way and I was worried they would be left out for another night without food or water, but Noah assured me they were not forgotten and at dusk they arrived at the doorstep. Our host, the mayor, proved to be a very gracious individual. The next day he drove us all around town, explained the history and future plans of the community that was populated by people who wanted to get back to a more traditional way of life. Because there was no flight out, we spent the next day following our varied interests, which for me was a long hike to the edge of the escarpment overlooking Richmond Gulf. I arrived back at the trailer just as the sun disappeared behind one of the Nastapoca Islands off the Hudson Bay coast.

The next evening I found David Peace, our pilot, at the bar in Auberge Radisson busy chatting up a very pretty barmaid. "Just trying not to lose the touch," said the very married fellow, perhaps a touch defensively. "I wasn't sure I'd ever see you again, I thought it was fifty-fifty" he added.[4]

SEVEN

Labrador's Fraser River, 1987[1]

I was back in Garfield Flowers' kitchen, finishing off the last morsels of a more than ample breakfast when my host announced the *Taverner* would be in shortly after lunch. Two summers previous, I had left my boat at Garfield's B&B, planning to pick it up on my way north from Goose Bay to Nain with the coastal supply ship to start a trip to the interior. As the summer approached, it became clear that I would have only three weeks at my disposal. And so, to make the most of it, I arranged for Garfield to forward my canoe to Nain with the first ship going north. This would allow me to fly directly to Nain and retrieve the boat there, a saving of three valuable days, compared to the longer journey from Goose Bay by ship.

The plan was to do a circle route starting in Nain, the most northerly settlement in Labrador. I was going follow the Fraser River upstream to the end of navigable water and then head south to the Kogaluk River watershed, follow the latter to the coast and return to Nain. I arrived at Goose Bay on July 9th at 5:00 a.m. after an overnight flight from Toronto and took the first plane north, a Labrador Air Twin Otter. These planes touch down at all the settlements along the coast. For at least six months of the year, while the sea ice has a firm grip on the shore, these hardy Canadian-made planes are the lifeline to the outside world for people across the North. This one, as usual, was loaded to capacity and a fierce wind made each landing and takeoff an adventure. When we landed at Hopedale, I scanned the scene outside, seeing just the usual activities associated with people getting on and off. And then came a slow recognition—the fellow refuelling the plane looked familiar. It was Garfield Flowers! I quickly rushed out to say hello and asked, "Did you send my boat to Nain?"

He replied, "No. We haven't had a ship in yet. But the *Taverner* is on its way."

The air crew was not amused when I asked them to dig out my gear from the jumble of luggage and freight in the rear of the plane, but with my boat still in Hopedale, there was no point in my going on to Nain and I told them as much. They complied, and I spent the rest of the day getting reacquainted with my canoe by paddling out to one of the offshore islands. Almost immediately I stumbled on a bit of local history, a lichen encrusted and deeply embedded in a ring of stones high above the present shore, testimony to its antiquity.

This year the ice had retained its grip on northern shores longer than usual and the first ship of the season was just now making its way north. Of the two ships that make regular runs from Lewisport in Newfoundland to Nain, the *Taverner*,[2] at six-hundred tons displacement, is much the smaller of the two and a bit long in the tooth. And now that my canoe was here, I was obliged to try to book passage on her for both of us.

There was an uneasy moment when the ship docked and the purser told me, "I don't know whether you should come on board, there is a lot of ice ahead and we don't know if we will be able to make it to Nain. Better go and see the captain."

Well—Captain French *was* agreeable and shortly I was exchanging gossip with a group of old friends and fellow members of the Wilderness Canoe Association, who had boarded the boat in Goose Bay and were on their way to the Torngat Mountains and the Koroc River, some four hundred kilometres north of Nain.

After a slow run to Davis Inlet in loose pack ice, we anchored for the night near one of the many islands that guard the mainland's eastern flank. With the first light of day we were on the move again, carefully manoeuvring among the ice floes at half speed or less. As time went on the sea became more and more congested and

The coastal supply ship *Taverner* is stopped by ice. Herb and members of another Wilderness Canoe Association trip opt to be lowered into the ocean from the ship about 18 kilometres east of Voisey's Bay.

the thumping noise of ice brushing against the hull came at more frequent intervals. Finally came the inevitable message: "The captain wants to see you."

On the bridge Captain French shook his head: "I am sorry, that's as far as I can go." The other group and I had discussed the possibility of this happening and now, having had the conversation about alternative plans, asked to be put over the side to make our way north under our own power. We were still more than 60 kilometres from Nain and about half that distance from the mainland, but we were confident that we could work our way to a nearby group of islands and there decide on the best way to proceed. The next hour was one of frantic activity for us and of more than passing interest for the rest of the passengers and crew. Cameras got a workout as the canoes were lifted out of the hold, loaded and hoisted over the side. Finally we were all in the water, the captain bid us goodbye with three blasts of the ship's whistle, the propellers started to churn and, ever so slowly, the *Taverner* turned and moved away.

A steady breeze from the northeast and the outgoing tide combined to confound progress through the tightly packed ice. It took several hours of pushing, shoving and prying to create tiny leads, which quickly closed up again. I was quite content and grateful to bring up the rear and follow in the openings created by the other boats. Eventually we reached open water in the lee of the nearest island and headed for the highest elevation to survey the scene. There was a curtain of pack ice to the east of the outer islands, but to the west, towards Voisey's Bay and the mainland, the path was relatively clear. For me it was time to say our goodbyes, but these were not without consequences. As we got ready to paddle, Dick Irwin, a member of the group, handed me his movie camera and asked me to film the group as they moved away. I was holding my map case at the time and put it down to accommodate the request. Several hours later I realized that the maps were still on the island. In the meantime, the tide was moving in and with it the pack ice. I didn't want to waste another half day to go back and, since I felt confident I'd find my way without maps, I carried on.

I was headed for the inside passage and the mouth of the Fraser River, some ninety kilometres away. It was a glorious sunny day but I quickly tired—evidence that pencil pushing and shuffling paper is not an adequate conditioning program for wilderness trips—so I stopped on Kiuvik Island for an early camp. The next morning started out well enough, but as the day progressed the landscape became obscured by fog and drizzle and a raw wind made things uncomfortable. Several times I went ashore and lit a quick fire to warm the shivering bones. At day's end I put up the tent at a spot where Ken Ellison and I had stopped for lunch five years earlier. Back then, glorious sunshine had etched the landscape in sharp relief; now, the world was small and grey and out of focus. Except for the muffled sounds of the shifting sea ice, silence blanketed this forlorn place and the cold fire provided no solace.

Ice, masses of ice en route to Nain and the mouth of the Fraser River.

The following afternoon the sun emerged for a brief hour. I was in Nain Bay and heading west, and for the first time I could see the tremendous cleft in the Precambrian rock that is the valley of the Fraser. Ten years earlier when I first came across Hesketh Prichard's account of his 1910 journey from Nain to the George River, a book called, *Through Trackless Labrador*, I was intrigued to hear how at that time the Labrador peninsula was still largely *terra incognita* and that Prichard had proceeded up the Fraser in spite of advice from the Inuit that the valley was too congested with rocks and alders to be a suitable route. I liked Prichard's independent and adventuring spirit, but what attracted my attention even more were the photographs of the Fraser Valley showing bare rock walls rising to impressive height on either side of the river. That was a sight I had to see with my own eyes I decided. It was well worth the long wait to see it in the flesh.

Nain Bay, as I found it on this occasion, was a tranquil place. Around me everywhere was evidence of the tremendous forces that ground and polished the steel-grey rock faces during the last ice age. The valley of the Fraser, carved out at that time, runs like a deep scar almost perfectly straight from west to east. Rock walls rise on both sides to a height of 600 metres with nary a gap to allow egress to the barren highland. The valley becomes a troublesome wind tunnel even in moderate winds, as I was to find out rather quickly. By evening the whitecaps were in full bloom, whipped by a northeasterly wind, a sure sign of bad weather in these parts, and my tent was safely tucked in among a stand of small tamarack. At four o'clock in the morning the rain came in gusty squalls and I was desperately trying to find an excuse to stay put, but the tide was coming in and it was time to move.

The long and narrow bays, which are so common in northern Labrador, give rise to strong tidal currents and one is well-advised to take advantage of them.

Before dissipating into Nain Bay, the Fraser River flows through a series of small intertidal lakes. Shortly after noon all but one of them were behind me and I headed for shelter. The wind had gradually intensified and the constant downpour had spawned numerous transient streams that plunged over the mist-shrouded precipices in wind-blown streamers to the valley floor. The rushing sound of wind and falling water had an unsettling effect, which was accentuated by the presence of many mutilated trees testifying to the force of past storms. It made for a restless night.

The next day, I entered the last of the lakes after a hard paddle up the last rapids and drifted along the south shore with a gentle tailwind. The sun had reappeared and sharp shadows etched the grand design. A short distance away, a large black bear was nosing along the shore with its back to me. The noise of a waterfall nearby must have masked the sound of my approach because it seemed quite unaware of my presence. The rushing sound of water offered an opportunity to startle the creature and so I stealthily approached to within ten metres, then slapped the paddle hard on the water and let out a yell. At this, Mr. Bruin slowly turned his head and looked at me. I instantly realized that if he took offence or recognized a meal in the offing, the joke was on me. Two leaps into the shallow waters and the bear would have been on top of me. And so, with uncommon speed and determined stroke, I retreated. The bear simply ignored me, and after some time, disappeared into the undergrowth.

Shortly thereafter, the wind picked up and I decided to camp nearby and wait for an improvement in conditions. It quickly became obvious that Mr. Bruin was not the only one of his kind in these parts. The shoreline was littered with droppings and in the tangle of vegetation beyond the shore was a network of bear trails that confirmed my imperturbable friend was part of a group. The idea of bear culture added an element of unease to my ramblings because my unattended food pack at the campsite was such easy pickings.

Tasisuak Lake, some 40 kilometres in length, is the last of the upstream lakes on the Fraser and a bad place to be caught in a storm. It occupies the whole valley floor and there is virtually no spot to put up a tent except near the two extremities. After two wind-bound but sunny days and an early morning dash in pouring rain, I reached the western end just in time for the next blow. I quickly burrowed into the vegetation and the debris from past storms with axe and saw, setting up shop at the base of two ancient trees near the water's edge. In little more than an hour, I was comfortably installed, and while the tempest roared outside my little cocoon, comfort and peace reigned within. I shall always remember the feeling of intense contentment, leaning against one of those gnarled old trees, soaking up the heat from the fire, and savouring the first meal in many hours.

From that point to the highlands, the Fraser is a small stream rushing along in braided channels at a rate of descent that increases from three metres per kilometre near the lake to more than three times as steep further west. As one travels upstream, the sandy shoreline near Tasisuak Lake gradually gives way to coarse gravel and finally, to boulders. Prichard's party ascended this section a little more than halfway towards the boundary between Quebec and Labrador. Here, at the only gap in the solid wall of rock on the south side, they made the difficult ascent to the barren highland above. On the way up the gap, Prichard shot one of several bears they encountered and called the place, "Bear Ravine." From the top of Bear Ravine, he continued west to the George River. My own modest goal was to make it to Bear Ravine, and even that was severely tested because a cold gale blew out of the west the next morning.

It was with some regret that I left the warm fire and took to the tracking line. Every few hours I stopped and started a warming blaze because I frequently had to get into the cold river to negotiate a difficult section. Two long days later I was stumbling along in the strong current at the foot of Bear Ravine. Two unscheduled swims in the numbingly cold water had dispelled any euphoria the grand setting might have evoked. The walls of the valley had gradually moved closer so that now the sun reached the valley floor for only a few hours of the day. Several streams tumbled noisily from lofty heights down the north wall of the canyon. Interspersed among the alders and scrub brush in the valley were large birch and massive, hundreds-of-years-old white spruce. Beneath a group of several of the latter at the water's edge, a flat spot presented itself and wearily I took possession. Fatigue has a way of undermining efficiency and it was dusk by the time the chores were done and I began to roam farther afield in search of dry firewood. Not 20 metres away were the remains of an old camp at the base of a large spruce.

Could this be Prichard's camp? I think it probably was. Certainly the Inuit never travel beyond the head of Tasisuak Lake because there is no game worth mentioning in the valley, save a large population of black bears. The caribou, which migrate in large numbers across the barren highland above, never venture into the valley. My original plan was to portage up Bear Ravine and head in a southwesterly direction towards the first of the large lakes in the Kogaluk watershed. With the delays at the start of the trip I didn't have enough time left to carry on, but there remained one ambition. Upon their return from the George River, Prichard's party abandoned a canoe at the top of the escarpment. I wanted to search for the remains.

From a distance, Bear Ravine looked harmless enough in the morning sun. Closer inspection revealed a boulder-choked, shrub-infested incline, the bottom of it occupied by a rushing brook; not what one might call prime portaging country. I decided to take a shortcut up a steep rock face and soon found myself

With maps left behind on an island soon after disembarking from the *Taverner*, Herb makes his way by memory to the mouth of the Fraser River. This is the view from the top of Bear Ravine.

trapped on smooth rock, scared to go on and equally reluctant to retreat. Looking at the depths below, I found myself engaged with the strangely dispassionate thought, "If I fall here, no one will ever find my bones." Eventually, I screwed up enough courage to cross a slippery section of wet rock and scrambled to the top, relieved to have made it and mad at myself for needlessly getting into difficulty.

After travelling for several days in an ever-narrowing corridor between smooth grey walls of bedrock several hundred metres high, I viewed the floor of a valley occupied by a crystal-clear stream of blue-green water as a truly awesome and visually pleasing spectacle, But the hard-won view across the top of the landscape was disappointing. To the south and west was a totally barren expanse of rolling hills extending to the horizon, but with no prominent landmarks to guide the traveller. The valley of the Fraser was a mere crack in this vast Precambrian hide. Cut into the stony ground along the edge of the precipice were caribou trails for as far as the eye could see. The search for Prichard's canoe came to a premature halt when my advance was blocked by a bear who showed no inclination to budge. I tend to feel rather vulnerable when facing a bear without an implement of intimidation at hand, and so I cautiously and slowly retreated. Who cares about remnants of canoes anyway? Once I was over the next hill, I set a course at right angles to the original direction to have a look at my intended portage route to the Kogaluk River. After an hour or so I came back, convinced that the delay at the start of the trip was very fortuitous.[3]

I spent another night at Prichard's camp, and in the morning made a feeble attempt to continue upstream on the Fraser to the last pond, beyond which the river disappears below huge boulders that fill the valley floor. The enthusiasm for the enterprise quickly disappeared in the face of the obstructions I faced, and I set off downstream. Four days with little rain were reflected in substantially lower flow volumes, and sections of the river where I had laboured hard to ascent were now barely deep enough to float the canoe. The journey back down to the western shore of Tasisuak Lake took barely half a day.

Five kilometres east of there, a small brook tumbles into the lake from the north. Up a steep scree slope and some fifty metres above the lake, I found a little space large enough and flat enough to put up the tent astride one of several bear trails in the immediate neighbourhood. Summer evenings in this part of the world are long, and this one was of rare quality. The place afforded a beautiful overview of the rock-encased lake and seemingly the resident bear appreciated it as much as I, because the place where he had rested and leaned against a tree was clearly imprinted on the ground; he had even recently broken off a small limb that interfered with the view.

While I attended to supper, a loon called from a distance and gradually moved closer as I answered, until he was right below me near the shore. Clearly he was starved for conversation and didn't care that I had a frightful accent. Overhead, the clouds changed from white, to pink, to red as the sun continued its descent. The air became cold as I moved closer to the campfire with my last cup of tea. My hope, as I turned in, was that the bear whose domain I had invaded would not pay his respects during the night.

Three days later I paddled back into Nain after an as nearly uneventful return journey as one is likely to have in these parts. The next day, out of the mists of pouring rain, the *Taverner* emerged and slowly approached the dock. It was only after boarding her that I found out that there had been some concern regarding the whereabouts and safety of a party of canoeists who had been let off among the ice floes and had not been heard from since.

EIGHT

Ancient Trails to the Coppermine River, 1988

For plodding types like myself the average gestation period for an extended canoe trip is several years. This was certainly the case for a trip in the summer of '88, which started just north of the village of Rae in the Northwest Territories and ended a month later at the mouth of the Coppermine River. For nearly ten years I had listened to accounts of trips on this river and seen pictures that put this watershed in the *must see* category. Eric Morse once mentioned that he thought it the finest trip he had ever undertaken; high praise indeed. On the negative side were two factors that had held me back: the high cost in time and dollars for a solo tripper to get from southern Ontario to Yellowknife and beyond, and the river was just too "in" with the paddling crowd to please me.

It was left to inveterate northern traveller George Luste to alter my tripping pattern, which for some time had focused on northern Labrador. In a wide-ranging conversation, the only kind in which George ever engages, he gently hinted at myopia when he declared with just a hint of condescension, "There are places other than Labrador to see!" Fortunately for me, George didn't leave it at that. A short while later he made arrangements to have my boat transported to Yellowknife—free. It was an offer I could not refuse.

Most wilderness trippers are a bit quirky in one way or another and I am told I'm no exception. One of my dislikes is following other people's routes, unless they have acquired the patina of history. The standard overland route to the Coppermine watershed is that taken by John Franklin in 1820–21.[1] It leads up the Yellowknife River, crosses over to the Snare River watershed, up the Winter River to Little Marten Lake and finally over another height of land to Point Lake.

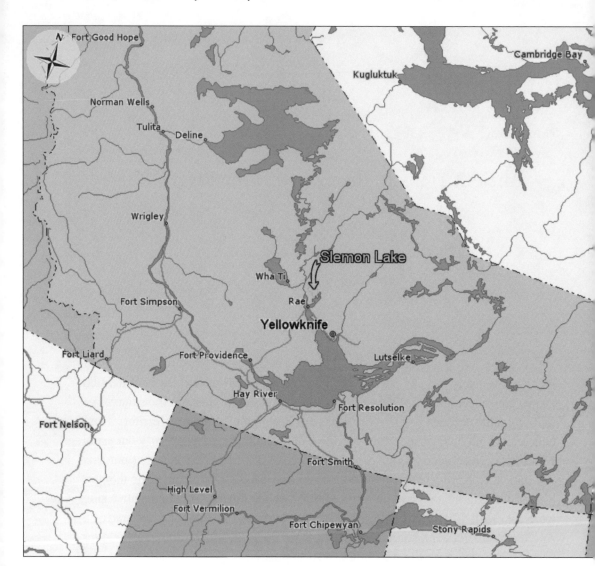

The Slemon Lake area, taken from Toporama, The Atlas of Canada Web site.

One variant of this route is to start at Rae and travel upstream on the Snare River to Winter Lake, a route taken by David Wheeler in 1912 and much more recently by Shawn Hodgins.[2]

A careful perusal of maps convinced me there was another and possibly easier approach to the Coppermine. I planned to follow the Snare River route as far as Kwejinne Lake and then cross over to the Emile River, which makes its way south from the Arctic height of land through a succession of lakes. Along its course the river receives only one substantial tributary, which originates as the outflow of Mesa Lake. At the small lake where the two streams join, I determined to strike out overland to reach Mesa Lake by the most direct route and from there portage over the Arctic height of land into Grenville Lake. The latter is drained by the Parent River, which then flows successively through Rawalpindi and Parent Lake to join the Coppermine at Red Rock Lake.

A complicating element in my plan was the uncertainty of the length of time it would take to finish the trip. After years of tripping I'm quite confident in assessing the actual travelling time, but on this route a substantial number of large lakes had to be traversed where one is at the mercy of the wind. One can make allowance for this potential delay by bringing extra food, but here the limited volume of my boat becomes the deciding factor. I can accommodate supplies for four weeks, anything more than that and I have to sit on, not in, my boat. So I decided to start the trip not at Rae, but at Slemon Lake, which shortened the journey by two paddling days.

So much for the plan. Now it was time to translate it into action. An early morning flight from Toronto had me in Yellowknife by mid-afternoon. Within two hours I was reunited with my boat (which had arrived a few days earlier) and heading northwest to Slemon Lake in a Cessna chartered from Bathurst Inlet Air Services. The boys at Bathurst Air assured me that as far as they knew, no one had ever followed my intended route.

After what seemed like a long time we approached a string of little lakes, which were the first features that I could identify on the map. A quick descent, gear hastily thrown ashore and I was alone. Well, not quite alone, the local populace was on the wing. Two hours later the first of many portages was behind me. With provisions for 38 days my outfit weighed a trifle under 150 kilograms, and it was awfully crowded in the little boat. The campsite that evening was way up on a bluff overlooking ridges of solid rock separated by long and deep grooves that had been carved by the ice sheet of bygone eons in its advance from the north. The flanks and tops of these ridges were sparsely populated with birch and jack pine that clung grimly to every crack in the solid mass, while poplar and black spruce predominated in the lower parts. The first evening was spent attending to repairs. My boat had gained a hole in transit and the baggage handlers of the air carrier managed to rip off the straps on one of the packs. As I finished my journal entry and a last cup of tea by the flickering light of the fire, I was keenly conscious of the enormous distance I had travelled in less than one day. Not so long ago it might have taken two years of hard travel. It's a magical world.

I was following an old portage route marked on the 1:50,000 maps, which bypasses a turbulent section of the Snare River. It leads due north from Slemon Lake, traverses a number of nameless bodies of water and rejoins the river at Bigspruce Lake. All the carries are along well-established trails, but I found the going hard. Two of my three loads were well over 50 kilograms, not that much less than my own weight, and it took a lot of resolve not to drop the loads before the end of the portage.

Most backcountry travellers I know tell me that within a few days after the start of a trip they are much fitter and thus find the exertions of the portage progressively easier to bear. I have always envied these individuals because at the end of a trip of two months duration they are bound to be Olympians. My own experience is that I get more and more run down and so even at the end of a trip when the loads are lighter, they are as onerous as ever.

Two days later, I put ashore at the most westerly bay of Kwejinne Lake in glorious sunshine. A portage of a little over two kilometres should get me to the Emile River watershed. What I could see from the top of a nearby hill was not encouraging—an alder-choked swamp flanked by fractured rock faces—but a short reconnaissance revealed an old and long disused trail. Hallelujah! It was a very soggy portage, not without obstructions and the blackfly population memorable, but what could have been a long and hard day was reduced to a few hours.

That evening I camped on a beautiful sandy point on Basler Lake next to the remains of an old grave. Despite the good example next door, I spent a restless night in the overheated tent, too tired to sleep. When I got up at four, the unwrinkled surface of the water already shone in the morning sun. Basler Lake is a beautiful body of water. High steep-sided hills dominate the northeastern shore. On the lower western shoreline, widely scattered evergreens, set in a mosaic of pale lichen and dark mosses, were pleasing to the eye. Yet, even from a distance, it was obvious that the vegetation was but a thin veneer over unyielding shield rock. I was on the water by seven o'clock and heading north into a gentle headwind. It was just enough to keep the bugs behind me. The boat seemed to move along almost without urging as I advanced unhurriedly. Despite the residue of aches incurred the previous day, or perhaps because of it, I had a most intense feeling of happiness.

The Emile River enters Basler Lake as a steep and boisterous stream. The short and easily found portage trail travels along the edge of a smooth rock face that ends at Mattberry Lake. A strong bear trail and numerous fresh claw marks on trees in the vicinity suggested that the shallow bottom of the rapids was a favourite fishing spot. A little further on a pile of scattered feathers, the remains of a grouse, was a poignant reminder of the uncertainty of life. By the time I paddled away from the head of the portage, the calm morning had changed to a blustery day. Mattberry Lake stretches some 60 kilometres from south to north. I didn't get very far against the strong wind before I decided to call it a day and set up camp on the highest point of a small, almost barren island.

It continued to blow all night. Anxious to move on, I set off in the morning into a heavy swell. By noon, I had advanced only ten kilometres in four hours of hard paddling and decided to stop at an island and wait for conditions to improve. Restlessness and curiosity soon had me scrambling about in the densely wooded interior of the island. Here, except for the rustling of the wind in the treetops, silence reigned. Faint sounds from the underbrush nearby informed me that I was not alone. I had stumbled upon a brood of newly-hatched chicks, little balls of fluff, and mother grouse was not happy with my intrusion. At her urging, the chicks scattered in an instant and she flew noisily onto a limb to face me. For a brief period silence returned, but one and then another of the brood began to call. To my adversary, this was a call to action. She flew up to another perch, head high and within arm's length and stared at me with a fierce look. "Don't you dare move!" it said. I could have grasped her easily and added her to the evening menu but instead remained motionless, captivated by her self-lessness and courage. After what seemed like a long time, my opponent was satisfied that I was harmless. She fluttered down to the ground, gathered up her charges and went on her way. And I wondered whether that pile of feathers on the last portage represented a similar encounter with a different ending.

When I woke in the semi-darkness of midnight the wind had died down and the silence seemed absolute. The aftermath of sunset, visible as an orange glow in the north, was reflected on the calm waters and served as a beacon as I quickly packed and pushed off. Canoe trips to me are sequences of magical moments, and this was as magical as it gets. The silence was palpable and accentuated by sporadic outbursts of bird calls that floated in from the dark-grey shore. The light breeze, which drifted frostily out of the north, banished curtains of fog to the sheltered bays along the way. Imperceptibly, the quality of the light changed and grew in intensity until the northern horizon was suffused with an orange glow that filtered through the swirling mists. Surely the Holy Grail was just around the next bend.

In a rare self-portrait, Herb cooks his supper on the way up the Emile River system, heading to toward the Arctic height of land.

Alas, the only thing around the next bend was a portage and sublime exultation was quickly replaced by muttered imprecations of a more earthy nature.
That evening I camped near the north end of Norris Lake. It must have been a
centre of Native habitation, for I came across the remains of no fewer than three
sites where substantial areas had been cleared of trees. This, together with the
total lack of the usual camp litter, suggested that these places were very old and
had been used for a considerable period of time. Much as these discoveries stim-
ulated my imagination, my attention was now focused on a narrow gap at the
northwestern extremity of the lake—my next portage.

The Emile River upstream from Norris Lake flows in a wide arc through several lakes. At a number of places this flow is interrupted by rapids. It seemed
better to bypass this section by cutting across a few small lakes before rejoining
the river at Brown Water Lake. Once again my luck held and after a brief search
I was panting along beneath my load in the deep groove of a centuries-old trail.
The day's travel went through the most forbidding looking terrain of the journey.
Rock faces rent with enormous cracks, huge boulders strewn helter-skelter
across the land—it looked like the battlefield of giants. In spite of the sun-
drenched day there was a sinister, evil feel to it all; the spirits were not far away.
Interestingly, I have found out in the meantime that the Dogrib Indians consider
this to be a spirit place.

Days later, at yet another portage, I came across the remains of a canoe.[3]
Except for the top of the bow it was completely overgrown by moss and lichen.
It was a powerful reminder to walk carefully, for whoever belonged with this
canoe did not forget it here. A short distance upstream from Rodrigues Lake, the
river flows quickly between high vertical banks of gravel and clay. I was preoc-
cupied with fighting the current when I heard a commotion overhead. It was a
black bear who was obviously intrigued by this strange apparition on the water
and wanted to take a closer look. He seemed rather precariously balanced and I,
scared he was going to fall right on top of me, veered away with determined
stroke. When I last saw him he was obviously no longer curious because he was
bounding away with remarkable agility.

The small lake where the Mesa River joins the Emile is ringed by sandy
ridges. Because my route went east and away from the river at this point I called
it, presumptuously, Nastawgan Lake in my journal (*nastawgan* is an Anishinabi
word meaning "the way" or "the route."). One could conceivably follow the circuitous course of the Mesa River to reach Mesa Lake, but a more direct overland
approach seemed the better choice. After a lengthy portage to bypass a series of
rapids, I briefly tracked up the Mesa River looking for the best place to cross a
range of steep-sided hills to reach the next lake. After some deliberation I started
out with the first load, convinced that this time I would have to make my own
way, but shortly I picked up a faint trail leading up a very steep incline. Years

later, I found out that the Dogrib called the portage from Nastawgan Lake on the Emile River (which they call "Sand All Around" Lake) to Mesa Lake the "See Far Away Portage," part of a trail system used for centuries to reach the Barren Lands for the fall caribou hunt.

A few hours later, I was standing atop a great hill and looked out over the wind-streaked expanse of Mesa Lake. In just a few kilometres the transition from boreal forest to treeless tundra had been complete. So far everything had gone much smoother than I had expected. The presence of old portage trails, although often difficult to follow after many years of disuse, had made portaging much easier than anticipated and the winds, which can pin one down for days, had not greatly interfered. So, when a stiff east wind made paddling difficult, I was not displeased. This would be wash day, I decided, and with good reason. The frosty night before I had stuck my head inside the sleeping bag to warm up and instantly realized the need for a good clean up.

Overnight the wind had moderated and I set off with the first light and without breakfast, anxious to gain the north shore of the lake without further delay. Along the way I stopped for a short reconnaissance to the top of a low rise, and upon my return found the fresh tracks of a grizzly who had strolled along the shore and past the boat during the few minutes I was away. It lent some urgency to my departure because the fellow was probably just a short distance away in the surrounding willows.

Now, only one major hurdle remained—the portage over the height of land that separates the Mackenzie River drainage from the Coppermine. The region before that portage, to the north and east of Mesa Lake, is an enormous undulating plain, not unlike the prairies. The few hills of modest height are not of bedrock, but piles of glacial rubble. Much of the low ground is filled with thousands of shallow bodies of water, wonderful incubators for mosquitoes and blackflies. After traversing Mesa Lake to the northeastern extremity, I continued through several small lakes to the gentle rise that constitutes the height of land. For the first time I could find no sign of human travel, which meant that this was not the Native route to Grenville Lake, where hunting camps were once again evident. With permafrost not far below the surface, the terrain was soggy even on sloping ground and walking on the soft hummocky peat was unusually tiring. The last campsite on the south side of the divide easily won out as the worst of the whole trip. After a fruitless search for a suitable spot, I pitched the tent on wet uneven ground amid clouds of blackflies that covered every fold of clothing several layers thick. Luckily, it turned cold during the night, which reduced the onslaught to tolerable levels in the morning, and after five hours of steady slogging I had my three loads over the four-kilometre portage and had lunch on the shore of a small lake. Strangely, there wasn't a blackfly around, nor did I see another one for the rest of the trip and, since I was thoroughly zonked, I settled for a catnap in the willows.

I reached Grenville Lake in late afternoon, intent only to find a decent camp-site on one of the many islands, have a good wash and lie down to laze the evening away. Of course it never works out that way. A dip in the ice-cold water revived the vital signs and I started to look around my little two-hectare island kingdom and came across some interesting things. In a low spot near the shore was a stack of poles, much overgrown, which had been used as drying racks. The poles must have been brought some distance as there were no trees for many kilometres around. There were caribou bones scattered about a large cuboidal erratic of basalt, polished to a glossy sheen by the ice sheet that had abandoned it here. A V-shaped split down the middle was oriented precisely east-west and was partly filled with caribou bones. I was trying to convince myself that there was some spiritual significance to all this, but more likely the Natives simply used the rock as a lookout since it was the highest point on the island.

The landscape in this region is quite flat and featureless and navigation required constant attention as both Grenville and Rawalpindi lakes are large and full of deep bays. After the relative confinement among trees and hills in the valley of the Emile, the horizon on this barren land seemed frighteningly distant, the overarch-ing deep blue sky immense, and one's self-importance miniscule. I passed the remains of several hunting camps and two lonely graves on my way to the well-hidden outflow from Grenville Lake. Rawalpindi, just a short pullover further on, is really two lakes separated by a short rapid. It is criss-crossed by several eskers that wend their way across the landscape, dipping below the surface of the lake here and there only to rise again some distance away.

After a long day of paddling, I reached the northeastern shore of Rawalpindi and set up camp at the base of an esker. It was a remarkable evening. Nearby the Parent River issued forth to start a steep descent toward the Coppermine. The rumble of an unseen rapid periodically drifted across a rise behind the tent whenever a slight breeze blew in from the north, a reminder of potential diffi-culties ahead. The vast expanse of the lake stretched west to a distant horizon. Pockets of clouds, occasionally trailing curtains of rain, loomed darkly in the sky, their images mirrored in the calm waters, brilliant shafts of sunlight pene-trated through the clouds in an ever changing pattern and once again the Holy Grail seemed within reach.

The Parent River, despite the large area that it drains, is a small stream—a reflection of the low precipitation and high evaporation in this region. As it emerges from Rawalpindi Lake, it races through narrow boulder-lined rapids. Gradually the slope becomes gentler and the riverbed wider. In total there are well over thirty rapids, all of them negotiable, although a number of them are so shallow that the canoe has to be dragged. Piles of detritus, sparsely covered with vegetation, are heaped up everywhere. At intervals the continuum of an esker interrupts the confusion of irregular hummocks, and during the advance toward the Coppermine, pockets of stunted trees reappear. Throughout the day storm clouds usurped the sky in an evermore threatening form. After nearly two weeks of perfect sunny weather, the wind increased and for two days kept me pinned down on Parent Lake. Downpours and sunshine alternated at fairly regular intervals and so it was a great opportunity to explore the country on foot. Parent Lake is bounded by sandy eskers and gently undulating hills. Trees cover the sheltered regions of south-facing slopes, their dark green foliage in sharp contrast to the subdued colour of the land around it. In the sunlight it was exquisitely beautiful, a place that invited contemplation.

On the evening of the sixteenth day of the trip I reached Red Rock Lake and made camp on a spit of sand. For the first time since the start of the trip the disagreeable sounds of "civilization" from Max Ward's fly-in fishing camp intruded into my cherished solitude. At five o'clock the next morning I quietly slipped away down the Coppermine. I quickly realized that the river was in flood. An enormous volume of water surged in smooth undulations at every constriction of the river's course like the muscular contractions of a giant serpent. The rumble of the first rapids below Rock Nest Lake was rather intimidating and I approached cautiously. The drop started with an enormous smooth wave at least 50 metres long, followed by columns of haystacks several metres high. I would have been quite happy to portage around this obstruction, but the river was running fast and deep through the tangled vegetation beyond the shore for a considerable distance, making this a very unattractive prospect. It seemed to me that by hugging a sharp eddy line after the first drop on what would normally be the eastern shore of the river, I should be able to skirt the worst turbulence.

It didn't quite work out as planned. As I was coming down the first drop the force of the river threw me against a bulbous rock, which buried itself with a resounding crash in the side of the boat. I sat there for some seconds, fully expecting to sink. In that short time, and convinced that the boat and all my gear were lost, I had already decided that I had to make my way back to Red Rock Lake, and worried as to how to attract the attention of the people at Ward's Camp on the far side of that lake. But then another wave liberated me from my anchorage and I continued on a wild ride through the willows and back out to the river. Almost immediately another nasty-looking stretch appeared and I put to shore at the first opportunity. By then the boat was riding rather low in the water.

Even a cursory examination of the damage revealed the need for extensive repairs—two cracks about half-a-metre long, where the hull had folded with the force of the collision, and a circular crack at the impact site.[4] What saved the boat from sinking immediately was the tightly wedged-in canoe pack, which acted as a pressure bandage. Fortunately, a nice campsite was nearby with plenty of dry firewood, a necessary commodity for the drying of the boat and the curing of the resin since it was damp and cold. By noon of the following day the

The first rapids below Red Rock lake was a near disaster. Another campfire repair!

repairs were done and I was back on the water in a decidedly less adventurous frame of mind. Thirty-five kilometres later I stopped for an early camp atop an esker some twenty metres above the Coppermine. It had been a fine afternoon on a river that alternately raced along boisterously and slowed at small lake expansions. My journal entry records that evening's mellow thoughts:

Frequently, by the time the chores are done, it's too late, I'm too tired or the gentle deeper spirit has withdrawn and cannot be brought back. So, now I sit atop a windy knoll of an esker and look out at the river stretching away beyond. All is peace and tranquility except the crackling of the fire, the hum of the teapot and the rustle of the wind. Bugs for once are nearly absent and the cold and drizzle of the morning has given way to an almost cloudless day and a mildness in the air which I would curse were I on the portage trail. That mighty body of water, the Coppermine, rolls by majestically and, for the moment, tamed to an unwrinkled but purposeful pace. Large hills, a whole range of them, line the horizon. Running north-south, they are ground-down remnants of granitic elevations, their rocky surface covered by trees and shrubs, which mask their rugged nature. Spruce trees line both sides of the valley to the highest points, but their growth and survival is challenged in a very visible way, sparse of living limb and short. Many times the current top is the latest in a line of unsuccessful tries to keep going."

This very remarkable campsite was transformed into a mystical fairyland the next morning. Excess tea once again forced me from the tent at four-thirty into the cold twilight of the morning to witness an extraordinary scene. Columns of fog swirled in from the river and settled as a thin veil upon the land. Through the mists the early sun emerged as an indistinct pale orb that gradually rose above the trees but almost disappeared from view in the ever-thickening fog. My first look at this scene had me instantly electrified, I grabbed the camera and rushed around madly. After a while the pain of cold feet became too much, the temperature was zero and my birthday suit not sufficient protection against the frigid air, so back into the tent I went for a few minutes in the sleeping bag before getting dressed and setting out again into the mystical landscape.

About noon on a gradually deteriorating day I looked back upstream and noticed to my dismay that I was no longer alone. My new neighbours were eight fellows from Wyoming travelling in two large rafts equipped with powerful outboard motors and whose only passion was fishing. On one level, their appearance was comforting; for hours the previous afternoon I thought I heard the sounds of a motor, perhaps the generator from an exploration camp close to the river I speculated, but the sound, faint though it was, never faded away until I worried it was all in my head. Fortunately, they were not of the gregarious mould, and although circumstances made us neighbours for several days we never exchanged more than a few words.

Rain and wind dominated the next three days, making travel at first difficult and then quite impossible, and the river rose and became laden with silt. The campfire, set in the most sheltered place I could find, was extinguished several times and I eventually abandoned it. It's a time like this when one really appreciates a good tent and sleeping bag to keep the elements at bay. During the fourth night a cold front moved through and the morning sun illuminated a frost-covered landscape not unlike that seen a few days earlier. After the enforced idleness this was definitely a moving day on a river that moved along purposefully and without obstructions. I had been told by earlier travellers that I would find this section boring, but I found it a delightful and relaxing float.

Along the way I passed a number of attractive spots that required investigation. Among them was an abandoned exploration camp, the walls of the structure were covered with the names of earlier travellers, which included that of a former prime minister of Canada. During lunch I became the centre of attention of a curious cow moose on the opposite shore. Trying to get down wind from me for a proper assessment, she moved upstream in several attempts to cross the river. Each time the current carried her past me and back onto the far shore. Unsure of her intentions, I shipped out before she succeeded in her endeavour.

Not far beyond Big Bend—where the river changes from a westerly course to head due north—I caught up with a group from Arctic Waterways. These were actually the people who had transported my boat from Toronto to Yellowknife, and I felt duty bound to spend the night with them. With the clarity of hindsight it was a mistake. One of their guides expressed an interest in buying my boat. It seemed a mutually beneficial transaction since the cost of transporting the boat

Looking north over Escape Rapids on the Coppermine River.

back from Coppermine to Toronto would have been considerable. And so I agreed to leave the boat, paddle and spray cover at the local hotel in Coppermine in return for $300 payable at the end of the season. During the many years since then I have gradually lost hope of getting that cheque in the mail.

There are a number of well-known rapids on the lower Coppermine River, which, by all accounts, warrant a careful examination by canoeists. The first of these is Rocky Defile, which I approached early the next morning with some apprehension. It was a remarkably clear, cool and nearly cloudless day. A short hike to the top of the nearest hill left behind the threatening rumble of the rapids and revealed an almost pastoral landscape, stretching away to the northeast with the bare hills of the September Mountains as a backdrop. There was an air of peacefulness and serenity that had me linger for some time before I reluctantly returned to the task at hand. From the cliffs above the defile it looked like a straightforward run and so it was, but the noise of the waves reverberating from the rock walls and the hiss of the many powerful eddies along the way made it a very nervous passage.

The rest of the journey down the river was a continual visual delight. To one used to the rock-strewn angularity of Labrador, the landscape seemed gentle and inviting. From here on I paddled only a few hours each day and spent the rest roaming far and wide, taking advantage of perfect weather. Especially remembered is a hike in the September Mountains amid the mists of a cold morning. Periodically, a little window would open in the wall of grey and allow the sun to illuminate a part of the landscape in a continual game of hide and seek. It was not difficult to imagine the presence of a supernatural force.

There are many more rapids on the river than are shown on the map and the descent to the ocean is one of great rapidity. They are all negotiable with care, except the last one—Bloody Falls. I spent the last night here and witnessed another remarkable sunrise. On the way to the village of Kugluktuk (formerly Copper-mine), the surface of the river downstream from Bloody Falls on this perfectly windstill day was like a giant mirror, reflecting the grey, furrowed clay banks and the wisps of clouds in the immense blue sky. A few hours later, I re-entered the domain of television, hot running water and internal combustion engines with a feeling of regret. An exciting adventure was over.

NINE

Umiujaq Circle—Wiachewan and Nastapoca Rivers, 1990[1]

The 1987 winter trip with Craig Macdonald was one of the most exhilarating journey I have ever undertaken. Extreme cold, exhausting labour, clear moonlit nights filled with the dancing lights of the aurora borealis and, most of all, the ever-present rugged landscape—frozen waterfalls, wind-scoured bare hilltops, the tree-lined lowlands buried beneath metres of soft clean snow—it all left a lasting impression. Long before the end of the trip, I vowed to return to this region.

There is always a little extra tension before the start of a trip, particularly when you are hostage to circumstances beyond your control. The drive to the airport at La Grande had an inauspicious beginning when a friendly member of the RCMP handed me a ticket for improper passing. Once at the airport, the assurance that I could take my boat as luggage onto the 737 for the flight to Kuujjuarapik was suddenly questioned and resolved only after an animated discussion. The flight from Kuujjuarapik to Umiujaq involved a change to a Twin Otter and here the same problem rose again. This time, the official reason was lack of space on the plane for the boat. Fortunately, the pilot came to my rescue by shifting some of the freight around to accommodate the situation. Once in Umiujaq, Noah Inukpuk, who had been so helpful in '87, arranged for me to stay with Eddy Weetaltuk.

Eddy, an army veteran and well-known Inuit artist, was a friendly and interesting host and his place seemed to be the local coffee shop, as a steady stream of visitors came and went. It was only much later that I realized that it was the itinerant canoeist who was the person of interest to the locals. The Inuk who unloaded my boat from the plane had clearly indicated his judgment of me when he heard of my travel plans. "Do you know what you are doing?" he asked. The condescension in his voice was telling. In his assessment, no doubt communicated to others, I was doomed. It cost poor Eddy at least a pound of coffee for everyone to pay their last respects, a wake if you like, while the body was still warm. In this congenial setting, and with transportation to my starting point arranged for the next morning, I could finally relax.

In the winter, the extreme north end of Richmond Gulf can be reached from Umiujaq by an eight-kilometre snowmobile trail. In the summer one can travel about half that distance by ATV to a gap in the escarpment that separates the Gulf from Hudson Bay. And here I was, below me and almost due east shimmered the waters of Richmond Gulf in the morning sun. On either side of the gap leading down to the water were steep walls of broken sedimentary rock, which rose to a height of more than 400 metres. In the centre of this sheltered valley was a small stream and, against the blue northern sky, the dark green of small spruce, the light green of willows and the pale colour of caribou moss interspersed with little ponds of meltwater and specks of snow left over from last winter, created a picture of peace and tranquil beauty.

Walking through such splendour turned out to be the worst portage of the whole trip. The squishy, ankle-deep cover of lichen, saturated with moisture from an all-night rain and rivulets of melt water made every step treacherous and tiring. Legions of blackflies and mosquitoes obscured the view, and what appeared a gently sloping valley from a distance proved to be a succession of little ravines partly filled with water and tangled willows. By late afternoon I had gained the sandy shore of Richmond Gulf, acutely and gratefully aware that for the next 50 kilometres or so I needn't worry about another portage. There was something else I became aware of at that moment as well—the fresh tracks of a large solitary wolf. It reminded me of the parting remark of the Inuk who had transported me to the top of the escarpment, "I should tell you that wolves around here seem to have lost their fear of man and there have been several attacks in the last while." I must confess that for the rest of the evening I never strayed too far without my axe.

Richmond Gulf, by any standard, is a remarkable place. The western shore is guarded by the steep ramparts of sedimentary rock that rise abruptly out of the brackish waters, giving it the appearance of turrets and castles of a race of giants. There is only one narrow breach in these fortifications at the extreme southwest end of the Gulf, and through it tremendous volumes of water surge with the rise and fall of the tides. The eastern shore, by contrast, rises more gradually and is largely Canadian Shield rock, overlain in many places by basalt. Several large rivers enter the Gulf in boisterous rapids or sheer falls. And the island-studded

Herb was mesmerized by the geology of the Richmond Gulf area.

waters are home to large populations of seals and waterfowl. Raised beaches extend far into the sparsely wooded valleys, evidence of post-glacial rebound, which exceeds 125 metres in this region. The whole visual impact of contrasting colours and physical grandeur, the evidence of the gigantic forces that have shaped the land, the enormous time scale embodied in the bands of sedimentary rock, all conspire to awe the solitary traveller and lend perspective to one's own relative insignificance in the overall scheme of things.

I was on the water with the first light of dawn and slowly made my way south. Not a breath of wind disturbed the surface of the Gulf. Soon the first rays of the sun illuminated the highest ramparts of the western shore, their amber reflections mirrored in the water. I paddled silently through this quiet world lest I break the spell. About an hour later I was jolted out of my reverie by a "Splash!" immediately behind the boat. Within a few seconds, the head of a seal surfaced a short distance away. I swear it was smiling. The creature obviously enjoyed the game, because the process was repeated several times over the next few hours.

By late afternoon I was camped at the mouth of the Caribou River and the magic was gone. I barely managed to cook supper before a deluge drowned the campfire. For the next two days I fretted while the waves pounded the shore and the wind worried the exposed tent. On the morning of the third day I pushed off into a heavy swell during a brief lull in the elemental assault, and struggled toward the mouth of Rivière de Troyes at the southwest corner of Richmond Gulf. A great amount of sand carried into the bay has rendered the last kilometre very shallow. Into this confining space the great waves generated in deeper waters broke with disconcerting force. It made the conclusion of an already exciting paddle even more tense.

Rivière de Troyes has been part of the Native route to the interior for many centuries. A.P. Low describes it in the Geological Survey report of 1888.[2] Within a few minutes after putting ashore at the mouth of the river, which the Natives called

Wiachewan, I discovered faint traces of an old trail leading up a steep embankment. This no doubt was the beginning of the four-kilometre portage that bypasses a 100-metre waterfall. After a few hundred metres, the trail emerges on a spur of rock and finally traverse a treeless plain. This plain, one of several raised beaches encountered on this portage, is remarkable for two reasons—it affords a beautiful view of the southern part of the island-studded Gulf and, even more exciting, it houses a score of shallow circular depressions scattered about, which the lush carpet of reindeer moss has not managed to hide completely. These teepee sites are of various ages and indications from the ethnographic literature are that not more than two or three were active sites at any one time, the latest occupancy being between 30–50 years ago. That evening, as I cooked my supper in one of the old fireplaces and looked out over the harshly beautiful land, I felt a spiritual kinship with the people whose moccasined feet had travelled this way for centuries.

Two days later, I was nearing the end of my journey on the Wiachewan River. For several kilometres a wolf had followed me along the shore, clearly curious about this strange creature on the water. By the time I reached the little tributary it was nowhere in sight. Taking my cue from Low, who states that the next portage "follows a small tributary stream to the north," I diligently searched both banks of the stream, sloshing through the marshy ground and tripping over willows for over an hour, all the while convinced that no self-respecting Indian would ever start a portage in this mess.

Solitary camp on the Wiachewan River, following the ancient Cree trail and in the footsteps of geologist and explorer A.P. Low.

Finally, I retreated a short distance downstream to a place that seemed better suited to the purpose, and before long carried the first of my three loads two kilometres up to a plateau a hundred metres above the valley floor and made camp near a small pond. Shortly after noon the clouds had disappeared and an indifferent day closed in a blaze of sunshine. In spite of fatigue and the discomfort of blistered feet I felt exultant. The tent was set up in the shelter of one of the few trees of any size, in a place where others had camped before. The ancient highway that had brought me here carried on, more felt than seen, up a gentle rise to the shore of a small lake, one of a number of interruptions in its eastward advance across lakes and streams toward the Clearwater River.

The next morning everything was covered with a thick coating of frost. Tiny columns of mist were rising into the pale sky from hidden bodies of water and forced into a spirited dance by the first golden rays of sunlight. It marked the beginning of a glorious day. Midday found me atop a high rocky spur. I had lost the trail among the large boulders near the shore of the last lake and as always in situations like this, I headed for high ground. The long, narrow lake I was aiming for was due east. To the west lay the deep blue waters of the small lakes I had traversed. The missing trail could be seen as a series of disconnected lines in the waterlogged plain below me. In spite of the extra work involved I decided to portage over high ground, motivated by the desire to see as much of the sun-drenched scenery around me as possible, but also to take advantage of the breeze of this exposed route because the mosquitoes were troublesome.

Overnight, more rain, signalling a change in the daily weather pattern that was to hold, with one notable exception, for the remainder of the trip: light precipitation during the night, cold foggy mornings, slight improvement with the odd hint of sunshine before noon and then progressive deterioration. Westerly winds increased steadily during the day such that by afternoon portaging the canoe over exposed terrain and paddling became difficult. Every day the long threatening storm would break between four and five in the afternoon with strong gusts of wind and heavy rain. While these squalls rarely lasted more than half an hour, they emphasized the need for a sheltered tent site and fireplace. The latter was normally placed in the lee of one or more large erratics, of which there was no shortage. It was the only way to avoid having the campfire drowned or blown away. More than once I was comfortably stretched out in front of the fire in the shelter of a house-sized boulder while the wind-whipped rain raced by a short distance away. Situations like these are always reminders that comfort and discomfort are never far apart. With temperatures between zero and ten degrees Celsius and a chilling breeze, one actually welcomed portages as a means to get warm. Even better, mosquitoes and blackflies were ridiculously clumsy and spent most of their time hiding in the ground cover where they were easy prey for the large number of jumping spiders. Yes!

The region immediately west of Clearwater Lake is criss-crossed by long water-filled troughs. Through a succession of these grooves in the shield rock the Clearwater River flows westward towards Richmond Gulf. Large expanses of flat water are interrupted here and there by boiling rapids and falls. I reached the river some 30 kilometres below its origin, and continued towards Clearwater Lake amid a steady stream of southward-moving caribou who crossed the river singly or in small groups, quite unconcerned about my presence. A week after leaving Richmond Gulf, I paddled out of the shelter of the high hills along the western shore of Clearwater Lake, and headed for the nearest of the islands that surround the centre of the impact crater of the meteorite that created the lake some 290 million years ago.

Even moderate winds give rise to high rolling waves on this large body of water and I was physically and emotionally drained when I stopped on the north-ernmost of the ring islands at day's end. Next morning, I crossed over to the north shore of the lake and after some confusion in dense fog, found the mouth of the small stream whose course parallels that of an esker that rolls eastward toward the Seal Lakes. A.P. Low called it the Noonish River in his 1896 report for the Geological Survey of Canada.[3] I began the ascent of the river under threatening skies, but by the time I had completed the first two portages, a hint of sunshine had me looking for a campsite. At one of several lake expansions, a little sandy oasis presented itself amidst the raw clutter of glacial debris. Soon the tent was up under the shelter of a tamarack. A small fire near the base of another tree provided heat for the weary traveller who was slumped contentedly against the trunk with his teacup in hand. On the far distant shore, a derelict and ancient canoe, propped up on sticks, was proof that the place had been a transient home to others. It was a poignant reminder of an almost extinct way of life.

The Seal Lakes are separated from the Clearwater watershed by a rocky ridge, which requires a half-kilometre portage. The lakes are spread out over an enormous area and connected by short sections of flowing water. Only a fraction of this area is water, however, owing to the presence of many peninsulas and islands. The view from the top of the portage was delightful, in no small measure because for one brief day the sun had returned and blue skies stretched to a limitless horizon. It also marked the beginning of the descent toward Hudson Bay. Up to this point signs of old Native encampments and portage trails had been encountered almost daily. By contrast, not a single campsite or axe mark was seen beyond this point (save for one small stone fireplace replete with little sticks of firewood cut into very short pieces with a saw, obviously the work of pale-faced urbanites). There was, however, plenty of evidence that Hydro Québec is set to drastically alter the landscape.

My advance on Seal Lakes toward the mouth of the Nastapoca River was soon barred at the head of a bay at a point where the map insisted a passage existed. Even though I had kept a close eye on the map during my advance past

numerous islands and was thus reasonably sure I hadn't made a mistake, I paddled back to my put-in point and started out again, with the same result.
Obviously, the cartographer had made a mistake because the low hill that
barred the way had never been a waterway. Not deterred by this experience, I
decided to make my way toward another channel indicated on the map, which
was equally non-existent. Experiences like this are not that unusual, but time on
this trip was in short supply and the waste of half a day had me muttering darkly
as I portaged to the open lake beyond.

The Nastapoca River exits from the most westerly arm of the Seal Lakes in a
long sweep of fast smooth water that terminates in a confusion of haystacks. In
its westerly course the river at first drops quickly over a number of bouldery
rapids. The large volume of water and speed of descent gives rise to large waves
and much turbulence. Nevertheless, the majority of these obstacles are negotiable albeit, in my case, not without some trepidation. For more than half its
length, the Nastapoca courses through gravel and boulder beds. At times the
river splits into channels separated from one another by eskers or other glacial
debris. Long stretches of utterly desolate country are interrupted by the occasional oasis of remarkable beauty. Finally, as sand and gravel are left behind, the
river runs confined between hills of solid bedrock and bouldery rapids give way
to sharp drops over ledges and spectacular falls. Trees become progressively
smaller and more widely scattered until only dense stands of willows remain in
sheltered places. Progress was severely slowed by constant headwinds and generally unpleasant weather conditions. Evenings were usually spent listening to
rain drumming on the tent rather than exploring the lay of the land.

One of these evenings is particularly clearly remembered. When I broke camp
in the morning the tent was uncharacteristically dry. All day I felt a certain
smugness—no matter what else might happen, I was going to have a comfortable dry abode. And because it was a particularly miserable day, it was a
sustaining thought that made adversity easier to bear. By mid-afternoon the sky
assumed an unusually threatening countenance. By a stroke of good fortune I
was in the process of portaging around an obstruction and quickly found a nice
sheltered spot, spread out the ground sheet on a thick layer of moss, unravelled
the tent to insert the poles into the sleeves—and then the deluge came. In a
minute the ground sheet was transformed into a miniature swimming pool upon
which floated my no longer dry tent. Despite my most passionate profanity, it
would not let up and continued to rain throughout the night. A fog-shrouded,
gloomy morning briefly spawned the idea of a layover day, but with no promise
of an improvement in the weather and time in short supply, I moved on.

The last 20 kilometres of the river are easily the most awesome. At the beginning of a large S-bend the Nastapoca thunders fifty metres into a deep
straight-walled canyon and continues with considerable agitation in a northerly

The Chutes of the Nastapoca. The river does not go quietly into the salt water of Hudson Bay. Next stop, Umiujaq, fifty kilometres south along the coast.

direction. Here it receives a large tributary that discharges its waters into the canyon in another sheer falls. The bend in the river, which brings it back to a westerly course, marks the start of a sharp and long rapid. It took more than half a day to portage around the falls and scout ahead before running the remainder of this section. When I put ashore at the head of the Nastapoca Chutes—the last obstruction before tidewater—it was with a sense of great urgency. Ever more threatening storm clouds, which had followed me for several hours, rendered the landscape dark and gloomy. A few drops of rain started to fall as I scrambled up the steep shoreline to look for a campsite. "Good grief, not again!" was the thought uppermost in my mind.

The view from the top of the chute was perhaps the most dramatic experience of the whole trip. In the foreground the river plunged from view with a muffled rumble sending up clouds of spray. Stretched out beyond was the immensity of Hudson Bay shimmering in the late evening sun. Spanning across this silvery expanse in a discontinuous line were the jagged, utterly black silhouettes of the Nastapoca Islands. The transition from the gloom and confinement of the canyon to the bright and wide expanse of the coastal landscape over such a short distance was truly incredible. The dark storm clouds, which had followed me all day like evil spirits, remained behind as if suddenly contained by an invisible wall.

The next morning the situation was unchanged—threatening skies upriver, bright and sunny on the coast. After a miserable portage past the last falls through spray-soaked willows all that remained was a fifty-odd kilometre paddle down the coast to Umiujaq. Soon I was riding the long swell of Hudson Bay with the gentlest of breezes urging me southward. Somehow I had expected the shore along the Bay to have the same inhospitable countenance as the region upriver, instead there were many small bays with bright sandy shores and ample driftwood. By mid-afternoon messages of distress from various parts of the body began to arrive in the brain, but I dared not stop lest I become windbound. A fog bank was creeping up the coast, the water became choppy and I began to worry—where the hell is Umiujaq? It was evening when I pulled the canoe ashore for the last time. In a show of bravado I humped up all my gear at once—three packs and a duffle bag—staggered up the village to Eddy Weetaltuk's place and knocked on the door.

"You look absolutely beat!" he said.

I was.

TEN

Kanairiktok River—from
Knox Lake to Hopedale, 1992

The pilot sounded exasperated, "I can't put down here, my friend, there is no water! I'll have to put down in the middle of the lake." We were circling above Knox Lake, some 85 kilometres east of Schefferville. I could have started this trip by paddling away from Iron Arm, as I had done in '82 and '84, but it would have taken at least five days to get here and, as usual, time was the limiting element. It was just as well that I hadn't planned to get here by muscle power, because from the plane we could see that Lake Attikamagen was still covered with ice. My plan for this year was to make my way east to the Kanairiktok River and follow it to Snegamook Lake.[1] From there, I intended to set off in a southerly direction over a height of land to the Naskaupi River and continue to Northwest River and Goose Bay. It was an ambitious undertaking for the 32 days of food that I brought along.

Like most lakes near the height of land, Knox Lake is populated by legions of boulders that lie in ambush in the shallow waters. After several minutes of searching for a safe place to land, the Cessna touched down with a resounding jolt. I was sure we had struck something in the water and was relieved to find it was only a sloppy landing. Within minutes I was alone on a vast expanse of water, the shore only a thin line of tamaracks and black spruce, not much help in trying to pinpoint my position on the map. It was an absolutely glorious day. A gentle wind out of the northwest was not sufficient to disturb the surface of the lake, which, like a giant mirror, reflected the wide expanse of sky. After the noisy plane ride the silence at first seemed absolute, giving way with time to the gentle sounds of undisturbed nature. Once again I felt the sense of spiritual homecoming, a feeling that seems to mark the beginning of every wilderness trip.

My immediate objective on this trip was to reach the headwaters of the Kanairiktok River. This would set me on an easterly course and require two crossings of the Quebec-Labrador border. I was determined to start at a leisurely pace in order to avoid the second- and third-day blahs incurred on previous trips. In this endeavour I was looking forward to a portage-free day, for all the interconnected lakes I had to traverse were shown as having the same elevation on the map. Alas, by afternoon I was struggling through the willows to bypass a lively rapid and strong current before making an early camp on Crossroads Lake.

It seems that on every trip, no matter how carefully I prepare, something gets left behind. This time it was the cutlery and so, before embarking on supper, I whittled away an hour and produced what to me was recognizable as a spoon. I thought it was a distinct improvement over my creation on the Notakwanon River years earlier, when I left my fork and spoon at a campsite and faced the same problem.

I was up with the first light of a cold, calm and cloudless day, packed away the frost-covered tent and was on the water by six. Morning brought a fairyland of swirling mists and utter silence, pierced occasionally by the call of a solitary loon. Gradually, the orange sun assumed dominion over the mists and opened the world around me to bald hills and inhospitable bouldery shores, lined with shrubs and stunted trees.

As I approached the eastern margin of Crossroads Lake, sounds of human activity drew me to a small peninsula. Several people were working on a frame dwelling destined to become a fishing camp. There was some urgency to their endeavour apparently, because the late break-up this year had delayed their efforts, and the first guests were scheduled to arrive within days. Over coffee, one of the fellows, who was from Northwest River, quizzed me about the abundance of fish along my route, and seemed pleased to hear that I saw many dorsal fins at the outflow of the lake. Of course, they chuckled when they heard about my intended destination and I soon departed. In my haste, I completely forgot to ask for a fork and spoon, the only reason I'd stopped there in the first place!

The next two days were spent working my way slowly upstream through a maze of channels and small lakes to the height of land and the western arm of the George River headwaters. In the backcountry, maps and reality have far less in common than one might hope, mainly because mapmakers have simplified the issue by showing clusters of small rock piles that protrude above the water as one larger island, or by only showing a few islands. Not sure of where I was caused me to retrace my route twice and the portage over the height of land involved a needless detour. But the journey through mirror images on the lake, and walking in the virtual absence of mosquitoes and blackflies was heavenly. It was an unexpected opportunity to allow large parts of the anatomy to get sun-burned and I took full advantage of it. The late spring had pushed back not only the emergence of insects but plant growth as well—willows and alders at the water's edge had barely begun to bud and the tamaracks were still bare.

The headwaters of the George River is a huge waterlogged plain. The underlying Precambrian shield is almost totally buried beneath poorly worked glacial till and large lakes and string bogs take up much of the surface. On the way down the western arm towards Lake Elson, and nearing the end of the day, I spurned the little island Jim Greenacre and I had camped on in 1986; it was now even smaller and less attractive. It was not a good decision, because later I spent hours making a worse site habitable. Campsites in this region tend to be on the soggy side and several times I had to build little platforms of brush to ensure a dry tent floor.

When one reads the account of Mina Hubbard in her book, *A Woman's Way Through Unknown Labrador*, one is left with the impression that this whole region was home to large numbers of caribou. This is certainly not the case today. The old trails are now overgrown and scarcely recognizable, nor are there any but the most rare signs of man. With the exception of birds, which are numerous and varied, the land seems empty and untouched.

The last body of water on the Quebec side before recrossing into Labrador is Lac Juillet. To reach it required tracking up the eastern branch of the George River, a task that was not appreciated either in anticipation or execution. Dense vegetation along the shore forces a traveller to stay in the river, stumbling and sliding among the slippery rocks in the rapids. It was thus with a sense of exultation that I gained the shore of Lac Juillet. The morning sun had transformed the lake into liquid silver. The backlit, bare hills beyond the far shore reached darkly into a pale cloudless sky. To the northeast the large expanse of water merged with the sky on the limitless horizon. The sandy southern shore arched away toward an esker, which disappeared into low hills. It was time for a stroll in the countryside.

The euphoria associated with my arrival on Lac Juillet was not sustained. My journal entry that night has a decidedly grumpy tone:

With very few exceptions, this is miserable Godforsaken country. Rocks upon rocks of glacial till, some covered with a thin veneer of vegetation, trees fighting against all odds to grow, mangled and leaning in various directions among the skeletons of the dead and half-decayed. The rest is water, stretched in shallow expanse over the bouldery floor. In between is the half-world of bog belonging to neither the land nor the water, the breeding ground of the legions of the devil. Eagerly they pursue their prey, miniature vampires not constrained by time.

After a day of paddling across Lac Juillet, a body of water that is really several lakes strung together by short sections of flowing water, I re-entered

Low-lying fighter jet on the horizon. Beseiged on this trip by these fighters flying out of Goose Bay, Herb wrote: "How I would like to have the Prime Minister and members of the cabinet subjected to the scream, swoosh and sonic booms of these instruments of destruction in *their* backyards."

Labrador by traversing the marshy height of land to Kenney Lake. The latter is scattered over a very large area. The deep bays, narrow channels and numerous islands mask the true extent of water. It's visually pleasing, with a backdrop of snow-covered mountains to the north, and teeming with fish. One could easily spend a day or two in quiet contemplation here except for the scourge of the Labrador skies, the low-level training flights of supersonic fighter planes stationed in Goose Bay.[2] How I would like to have the prime minister and members of the Cabinet subjected to the scream, swoosh and sonic booms of these instruments of destruction in *their* backyards.

Two days later, I was stood on a bare rocky hill taking in the Labrador Plateau as it rolled away to the east in gentle undulations, low spots filled with detritus and all covered with a hint of vegetation. Just a short distance away the tributary I was travelling on joined the Kanairiktok in a foaming cascade of whitewater, the first of several portages over the next two days. In contrast to the valleys of the more northerly rivers in Labrador, which have been gouged out of solid bedrock by glacial action, the valley of the Kanairiktok is entirely the product of post-glacial erosion. It begins as a shallow boulder-lined depression through which the stream runs an uncertain course. Over the span of 30 kilometres, during which the river loses between four and six metres per kilometre in altitude, the valley becomes a narrow canyon more than one hundred and fifty metres deep. Beyond that section, it assumes an easterly course through alluvial depositions. The almost continuous rapids in the canyon demand precise manoeuvring. The problem isn't wave action, but a fast current between closely-spaced boulders. Strong back paddling to slow the pace is essential.

Despite my best efforts, I had to dig out the patching kit early on this trip and thereafter proceeded with more than the usual amount of apprehension, for one is keenly aware that losing the boat in this part of the country lowers the chances of survival of a solo traveller considerably. At one point, faced with a nasty stretch of water confined between vertical rock walls, I took to high ground. The portage up to the rim of the canyon through an old burn was easier than antici-

pated. Still, by the time the third load was back at the water's edge, 500 metres downstream, it was time to look for a campsite. In spite of a willingness to settle for something marginal, I couldn't find a spot large enough to pitch my tent. I ended up lugging my gear back up to level high ground and spent an uneasy night. During the afternoon a cold front had moved through with a bit of rain, fierce gusts of wind and a noticeable drop in temperature. Sometime during the night I woke shivering and started to worry whether I was coming down with something, but before long realized it was only the cold wind blowing through the tent. It was −7° C in the morning and the ground was covered with hoarfrost.

It was but a short distance downstream from this campsite that Karl and Peter Schimeck had come to grief in '83, as I found out later. They were lining their 17-foot Grumman canoe past a turbulent section of river and couldn't hold on to the ropes in

Paddle or portage, either way, descending the Kanairiktok River is not for the faint of heart.

the strong current. The boat drifted away and became pinned against a large boulder in the middle of the river. In a desperate attempt to free the boat, son Peter floated down the ice-cold water to the rock. He could not dislodge the canoe but managed to extract one of the packs from the badly deformed hull. By then, Peter was suffering from hypothermia and just barely made it back to shore. Fortunately, the pack contained their tent and sleeping bags and they spent a hungry and worried night high above the river. The next day, Peter still had not quite recovered from his ordeal. At first he refused to get back into the water, but there was little choice, as he was by far more robust than his father, and strength was essential to free the craft from its confinement. By means of a long and stout pole, Peter managed to pry the boat loose and they spent most of the day trying to restore the aluminium shell to a semblance of its original shape.

They continued downstream with their demolition-derbied canoe, which stayed afloat only through liberal use of duct tape. Their most serious loss, however, was a food pack and their only set of maps. Despite their best efforts, they rarely caught enough fish for an adequate meal. No maps complicated the issue because trying to find Hopedale, 75 kilometres from the mouth of the river, among many islands and bays, would be impossible. And so, when they reached Snegamook Lake, they decided to stay there in the hope of attracting the attention of a passing aircraft. A week later, they heard a plane and immediately lit the long-prepared smoke fire to attract the pilot's attention. The float plane passed overhead and continued on a southerly course. Just about the time they had given up hope that they'd been seen, the plane turned in a wide arc and made another pass low overhead. Three hours later, they sat down in Goose Bay for their first real meal in two weeks.

Once past the canyon, the river continues to race along in a wide gravelly stream bed, past the cutbanks of old riverbeds, sometimes wide and shallow, sometimes narrow and deep. And lower down, there is a profound change in the landscape. The outer limits of the valley are the sides of a huge trough of Precambrian rock. The alluvial deposits that once nearly filled this basin have been gradually carried downstream so that now the river's course all the way to the sea wends its way through beds of gravel and sand. Occasionally the river's flow is obstructed by outcroppings of shield rock over which the waters tumble in sheer falls or intimidating rapids. Except where forest fires have ravaged the land the whole domain is covered by dense boreal forest, a nearly impenetrable barrier to cross-country travel and a serious impediment to exploration on foot. Even short excursions required considerable effort for little reward, as even the higher elevations are densely covered by vegetation and thus afford no overview of the country.

As soon as I left the canyon of the Kanairiktok behind, the weather began to deteriorate. Dark clouds gathered in ever more ominous patterns and strong gusts of wind signalled the end of the travelling day. Within an hour after camping, I was comfortably ensconced in the large vestibule of my Cannondale tent and cooking supper, while torrents of water lashed my abode. And then things took a turn for the worse. Mosquitoes began to appear in astonishing numbers. Hundreds perished in the gas flame and formed a ring of corpses around the stove, but more kept coming. A glance into the tent revealed the genesis of a small lake in the middle of the floor. While I hastily unzipped the screen to attend to this problem and save the sleeping bag from drowning, clouds of mosquitoes resolutely took up residence in the inner sanctum. Some two hours later, with the tent repitched, the floor reasonably dry and most of the intruders eliminated, a short-lived sense of equanimity returned. Short-lived because soon stretch receptors reminded me of the limits of my fluid storage system. Hmm, what to do?

I had no intention of venturing outside again and fight another battle with intruders and so cast about for suitable alternatives. And then I noticed the plastic bag that, until recently, had contained my supper. Eureka! I have since been told by several experienced individuals that they are well-acquainted with the fluid transfer method I was so proud to discover. I guess it's proof that I am a slow learner. Unfortunately, the learning process still wasn't quite complete. Several nights later, while happily practising the new technique, I was slow to notice that the fluid level in the bag remained remarkably constant throughout the operation. Henceforth, the last task of the evening involved testing a plastic bag for fluid retention capability.

The storm blew itself out overnight, but for several days the clouds remained low and darkly threatening above the river. Like a fringed curtain on a window they provided a sombre frame through which one could glimpse a succession of rocky hills beyond the northern shore. The pale colour of lichen that covered their flanks gave the hills a luminous quality reminiscent of paintings by Rembrandt.

Early the next day, on a wide stretch of river, I passed a small black bear wandering aimlessly along the shore. He seemed rather disconsolate and I suspect he just got his walking papers from mom and now had to look for sustenance on his own. I lingered alongside him for awhile but he paid no attention. A few hours later, a little opening in the dense vegetation along the north shore aroused my curiosity, and I went ashore to investigate. The remnants of several hunting blinds suggested the place had been a goose camp. Scattered about were bits and pieces of a wooden box and its contents. The many tooth marks indicated that the box had aroused a bear's curiosity and I was thankful for it because among the scattered items were a fork and spoon.

Not far downstream was the place where I'd planned to leave the river and portage 250 metres up to the height of land that separates the watersheds of the Naskaupi and Kanairiktok rivers. There were a number of small lakes along the 35-kilometre traverse, but for most of the distance I would have to carry my three loads. I watched the southern shore of the river with growing apprehension

Once again, by choice, Herb carried his gear from the George River watershed, over the divide into Labrador, and then down over countless portages to the sea. To Herb, a canoe this far above the water was a point of privilege.

as I slowly continued downstream. The region had been devastated by at least two forest fires. The first fire, which happened some 70–80 years ago, had burned what must have been a mature forest, and the remaining trees trunks were scattered chaotically across the landscape. The next generation of trees had suffered the same fate 30–40 years later, and their skinny skeletons were standing like a grey wall amidst the latest dense generation of green. The only way through this mess would be by cutting a trail and one would be lucky to advance one or two hard-won kilometres a day. I had allowed five days for the crossover, and it was clear that it would take more than twice that long under these conditions, too long for my supplies of food. And so, without long deliberation, I decided to stay on the river and paddle out to Hopedale because, unlike Karl Schimeck, I had maps for this alternative.[3]

The change of plan was not totally without consequence. Years earlier, I had met Frank Moriarty aboard the *Taverner*, and he had invited me to stay at his place in Goose Bay. A few years later, Frank moved away and it was some time before I located him in Nova Scotia. He was surprised to hear from me, and went on to explain, "There was a story going around Goose Bay that a fellow from Ontario named Herb, started a trip down the Kanairiktok and was never heard from again. I was sure it was you, and thought you wouldn't mind finishing that way." The story no doubt originated with the people I had met on Crossroads Lake, and points to the readiness with which the locals embrace disaster stories of this sort. And, just to set the record straight, I'd rather die in a comfortable bed.

I was nearing Snegamook Lake, the only substantial body of water along the river's course, when the sun returned. It was only mid-afternoon but fatigue had me looking for a campsite. I spotted sandbars extending from both shores not too far ahead, a welcome prospect after kilometres of dense bush and marshy ground. Drawing near, I noticed a large black bear patrolling the southern shore. He was the centre of attraction of two wolves who occupied the northern shore—until they noticed me. As I drifted along near the shore, trying to decide on a course of action, the wolves kept pace with me at the edge of the water not more than ten metres away. It seemed a good opportunity for a picture. Alas, the clicking noise when I opened the camera case startled them and they withdrew far enough to spoil the chance of a close-up. With some apprehension—I am a confirmed coward at heart—I went ashore, put up the tent and soon had a camp-fire going. At this point I felt a little more at ease, although all the while the wolves kept a close watch. Periodically during the evening, and several times during the night, they serenaded me with their melancholy howls. In spite of the beautiful setting I wasted little time breaking camp in the morning. Only when I was back on the water did I realize that my departure was watched not by two but seven wolves. Further downstream I was to witness the chilling spectacle of a pack of wolves pursuing a caribou. Mother Nature is a remorseless lady.

The Kanairiktok River below Snegamook Lake is characterized by a number of rapids and falls. The latter can always be instantly assessed on approach as either utterly unrunnable or negotiable, there is no middle ground. As everywhere in northern Labrador, there are no trails around obstructions, but in many instances bare bedrock along the edge of the water affords an easy passage. The last few kilometres are particularly striking. The influence of the cold current of the Labrador Sea can be seen in a diminution of the lush vegetative cover and the rocky hilltops bare of trees. Just above tidewater the river plunges a total of more than 40 metres in two tremendous cataracts before being swallowed by the sea.

The Labrador coast can be a very inhospitable place, but I was fortunate. Morning dawned in cloudless brilliance. A strong quartering breeze and the incoming tide delayed my departure, and it was eight o'clock before I pushed off into Kanairiktok Bay. Fighting wind and waves was hard work, and when I spied a nice sheltered cove, I headed for shore. The place had obviously been home to someone for many years. The remnant of a dwelling, the derelict hull of a fishing vessel and many sheet metal containers littered the ground. When I later talked to George Bromfield in Hopedale, he explained that they used the place to hunt harp seals when they come up the bay in the spring.

Because I had plenty of time and the wind continued to blow, I took an extended hike to high ground. I don't know what causes the excitement I feel when I look at a raw, wild and bouldery landscape, ice-scoured and wave-washed bedrock, wind-mutilated trees, yawning canyons. The Labrador coast has all these elements and more. Today, the sun added contrast and definition, which only intensified my joy in rambling. During this time, the wind had lost none of its force, and, when I got back on the water, it provided excitement of the roller-coaster kind. Progress was slow and it was five o'clock by the time I pulled into the sheltered bay of a five-hectare island, a mere 20 kilometres away. Set in an arc of sheltering trees were stones of a large tent ring, a perfect enclosure for my own accommodation. A profusion of flowers coloured the ground; it would have been sacrilegious to damage this carpet with a campfire, and so I cooked my supper on the stove.

Some time during the night I awoke to the sound of rushing waves. The sea had been distant when I landed at low tide, but it now seemed very close. The worrying thought, "Did I pull the boat up high enough?" was instantly followed by a mad rush outside to find the boat well above the waterline. Nevertheless, I pulled it up next to the tent. Overhead, a dark canopy of stars sparkled in cloudless splendour above the muted northern lights. All around, the wrinkled sea shimmered faintly and all was peace. Despite the quiet it took a long time for sleep to return. The thought of being marooned on a tiny island off the coast of Labrador continued to niggle away in the back of my mind.

The next morning, even with a cold breakfast (the only time on this trip that I started a day without bacon and pancakes, my journal informs me), I soon began to sing. The sea was calm, the sun was shining and the scenery filled my soul. For a while, a shark kept me company, perhaps he thought the sound waves indicated distress and the promise of a meal. A derelict building came into view. It sat on an exposed rocky point near the shore, a sure sign its use went back to the days when hundreds of schooners converged each year on the shores of Labrador and dropped off part of their human cargo to pursue the onshore fishery. The building was constructed of local timber. Hand-sawn two-inch planks, edged with an adze, were used throughout. A rickety ladder led from the one room interior to the loft. The substantial cracks between adjacent boards indicated that the lumber used was freshly cut when they slapped the structure together. By the end of the first season, the consequent shrinkage must have made the place draughty and uncomfortable, even in good weather. Later on, I met a local fisherman who volunteered to take me along on his return journey to Hopedale. I had the feeling he was offended when I politely declined the offer.

As it turned out, I had to spend more time in Hopedale than I liked. My old mentor Garfield Flowers was out of town and the local hotel was a much more expensive alternative as I had to wait four days for the coastal ferry. The *Taverner* had called here five days earlier and, unable to get through the ice as in '87, Captain French had turned back. She wasn't due back for another week.

Reluctantly, I shipped out on the second ship that also makes the run. The *Northern Ranger* is a much larger and newer vessel,[4] but she lacks the rustic appeal of the *Taverner*. I think many of the regulars on the route, including paddlers like me, were saddened when the *Taverner* was taken out of service a year later, a mere 54 years young.[5]

ELEVEN

First Descent of Rivière du Nord, 1993

Sometime during the winter of 1992–93, the illustrious George Luste, that tireless wilderness traveller and occasional bookseller, allowed me to glance at a book he thought might be of interest to me—*Northern Quebec And Labrador Journals And Correspondence 1819–35,* published by the Hudson's Bay Record Society.[1] With bait like that I'm helpless and George knew it. What he didn't know, was that my wife was looking for a birthday present for me. So, unselfish and anxious to please as always, I played the intermediary and made both of them happy. The inevitable consequence for me was a rekindled interest in the region north of Radisson, the northernmost town in Quebec with road access. In particular, I wanted to go back to the Seal Lakes, cross from there to Clearwater Lake and then follow either the Caribou River or Rivière du Nord to Richmond Gulf and finish by paddling south along the coast of Hudson Bay to Kuujjuarapik.

As always, the challenge was to find the most economical way to get there. Several days spent in the map library confirmed that it was possible to paddle from the end of the highway near Radisson, follow the Kanaaupscow River upstream to its nearest approach to the Great Whale River and, from there, travel due north past the Great and Little Whale watersheds to join the Nastapoca River upstream from the Upper Seal Lakes.

There was only one small problem—it would take 45–50 days to complete the trip, well beyond the length of time at my disposal. To shorten the trip I decided to fly into Lac Lenormand, one of several large lakes in the watershed of the Little Whale River. In an attempt to assuage the financial pain of this alternative, I invited two other members of the Wilderness Canoe Association, Rob Butler and Mike Jones, to join me on this journey.

The two-hour flight from the seaplane anchorage of Air Wemindji at La Grande began in perfect sunshine. As we headed north across a vast expanse of drowned land—the storage basin of Hydro Québec's LG 2 power complex—sunshine gave way to ominous clouds, strong turbulence and rain squalls. Despite my conviction that the pilot was hopelessly lost among the uncertain outline of hills and lakes, he put the plane down right on target at the base of a sandy esker. With firewood from an old campsite nearby providing warmth and a quickly erected rain shelter offering protection from the elements, we spent the rest of the day trying to sort and organize food and equipment into a manageable configuration. For the next three days we paddled in a northeasterly direction through a region of open woodland and large lakes. Despite the presence of many outcrops of shield rock that rise up to one hundred metres above their surroundings, the feeling here is one of endless open space. The lakes we traversed were connected by short sections of flowing water, which occasionally demanded a short portage or walking the boats upstream. While paddling on Lac Saindon, however, we unexpectedly found our upstream journey transformed into a downstream float towards Lac D'Iberville. Some of the Little Whale River headwaters apparently spill over into the Nastapoca River watershed.

Lac D'Iberville is bisected by an esker that starts as a massive pile of sand and gravel on the western edge of the lake and runs in ever diminishing height towards the eastern shore. We arrived there just as the swirling mists evaporated in the morning sun. The combination of warm sun and gentle breeze, shimmering lake speckled with tiny islands and a kaleidoscope of colours was a joy to the senses and balm to the soul, ample reward after the generous precipitation

Loading up at La Grande for the flight into Lac Lenormand.

that preceded it. Progress through the rest of the lake was slow, largely because a maze of frost-shattered rock piles, which the map-makers arbitrarily lumped together as islands, created some confusion. We stopped for the day near the remains of an old encampment. The poles of a large teepee had collapsed inward but still showed that all the structural components had been carefully tied with split spruce roots. There were also remnants of a canoe but absolutely no sign of European artefacts. It must have been occupied for a considerable period of time as there were virtually no trees left in the immediate neighbourhood, even though the area in general was well wooded.

Early the next morning, after a short carry past the rocky outflow of Lac D'Iberville, we launched our boats into Upper Seal Lakes and headed for one of the many high mounds of glacial till. Climbing to high ground and looking over the lay of the land is an important and satisfying component of my outdoor experience, but this time there was a little more tension than usual associated with this process. In 1820, James Clouston passed through here on his way back to Hudson Bay from the Kanaaupscow River.[2] In the course of his exploration of the region at the behest of the Hudson's Bay Company, he produced a crude map that showed his route from the Upper Seal Lakes to Clearwater Lake. Since he was travelling in the company of a large group of Natives, I presume he was following a well-established track. It was my hope to find and follow that portage route to Clearwater Lake.

In spite of the short distance that separates Lac D'Iberville and the Upper Seal Lakes there is a pronounced change in the landscape; trees are confined to sheltered areas and the barren, boulder-strewn hills are higher. From our vantage point we could see a shallow tree-lined depression that concealed a creek, the outflow of a lake situated further northwest. I was confident this was the beginning of Clouston's overland route. Our campsite that evening was a sombre place, bare rocky desolation, and yet, in the last orange rays of the sun, the place was wildly beautiful.

Three long and sweaty days later we floated out into Clearwater Lake. All along we had seen absolutely no sign of anyone ever having travelled the same way. So much for my route finding ability. I have since acquired a copy of a map produced by George Atkinson,[3] who seemingly travelled Clouston's route in 1818 but in the opposite direction. It suggests a more westerly course than we pursued.

Clearwater Lake is a huge body of water that occupies the site of twin impact craters. The two halves of the lake are separated by a string of islands that rise 150 metres above water level. It's a place of extraordinary visual appeal. The bare, light-coloured hilltops, the dark green seams of stunted trees in miniature valleys, the light green and unusually transparent water, the dramatic cloud patterns on the huge expanse of sky, all combine to create a sense of awe. Just as we entered the lake a brief and violent rain squall sent us ashore. Not long thereafter we stopped for the day on the north shore near some old Native campsites. The weather remained unpredictable with frequent showers throughout the night. The lake was rather unruly in the morning and we made a cautious crossing to the south shore, using the islands as shelters from the worst wave action. We stopped early on the last tiny island in a sheltered bay and spent a memorable evening watching a number of storm cells pass by in quick succession and culminating with a magnificent double rainbow.

Two days later we entered the long narrow channel that was the starting point of Craig Macdonald's 1987 winter trip. I had planned to visit the first campsite of that memorable journey, but at the end of a hard day's paddle, nostalgia took a back seat to practicality. We opted instead to set up camp on a sandy beach, applied soap and water to skin and clothing and basked in the sun.

Canoeists have several routes from which to choose when travelling between Clearwater Lake and Richmond Gulf. The early travellers of the Hudson's Bay Company used the Caribou River to travel upstream to Clearwater Lake but preferred to use the Clearwater River when going downstream. Another route, described by A. P. Low in his GSC report of 1888, which I had followed in 1990, uses in part Rivière de Troyes as the connecting link between the two bodies of water. Lastly, there is Rivière du Nord, which has its origin in an nameless lake a short distance from the northwestern shore of Clearwater Lake and flows into the most northerly bay of Richmond Gulf. It became the river of choice primarily because I could find no reference that anyone had ever descended it. The thought of making a first descent appealed to us all.

Two short carries brought us to the small lake from which rises Rivière du Nord. It was an exquisitely cloudless day and the sense of travelling in "unknown" territory added excitement to the venture. I was quite prepared for a day of wading and portaging, but we had only two short impassable stretches and a surprisingly strong flow of water immediately below the headwater lake before we entered into a plain of low ridges of sand and gravel, through which the river makes its way west in a series of long narrow channels. A fire some 30–40 years ago had burned off most of the vegetative cover and only now were widely scattered trees making a hesitant return.

Successive river channels were separated from one another by outcrops of shield rock or boulders requiring short lift-overs. The first camp on the river was struck on a sandy bay among a few weather-beaten tamaracks. Mike disappeared with the fishing rod and came back empty-handed but with a "big one that got away" story. Except for a 15-centimetre trout that Rob snared the next evening, it was the closest my companions came to success at fishing on the whole trip. Mind you, there wasn't a lot of spare time. During the night I woke to the sound of clacking hooves and the grunts of a large group of passing caribou. At daybreak only their tracks remained, save for a solitary bull who observed us at close quarters while we broke camp. It was the only caribou we actually saw on the whole journey.

With each succeeding day the river gradient increased. By the end of the next day gravel and sandbars had been replaced by boulders and rock, and lift-overs by portages of increasing length and difficulty. The river became more and more recessed and hills of bedrock became more and more austere. Anyone not into wilderness travel would have found the landscape intimidating, but our frequent hikes to high ground only evoked a deep sense of joy to be wandering in such an unpeopled place. Except for one very old teepee site about halfway down the river, we came across no sign of human presence. This added to the sense of adventure, as the best route for each carry had to be "discovered."

To all these (imposed) challenges my companions rose without complaint. The most memorable of these was a portage, which was no more than one-and-a-half kilometres as the crow flies. It started with a steep ascent up an alder-clad embankment to more level ground above. To ease the process I cleared a route with my axe. After an exhausting scramble through more alders and willows, we changed tactics and moved to still higher ground. Evening found us encamped a long way from a source of water but with a wonderful view of the river below, the roar of the rapids just a faint murmur and the dark silhouettes of the western ramparts of Richmond Gulf painting the horizon.

Companions on this journey were Rob Butler, *left,* and Mike—"Laurence of Eastmainia"—Jones.

It was enterprises like this portage that made me forget my preference for solitary travel. There is something reassuring about the grunts and heavy breathing of your companions when you yourself are labouring under a weighty load on the trail. There is something consoling about seeing their sweat-soaked, tired faces at the end of the day. It was nice, too, not to have to do all the chores by yourself every day. But there was one aspect of my companions that cast a pall on everything—it was the disproportionate distribution of blackflies. If I had been travelling alone I would have simply accepted the presence of large numbers of this scourge as an unavoidable price that must be paid. But here I endured bloody discrimination; while I was constantly besieged and grievously wounded, my companions rarely attracted the attention of my tormentors.

Our return to river travel the next morning started with a bit of adversity. The boys managed to sink their canoe while lining down a stretch of fast water. I saw Mike's life jacket float away and took off after it, but to no avail. Looking back at it now, the poor fellow must have had some anxious moments later on when we were paddling in some dicey situations, and he without supplementary flotation. We didn't cover very much ground the rest of the day. Fortunately, it was a beautiful sunny day for drying everything.

The last obstruction on Rivière du Nord is a 4.5 kilometre rapid with a drop of more than 80 metres. We didn't have to scout it to know it wasn't negotiable. A close look at the map revealed a shorter portage route to Richmond Gulf through a gap in the rocks some distance south of the present channel, which appears to have been the original outlet to the Gulf. Two short portages brought us to the shore of the last freshwater lake where we set up the tents and made the obligatory hike to high ground from which we could observe the rugged landscape of Richmond Gulf.

The three-kilometre portage to saltwater the next morning was remarkably painless. Well-trodden game trails breached the dense jungle of vegetation at the base of the escarpment, then sloping bedrock of smooth basalt made progress even easier. Only the last few hundred metres of willows posed an obstacle requiring axe work. But there was, in the end, a disagreeable element—timing. There are extensive foreshore flats along parts of the eastern shore of Richmond Gulf and now the tide was going out. No matter how speedily we tried to return with the next load to the boat left at the water's edge, it required dragging across oozing, fetid muck to catch up with the constantly receding waterline.

On our way south to the mouth of the Caribou River, we experienced one of the sudden blows for which Richmond Gulf is known. In minutes, a strong westerly had rows of whitecaps marching in the most disturbing manner. With a fractured shoreline discouraging any attempt at landing, we were forced to ride the watery roller coaster for an hour or more until the wind died as suddenly as it started. The next day, while approaching the narrows that separate Cairn Island from the south shore of the Gulf in perfect calm, another sudden blast had us scrambling ashore barely in time to observe the fury of the elements from the shelter of house-sized boulders.

Richmond Gulf is connected to Hudson Bay by a deep channel barely 100 metres wide in some places, and for much of its three kilometre length it is bordered by vertical rock faces. Strong tidal currents give rise to considerable turbulence, and early European travellers report that the Natives preferred to portage rather than face the whims of the spirits that inhabit the place. Its name—Le Goulet—does little to reassure the traveller. Dominating the entrance to the channel from the east are the ramparts of Presqu'île Castle, a rocky peninsula whose near vertical walls rise nearly four hundred metres into the sky. After a damp night and a foggy morning we approached this imposing place, just as the emerging sun began to dissolve the mists. Light transformed the monotone landscape into sharp and colourful relief and me into photographic improvidence. Our passage through the channel to the wide horizon of Hudson Bay was entirely uneventful and did not warrant the nervous tension with which I approached the task. Once out on the bay, a light westerly breeze was sufficient to create a confused slop that made paddling slow and tedious, so we went ashore at the first sandy bay that came equipped with clear running water and plenty of dry firewood.

The eastern shore of Hudson Bay, travelling south from the mouth of the Nastapoca River to the Great Whale River, offers many attractive campsites although most are exposed to the prevailing westerlies, which can make landing and launching in the waves an interesting experience. One can be windbound for extended periods in bad weather, but we were fortunate and only had to put to shore for a few hours when the waves became too ominous. Evidence of human presence manifests itself in Inuit tent rings near the shore, Indian hunting camps further inland and the accoutrements of western civilization everywhere—rubber boots, bits of plastic, empty oil cans, even disposable diapers. We arrived at our last campsite before noon with the intention of having a good wash in privacy at the last creek before town. We quickly found out that privacy was in short supply. It was Sunday and half the population of Kuujjuarapik roared up in their ATVs to spend the day at their favourite picnic ground.

The return flight to La Grande the next day proved to have another surprise in store for us, this one much more appreciated. Canadian Airlines charged us only by weight for our boats, not volume. That saved us at least $300,[4] which was enough to put a smile on Rob's face for most of our flight back.[5]

TWELVE

Retirement Odyssey in the Great Northwest, 1994

In the years following the trip down the Coppermine River, others parts of Canada's great northern playground beckoned, delaying my return to the Northwest Territories until 1994, the year of my retirement from McMaster University. The university had, for some months prior to that fateful day, arranged for me to attend workshops and counselling sessions to help retirees cope with the transition. Apparently, for many people, the change from a prescribed set of activities to one of your own choosing is quite traumatic. All *I* could see was permanent, paid holiday with backcountry travel no longer restricted by time. I thought that occasion might be marked and celebrated with a longer trip back in the Great Northwest.

In spite of dramatic increases in recreational canoeing in the Northwest Territories in the last twenty years, there are still large areas that are lightly travelled and about which, apart from the reports of the Geological Survey of Canada, little has been written. For me, this in itself constituted enough justification to take a closer look. In this particular case, an additional impetus was my fondly remembered 1988 trip, which took me from Slemon Lake to the mouth of the Coppermine River. Nevertheless, in that interval and after many trips to the map library, I decided that a route I'd found in consultation with the maps and my friend John McInnes[1] best satisfied several of my criteria—inexpensive, variety of terrain and away from popular routes. The most important element of all was the ability to fly supplies via scheduled carrier to two Indian villages along the route. This allowed me to exceed the five-week limit that the carrying capacity of my boat imposes. It also meant that the loads on the portages could be a little lighter and more appropriate for the ageing frame of a senior citizen.

I arrived in Rae in the first week of July. Because of several reports of the high incidence of vandalism in the community, I visited the local detachment of the RCMP and asked whether I could leave my car at their post during my absence. "No problem," said the man at the desk, "as long as you understand we take no responsibility. We also have to know exactly where you are going and how long you expect to be away!"

"Well," said I, "it's a bit complicated, but in bare outline my first target is Rae Lake, then Rawalpindi Lake, Snare Lake and back here. As to time, somewhere between seven and ten weeks." That seemed to be exact enough and was duly entered into the computer.

Rae is located northwest of Yellowknife on a small peninsula at the southern shore of Marian Lake, a large shallow body of water nearly 40 kilometres long. It receives the waters of the Snare River, which enters from the east, and from the Marian River at its northern extremity. These waters are then dissipated into Great Slave Lake through several short channels. My immediate goal was to reach the mouth of the Marian River and follow it upstream to Mazenod Lake. As always at the beginning of a trip I was anxious to get started, but my departure was delayed by the brisk wind that had churned up the silty lake bottom and turned the water into grey-brown soup. By the evening of the second day, with no change in sight, my patience was gone and with some misgivings I pushed off. I only made it to the first island some seven kilometres away before courage failed me, but at least I was underway. In the morning the wind blew with unabated vigour out of the southeast and pushed me with surprising speed toward the mouth of the river, past an abandoned Indian village into a landscape that featured little change over the next few days.

Near the end of the last Ice Age the whole region from Marian Lake to just south of Great Bear Lake was occupied by a huge meltwater lake. The run-off from the ice sheet, centred near the headwaters of the Back River, brought with it a great amount of sediment, which settled on the lake bottom. With the disappearance of this lake the region is now a huge plain through which the highest elevations of the underlying shield protrude in sculpted grandeur. In its lower reaches, the Marian River has carved a course through the sediments of the old lake bottom in a process of continual erosion. Much of the surface beyond the riverbanks is occupied by shallow bodies of water, a veritable haven for fish and fowl, muskrat and beaver, as well as their predators—eagles, otters and wolves. The predominant tree species are poplar and birch, which are gradually replaced by spruce and jack pine as one travels upriver. The Marian is a small river with a gentle current, making upstream travel easy. By mid-afternoon, the hot sun and plain fatigue had produced the lethargy that had me looking for a campsite. When I reached the base of the second falls, I decided to set up camp. For a while, a pair of wolves on the opposite shore watched the proceedings before sauntering off

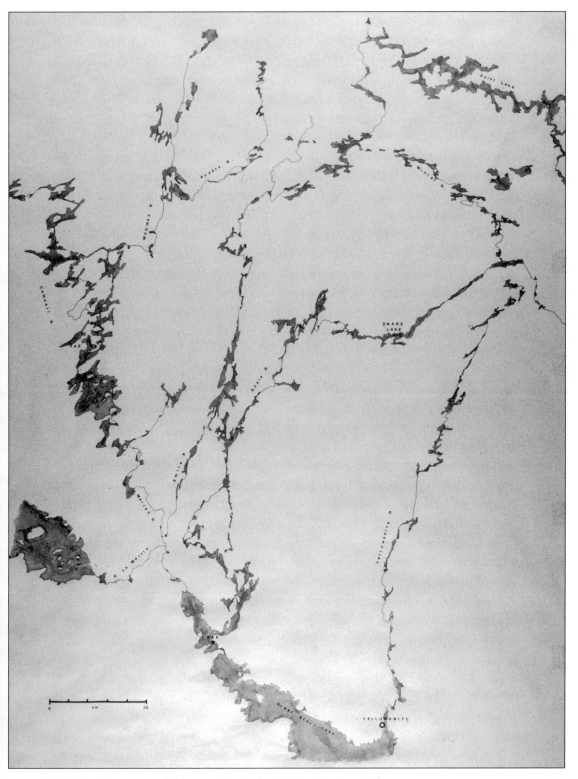

Herb's hand-drawn map of the unusual route for his Great Northwest trip.

into the bush. It was the first of a number of encounters with wolves; all of them were in splendid condition and not overly concerned about my presence.

By the end of the third day, I had passed the two major tributaries of the Marian, the Emile River and Rivière La Martre and several trapper's cabins, one of which had been used until very recently and contained homemade snowshoes, toboggans and what is referred to as a "ratting canoe" by the Dene—perhaps three metres long and very slender, enough to carry one person and little else.[2] Upstream from the confluence with the Emile River, the Marian is reduced to a tiny, muddy trickle. The mud is due to the activity of literally countless muskrats and beavers that continually stir up the silty riverbanks. I normally don't worry about water quality, but here I drank only tea. Further upstream the river not only gets cleaner but, surprisingly, also larger. Presumably the boggy sections act like a sponge during periods of low precipitation.

After a succession of short carries across well-maintained portages I reached Hislop Lake and camped at the base of a high hill on the western shore. I had planned to get to the summit with the first light of dawn and come away with some decent pictures. Alas, by morning the haze of a distant forest fire obscured the horizon, a forerunner of things to come, which dogged my efforts at photography throughout the trip. Above Hislop Lake the river is a delightful mix of placid stream and boisterous drops, the shield rock becomes more prominent, and at several points the river separates into two or more rocky channels. Wading and dragging the boat over the many shallows and ledges soon proved to my dissatisfaction that the abrasive quality of the shield rock was excellent. Finding portages became more time-consuming as well, and I was glad when at the end of the first week I reached Mazenod Lake. It is a beautiful, island-studded sheet of water. The largest of the islands rises steeply to a flat summit some 70 metres above the lake. It provided not only a lovely campsite but afforded a remarkable overview of my "kingdom for the day." A pair of bald eagles soared and dipped in the wind; the flecked and streaked surface of the lake, almost black when viewed in one direction, was magically transformed into quicksilver when looking towards the setting sun. Could heaven be any better than this?[3]

In contrast to the vast majority of wilderness trippers, who insist on gathering as much information about their intended route as possible beforehand, I consciously limit myself to a careful examination of existing maps, the rest of the information gathering happens during the trip. This approach maximizes the *discovery* aspect of the journey. It does occasionally incur the additional expenditure of nervous and physical energy, which could be avoided by a through pre-trip research, but I find that this just adds a bit of spice to the enterprise.

The next portage was a case in point. The watersheds of the Marian and Camsell rivers have their closest approach between Mazenod and Sarah lakes. I had spent a great amount of time staring at the map to try and anticipate where the old Native portage was likely located. There was no doubt that one existed, but I had no idea how easy it would be to find and follow it. At any rate I was prepared for a three-kilometre carry. It turned out that instead of one long carry, the old trail crossed several small ponds and was quite painless, exactly as shown on the map produced by the Geological Survey, as I found out later.

The Camsell River is the connecting link between a number of large lakes, remnants of the ancient meltwater lake, which are in close proximity to one another. The most prominent landmark in this land of distant horizons is Mossy Island, which rises 160 metres above Faber Lake, a fabulous lookout, well worth the effort needed to climb it. A short river channel connects Faber Lake with Rae Lake and is the standard route of the Natives today. My interest, however, was piqued by a portage route indicated on the 1: 50,000 topo map, which reaches Rae Lake from a deep bay in the northeast corner of Faber Lake.

Old and now unused portages are sometimes difficult to locate and follow. I find the process extremely stimulating and satisfying, although in this particular case the script was not entirely to my liking. The barely recognizable trail traversed a marshy region with shallow ponds and passed the remnants of old winter camps. Along the way I stopped again and again to feast on blueberries. On my approach to the end of the portage with my last load, I found a black bear engaged in trying to extricate one of my food packs from the boat. What concerned me more than the impertinence of the action was the fact that the creature only moved off about 25 metres.

Well, I had a cure for that!

I had brought along a little plastic flare pistol for just such an occasion. It makes quite a loud report, akin to a shotgun. I quickly loaded it and fired the flare out over the water, all the while keenly observing the bear. I instantly recognized this animal had a problem, there was absolutely no reaction—obviously this was a dumb creature. At this point I decided that one of us had to move and so I purposefully tried to launch the canoe. As the devil wants to have it, the water was rather shallow, even 50 metres out it was hardly deep enough to float my conveyance. Worse still, the bear had moved closer and was matching my progress step for step. It would be an understatement to say I was nervous.

Damage assessment at the next lunch spot revealed a badly shredded food pack, several punctured containers and a crack in the boat, but nothing that duct tape couldn't handle in the short run. Later that day I retrieved my food supply for the next 25 days, which had been flown in to the village of Rae Lake, a Native community of approximately 200 inhabitants. It was an excessively hot day and I wasted little time getting back onto the cool water. For the next two days, my route took me through Rae Lake, Lac St-Croix and Margaret Lake to the mouth of the Wopmay River. Many parts of these lakes have shallow, marshy sections well-populated with moose. The boulder-clad bedrock hills showed old scars of forest fires. I was getting increasingly concerned that my way might be blocked by one of the many fires that were burning at the time, as smoke frequently obscured the landscape. As it turned out it was a needless worry.

The Wopmay River[4] is the major tributary of the Camsell River and carries a substantial amount of water. It's a drop-and-pool river with little current in between drops, at least as far upstream as I travelled. The 1:50,000 maps indicated portage trails around many of the obstructions. The actual existence and location of these portages, however, rarely coincides with the map location. The condition of the trails appears to depend on the local fauna—if there were moose in the region, the old trails were easily recognized; if not, they were almost impossible to find.

Just below Grant Lake I left the Wopmay and followed the southern branch of the Acasta River to Little Crapeau Lake. With it I entered a noticeably different landscape. The lower river is an enormous collection of sand—the plain of the old lake floor interspersed with partially eroded sand eskers flanked in places by high vertical cliffs of frost-shattered rock. The dark lichen and the bright sand provided a curious contrast, a metaphor of evil and good I thought. It was here that I came across an old Indian encampment, seemingly a canoe-building site, for I found many canoe components including pieces of birchbark beautifully stitched together with spruce roots. Nearby were also the remains of a cabin that contained a cast iron stove. What was once a canvas-covered freighter canoe was scattered in little pieces over a large area, obviously the victim of the wrath of the local bear population.

Further upstream, the land shows all the markings of a gigantic meltwater spillway. Large fields of boulders, of distant origin and tightly packed, lined the shallow and poorly defined valley floor. The river became a succession of obstructions and I spent very little time paddling. It took three days of almost continuous bushwhacking to reach a wide, marshy plain. All along the way the country had been attractive in a wild sort of way, but here a sense of tranquillity reigned supreme. From one of the low hills, I could see glittering outlines of

Carrying a canoe up one side of a thousand-foot mountain and down the other can be hard on the footwear. This was Herb's kind of trip.

shallow lakes stretching to the far horizon, and I could feel the soothing silence of the place. At the far end of the plain, the sluggish and circuitous flow of the river assumed a more purposeful pace between banks of gravel and sand and trees became more abundant. I watched the passing scenery with a growing mix of apprehension and excitement as I was approaching the point where my route left the river and continued east overland toward Rawalpindi Lake. All of a sudden I wasn't so sure it was a sensible undertaking.

I had spent a great deal of time looking at maps before deciding on an overland route that would take me from the Acasta River to the Winter River headwaters at Whitewolf Lake. The plan was to leave the Acasta at a point where a poorly defined esker, running east-west, was bisected by the river. Now, with mounting excitement, I was nearing the area and worried whether I would recognize the place. Right on cue the river widened, revealing mounds of sand and boulders beyond a little bay on the eastern shore and a narrow, shallow opening, which led to a series of interconnected ponds. This looked much better than I had dared to hope. The esker, rather than one continuous ribbon, was a series of anastomosing heaps of gravel and well-rounded rocks that separated the water into discrete entities. Spruce trees, hundreds of years old and much larger than anything I had encountered heretofore, dominated the high ground. I had actually planned to camp here and do a bit of reconnoitring, but a nervous restlessness and the ceaseless complaints of a sandpiper urged me on. Several short portages brought me to the last pond draining into the Acasta River. By now it was too late to continue and I reluctantly made camp on the south shore. Just behind the tent a dark wall of rock loomed and all around there was an air of desolation. There was no evidence that anyone had ever visited the place and one could almost feel the presence of the spirits.

Progress from here would be mainly by shank's mare and, in spite of fatigue, I proceeded to the top of the highest hill to see what the morrow held in store. Below me, the land stretched eastward in gentle undulations, hummocky bog intermixed with gravelly higher ground upon which widely scattered clumps of small spruce shared space with a profusion of low shrubs. Except for a small pond at the base of the hill I was standing on, there wasn't a sign of water anywhere. Somewhere towards the east was a small narrow lake, which was my next target, but it was hidden from view. The only prominent landmark was a line of ragged low hills that ran from my lookout to the horizon. According to the map their alignment was south-east, but the compass insisted it was east. This was anything but reassuring and I returned to the tent a worried man. During the night a cold wind blew in from the north. In the morning the air was sharp and clear, perfect for portaging. I found the next lake within two hours, then the next and by late afternoon looked down on Irritation Lake, a sheet of water that looked rather beautiful to me. The evening was warm and the campsite remarkably bug-free. An abundant supply of firewood beckoned in the form of a dead tree some distance from the tent. So off I went with my axe, clad only in socks and shoes, to bring home the bounty. And then a remarkable thing happened, which reminded me of the ringing of the triangle at meal time in the bush camps where I had worked many years earlier. Each stroke of the axe seemed to bring out large numbers of mosquitoes, as if it were a call to dinner—and so it was. For a while I held out manfully, but finally reason won out and I raced back to the tent and put on some clothes.

The next day was spent portaging across a wild confusion of glacial debris, pockets of trees, bogs and humps of bedrock. By mid-afternoon I was standing atop one of the high hills lining the valley of the Emile River, which at this point widens into a lake. The shadows on the vertical rock faces beyond the far shore contrasted sharply with the bright sand at the deep blue water's edge. Caribou were wandering about everywhere. The land radiated peace and silence and I was happy beyond words.

At the Emile River the last trees were left behind, and for several days I carried on through a succession of ponds, across Rawalpindi Lake eastward to Whitewolf Lake. This was truly a barren, almost featureless land. Most bodies of water were so shallow as to barely float the boat, and full of sharp-edged rocks. Also, the transition from boggy land to water was so gradual that landing and launching the canoe was often more work than simply carrying past. Most unexpected and much appreciated was the almost total absence of mosquitoes and blackflies. The only fly in the ointment was the presence of high-level smoke from forest fires farther south and west, which rendered the sky a peculiar shade of grey through which the sun shone only dimly.

The most prominent feature of the Winter River watershed is the presence of several eskers that snake across the landscape in a generally east-west orientation. Their outlines define not only the horizon but also the boundaries of many of the large lakes covering much of the surface. Along the way I developed a decidedly hostile attitude towards the people who had produced the maps of the region. Virtually all river sections, which connect adjacent lakes, were impassable boulder fields through which water percolated in the most discreet way. Yet, many times the map would show a broad channel free of obstruction or, at most, a bar or two across to indicate all was not well. Every wilderness traveller is aware that maps are not always accurate, but here the discrepancies were numerous.

All along the way, caribou wandered over the land and several times they were clustered around the tent during the night, as if it were a refuge from the wolves whose howls periodically pierced the silence. After a week of picking up every little piece of dry brush along the way to cook my meals, I stumbled upon some real firewood at the base of a large esker. It was all the fuel needed to transform a weary traveller into a happy camper. The day had been dominated by a cold north wind that sent the temperature close to the freezing point. Now I could

An esker and sandy beach on the Winter River.

luxuriate beside the warming blaze and linger over an extra cup of tea; my soul filled with gratitude. That same wind also blew away the smoke of distant fires and the morning was crisp and clear. The delicate pink light of the morning sun transformed the drab landscape of yesterday into a fairyland and I raced around for an exhausting hour trying to capture the magic on film.

It was below Little Marten Lake that I finally managed to run a rapid without scraping and bumping. All the way to Winter Lake, however, most drops were carries over boulder fields with treacherous footing. Perhaps it was just the realization that it was the last carry on the Winter River, but the view of Winter Lake from the top of the portage was extraordinarily beautiful. Beyond the bay into which the Winter River discharges lie several small islands, little jewels of sand and stone. Scattered stands of trees dotted the landscape and gave it texture. This day, the haze of smoke put a soft dreamy focus on the scene.

Under vastly different circumstances, Franklin had surveyed this landscape on his disastrous journey to the Arctic Ocean in 1920–21. I was now only a few kilometres from the site of his winter quarters located on the Snare River, a short distance below Winter Lake. When I put ashore in a little bay just to the north of the mouth of the river, having read and reread Franklin's *Journey to the Polar Sea*, I was more than a little excited. The area is criss-crossed by many strong caribou trails, which partially obscure the old portage trail, but there was no mistaking the marker on an ancient spruce, a tree that must have witnessed the comings and goings of Franklin's men. Near the end of the portage dozens of stumps of large trees, their wood still solid, show the axe marks of the voyageurs. However, except for a few scattered logs, nothing remains of the three buildings that once was Fort Enterprise. When I departed several hours later it was with a new sense of urgency. For the first time on the trip large numbers of blackflies had made their appearance. In my excitement I had ignored their persistent efforts and paid the price.

A short distance below Fort Enterprise, the Snare River enters the first of two long and narrow lakes—Roundrock and Snare—both of which occupy a groove in the shield rock, which runs from northeast to southwest for nearly 100 kilometres. A range of high rugged hills dominate the southern shores; by contrast the low northern shores are delimited by parallel eskers that offer a continuum of beautiful campsites. Sadly, there is a disturbing amount of garbage at all the most scenic spots, which can only be attributed to the proximity to the village of Snare Lakes. The latter is a permanent settlement of very recent origin and undergoing rapid expansion. At the time of my passing by, construction of a number of buildings was under way and a new runway had just been completed. Confronting "civilization" on a wilderness trip to me is always an unsettling experience, and I wasted little time collecting the food pack flown in earlier at the band manager's office and paddling on.

The Snare River below Snare Lake drops sharply into an impassable canyon. To bypass this section I portaged through a number of small lakes to the south of the river, a route I believe to be identical to that taken by Eric Morse's party in 1964.[5] The curious aspect of this route is that some of the small lakes are connected by readily recognizable old portage trails, while others show absolutely no sign of human travel. I rejoined the Snare a short distance above Indin Lake, more than a little fatigued from the exertions of the previous two days. When an attractive campsite presented itself on the north shore of the river, it was all the excuse I needed to stop for the day, even though it was barely after noon.

There is something immensely satisfying about a nice campsite and I certainly loved this one. A thick carpet of lichen covered the sandy, level ground. Ancient, widely scattered spruce provided shade from the burning sun, the sound of rapids downstream rose and faded with the halting, gentle breeze. With nary a mosquito around I stripped down for a good wash, did the laundry, attended to a leisurely supper and finally conveyed my feelings of happiness to my journal. By then the sun was setting in the west and while the spirit was one of contentment, the body was aching for rest.

Turning in for the night is a rarely changing ritual. Some kindling and one of the food packs is placed under the boat, a pot of water for breakfast is left at the fireplace. The vestibules, repositories of the rest of the gear, are left open in fair weather to allow the air to circulate and reduce condensation. I was just drifting off to sleep when I heard a scratching sound—something was at the boat. Instantly, I was wide awake, sat up and saw a dark furry head peering into the vestibule. Things happened rather fast after that. I let out a tremendous yell. The head disappeared. I unzipped the mosquito screen and looked out just in time to see two cubs running away. In the same instant I felt the tent shake violently and realized that mama bear had joined me in my abode. Her interest was seemingly focused on the same food pack that had been mutilated a few weeks earlier. Without so much as a "May I?" she grabbed the pack and walked nonchalantly away.

Readers will recognize that this is a script straight from Hollywood: Yogi Bear with Boo-Boo and the picnic basket, only now it wasn't funny. I was scared and mad and the one thing I wanted to do was fire one of my flares right up mama bear's butt, but I had no such luck. The first try missed by a wide margin, the second, though closer, never worried her and by the time I had reloaded for the third try she had disappeared behind bushes some 60–70 metres away. Then I noticed to my considerable chagrin that one of the cubs had climbed up a small tree only a few metres away. I could just visualize mama returning angrily to claim her charge, so my third shot was aimed to speed the waif on its way. It too missed, hit the tree and ricocheted onto the ground where it immediately started a fire. It only took a minute to put it out, but, I dare say I was never more scared, scampering about within reach of the cub and mama just a short distance away.

At this point I came to the reluctant conclusion that I had to get the hell out of there. Within minutes everything was thrown helter-skelter into the canoe and I shoved off. None too soon either, for shortly thereafter the dark form of a bear emerged at the campsite, looking for seconds. By now it was almost totally dark and, with a rapid downstream blocking my way, I had nowhere to go. Fortunately, there was a marshy bay on the opposite shore. I eased the boat into the vegetation and there I sat for five shivering hours waiting for daylight. As time went by and the temperature fell, the starry sky became obscured by the rising mists. With some unease I became aware that there were other creatures afoot or afloat in the neighbourhood. With the first greying of dawn I hesitantly floated downstream in shallow water near the shore, almost within reach of a towering moose that had materialized out of the dense fog and put ashore at the head of the rapids. A short carry later I floated out into Indin Lake.

Camp that evening was a good distance down the lake. Against all expectation I slept soundly that night, but for the rest of the trip there was a heightened awareness of one's vulnerability. In terms of calories the loss of the food pack was not a problem. I had enough dinners left in the second pack and plenty of pancake mix and bacon, but little else. On the positive side, I was now able to portage my gear in two trips. The section of river between Indin and Kwejinne lakes contains a number of significant drops and is delightfully wild. In one stretch the river runs deep and slow between glacier-polished hills of bedrock that rise steeply on either side. When I drifted past here early one glorious morning, the sun's rays were streaming obliquely through the swirling mists and I was lost in the magic of the moment. In the process, I nearly collided with a bear that was out for a swim. We must have noticed each other at the same instant, little more than a boat length

Quiet camp on the Marian River.

apart. I put on the brakes, and he headed for shore where he stood up to take a look at me. It was the biggest black bear I have ever seen and I was thankful he hadn't paid me a visit at the campsite just a kilometre upstream.

At Kwejinne Lake I left the Snare River and portaged to the Emile River at a place where I had crossed six years earlier on my way north to the Coppermine. I like small streams and the Emile fits the bill admirably. Despite its length it never seems to gain in volume and offers an interesting mix of scenery. Just downstream from where I joined it, the river drops 60 metres in two kilometres as it cascades over solid bedrock. To my surprise I couldn't find a portage trail, but the carry through poplar and jack pine was not difficult (as it turned out I didn't look in the right place). Below this section the river enters a region that shows little evidence of glacial abrasion; rock faces are sharp and angular and there is little sand or gravel. Stretches of flat water and small lakes are separated by steep cataracts requiring carries. Below Lac Labrish the portage trails around these obstructions are veritable highways and one finds many signs of previous human occupation. Among the latter was a deserted prospector tent on an island. It contained a small supply of groceries including a, *to me,* highly valued commodity—tea. I absconded with a few bags, wrote a note admitting the offence and left without remorse.

Two days later I entered the Marian River and, with it, familiar territory. When I reached the portage where I had spent the first night on the river, the pair of wolves that had greeted me then, were there again. Just to say hello I gave them my best imitation of a wolf howl and they answered in kind. For the next 20 minutes, while I carried my two loads across the trail, their melancholy chorus persisted and followed me downstream. When I reached Marian Lake a few hours later the surface of the water was like polished glass. At noon the following day I could see the steeple of the Catholic church in Rae reaching above the horizon, and felt like a voyageur at the end of the summer's journey. I had covered a little more than 1,100 kilometres, carried over nearly 150 portages and wore out a pair of new boots. Of course, I checked in at the RCMP detachment to tell them not to worry about my whereabouts.

It seems there was no record of my journey on their computer.

THIRTEEN

Unfinished Business on the Quebec-Labrador Border, 1996[1]

Perhaps it's just the feeling of relief one experiences when crossing a height of land—the uphill part of the journey is done—but, on my trips from the George River side of the watershed to the headwaters of one of the northern Labrador rivers, I have always considered the region straddling the Quebec-Labrador boundary extraordinary. There are one or more ranges of bare hills oriented in a north-south direction, which dominate an undulating plain dotted with bodies of water. These ranges have been breached in a number of places by glaciers that advanced from the centre of the ice cap that occupied the Labrador peninsula during the last ice age. The many eastward trending eskers and profuse erratics indicate the scale of the forces that shaped the land. Visually, there is a raw edge to it all, exquisitely beautiful when the sun shines and the horizon is at infinity; hostile and bleak when rain and fog dominate the scene.

In the summer of 1996, I decided to spend several weeks in the Quebec/Labrador highlands following a course through small lakes and ponds in a generally south to north direction. The idea was to touch on areas with inter-esting geographical features away from the main travel routes while keeping the portaging within tolerable limits. Last, but not least, it had to stay within the bounds of a modest financial budget. Retirement had removed the strictures of time in my travel, so I left southern Ontario on Monday, July 22, with visions of a leisurely drive to Labrador City. The weekly train of the Quebec North Shore and Labrador Railway to Schefferville leaves Labrador City on Thursdays at noon and so I was looking forward to an unhurried observation of the country-side along the way, particularly the stretch of road beyond Baie-Comeau, which I had not travelled before.

Unbeknownst to me, my departure coincided with the occurrence of torrential downpours in the region north of Quebec City. The first inkling that all was not right were frequent signs of washouts on Highway 138 and finally a roadblock by the Quebec Provincial Police. The message: No point in going any farther, roads and bridges ahead are washed out and it will take as much as a week to repair. They didn't insist that I turn around, and so I continued past more road-blocks and newly bulldozed detours, and by Tuesday afternoon, reached Baie Comeau and turned north. Driving on Highway 389 to Labrador City was an adventure. Full of ups and downs and hairpin bends, it begins by traversing some of the most intimidating landscape imaginable. The sole reason for its construc-tion was to bring in supplies for the construction of five massive hydroelectric dams. The last of these, at Manic-Cinq holds back the waters of the Manicoua-gan Reservoir. It is also the end of the pavement. The highway was later extended as a gravel road to Gagnon, a mining community still shown on the map, but which is now completely erased from the landscape. In this section, I experienced my last delay. A transport truck had spilled part of its load across the road and it took hours for a crane to arrive and clear away the debris.

Home for the night was the Provincial Park at Lac Dudley, a beautiful spot with a memorable blackfly population. It was perhaps the reason why I was the sole resident of the place. The next morning, I reached Lab City in time to load my gear in the freight car and with quiet satisfaction, took a seat in one of the passenger cars on an adjacent track—perseverance had won the day.

Well, not quite. In a few minutes the coaches started to move forward, just to the next switch, or so I thought, expecting that the train would back onto the adjacent track to hook up with the freight cars. Alas, the passenger part of the train merely gathered speed and kept going. As the conductor explained it to me, I was participating in something of an historic event. Responding to complaints about the leisurely pace of the passenger train, authorities had responded by sep-arating freight and passenger traffic. As it happened, I was on the first segregated train. I was assured, in response to a rather sour attitude to this unexpected devel-opment, that my gear would be on its way to join me within hours of my arrival in Schefferville. Somehow I was not convinced that this new strategy by the QNS&L represented an improvement in service. True to form, the passenger train chugged into Schefferville at 11:00 p.m.—same as always. The freight arrived two days later!

Fortunately I was the beneficiary of the kind hospitality of the people of George River Lodge during the waiting period, particularly Jackie Courtois who went out of his way to find alternate transportation when the promised Cessna 185 failed

As always, Herb takes the time to find a point of prospect to really see the landscape through which he is travelling. Here, he takes in the esker snaking between Resolution Lake and Lac Raude.

to materialize. The alternative turned out to be an ancient Beaver operated by Saguenay Air out of their Squaw Lake[2] anchorage. My third morning in Schefferville dawned cool and cloudless, perfect flying conditions, and with the usual eagerness to get away, I looked forward to an early departure. Alas, at Squaw Lake, a number of other hopefuls—prospectors, guides and fishermen—all had the same intentions. I clearly wasn't very high on the priority list and my departure was pushed back hour after hour. The intervening time was spent in conversation with an interesting collection of other travellers, most of them guides with local outfitters who had many stories and knew how to tell them. I had almost given up hope on a gradually deteriorating day, when it was finally my turn.

I always find flying in small planes exciting, primarily because it adds perspective and widens the horizon. In this particular case there was the added intrigue of trying to identify specific landmarks passed on previous trips. Within an hour we had reached the upper George River watershed and approached the esker that connects Resolution Lake to Lac Raude. In 1985, Jim Greenacre and I had portaged across this very same esker on our way to the Ugjoktok River.

At my request, the pilot deposited me at the base of the esker on the south shore of Lac Raude and quickly disappeared in the overcast. The place had all the prerequisites of an ideal campsite—dry firewood, level tent site, exposure to the prevailing breeze, a nice view from the top of the high esker. There was only one distraction—numerous very fresh bear tracks. Normally, I would have put up the tent, with some unease to be sure, for bears and I seem to go together, but I had been sensitized by the many bear stories told by the guides, some of them rather worrisome. And so, despite the late hour, I shipped out to the north shore of the lake and a place much less endowed as a campsite. Just as I landed, a little seam opened in the gloomy cloud cover on the western horizon and allowed the dying sun to gild the low hills, a bit of magic that brightened the mind well beyond daylight.

Lac Raude is connected to the lake immediately north of it by a short bit of turbulence. That lake, a thin watery cover over glacial till and nameless on the maps, receives a stream on its eastern end, which is the outflow of three large lakes situated immediately west of the height of land that separates Quebec and Labrador. My expectation was that this stream would allow relatively easy access to the height of land—a 50-metre elevation change over 20 kilometres to get to the first large lake (Lac Aismery)—and good flow because of the large drainage area. A first look at the river confirmed that I was dealing with a substantial volume of water. There was only one small problem—the stream bed was wide and bouldery, and only occasionally was the water deep enough to float the boat. The "easy access" was going to involve some hard labour.

The end of the first day found me encamped on the shores of what looks deceptively like a lake on the map. After supper I climbed a high, barren hill, more by habit than inclination, because it promised a good overview of the region. To the west the wide, waterlogged valley of the George River was overlain by billows of clouds through which rays of light from the evening sun burst forth in ever changing patterns. A thunderstorm in the northwest darkened and rippled the surface of White Gull Lake. It was a scene that called for contemplation and reflection, were it not for the presence of a multitude of winged creatures who clamoured for blood. Their angry, relentless chorus spurred me on to an early retreat into the tent.

By early morning of the third day I had gained the western shore of Lac Aismery, happy to exchange the tumpline for the paddle. The landscape in this region is dominated by barren, rounded hills that rise a hundred metres or more above boggy lowland. Despite the modest increase in altitude from the valley of the George River to the height of land, there is a marked change in the vegetative cover—dense growth of black spruce, alders and Labrador tea is replaced by a covering of lichen among widely scattered tamaracks. The high ground is ideal hiking country, particularly if the wind is strong enough to keep the bugs in check, and I frequently availed myself of the opportunity. The reason for that was not only to get a better view of the surrounding countryside, but also to get a bit of respite from fighting the waves generated by a strong quartering wind, which blew relentlessly during the next few days—and stopped as soon as I decided to put up the tent. As any northern traveller knows, the biting fraternity's attraction to warm-blooded feeding stations is directly proportional to the length of time they have been confined to their hiding places. This unwelcome behaviour made life at campsites considerably less enjoyable.

Of all the bodies of water traversed on this trip, I remember Lac Beaupré with particular fondness. My campsite was at the base of a large hill jutting out into the lake from the north. During the night I was there a storm blew in from the west; morning dawned wet and dreary under threatening clouds. With some reluctance I retrieved the dry firewood from beneath the boat and started preparing the usual breakfast of pancakes and bacon. Halfway through the process I realized that all around me a remarkable change in the weather was taking place. While the western sky appeared dark and threatening like the gates of Hades, a magical brightness was beginning to emerge through the shifting mists in the east. An extraordinary visual spectacle was in the making, of that I was sure. Quickly grabbing tripod and camera I headed for high ground; breakfast would have to wait.

As too often happens, the photographic evidence was far from adequate in conveying the wonder and excitement of the event. Within an hour, the sun had assumed dominance and whitecaps dotted the lake. My course from the north-eastern end of Lac Beaupré was due north and despite a number of portages an euphoric sense of well-being lingered. During the next four days I crossed the headwaters of the Ugjoktok and Notakwanon rivers in quick succession before

Wild wind, wild rain, wild skies—Labrador, Herb's favourite place on earth.

reaching the region drained by the Mistastin River. In the process, euphoria was gradually replaced by fatigue; the keen appreciation of the glorious wildness of the country superceded by tired indifference and the body goes on autopilot as lakes and portages come and go. I usually have a vague target for the evening camp, and that becomes the motivating goal on a difficult day.

I was now following a drainage northwards through a series of small lakes to a point where it joins with another creek flowing in from the west. The combined waters of these two streams continue a turbulent northerly course to Mistastin Lake some 15 kilometres away. My course lay to the west and towards a long shallow groove in the bedrock that runs westward from the height of land.

Half-a-day's travel past the juncture of the two streams, I rounded a point in the narrow valley I was travelling in—the day had been squally, the labour hard and the mood sullen—and unexpectedly found myself confronted by a scene of exquisite beauty. Eskers converged from several directions to a high focus amid shallow bodies of water that shimmered in the afternoon sun. Just a kilometre to the east the surface was dotted with erratics, but here a covering of sand had softened the contours of the wide treeless plain. Far away on the southwestern horizon a range of high hills reached darkly into the blue sky. And once again, as on Lac Beaupré a week earlier, I was trying to photograph a panorama which filled me with awe.

The next day I was faced with a portage over a spur of the high hills that had provided such a beautiful backdrop the day before. On the map it seemed a straight forward carry, but bog and rock faces dictated a much longer circuitous route. Trying to hang onto the canoe in the strong wind was hard work and at day's end I was exhausted and footsore. An hour's search had produced a few meagre sticks of firewood, enough for a quick breakfast at best, and so I settled for a cold supper. During the evening a threatening sky gave rise to a full-blown storm that worried the tent for most of the night, but morning dawned serenely beautiful.

The lake I was camped on was completely landlocked except for a tiny outflow over a high rock ledge. Nevertheless, it was populated by large numbers of fish. During the morning chores a pair of resident loons approached quite closely as we carried on an animated conversation. What made this unusual was that it was the only time on the whole trip that I encountered another animal other than a few song birds—no ducks, no geese, no caribou, no bears, no wolves—the land seemed empty. Equally surprising was the total absence of signs of human occupation, old or new, in spite of a careful examination of potential camping spots along the way. It left the impression that I was travelling beyond an invisible barrier, removed from the everyday world.

For the last few days, walking had become increasingly painful. I thought a change of footwear might relieve the creeping fasciitis, so I switched to my hiking boots before setting out on the way to the next lake. From the top of the next portage I had a wonderful bird's-eye view of the glacial groove in the bedrock

The manager of Tuktu Lodge in Schefferville had agreed to fly in a cache to their lodge on Mistinibi Lake. "Decision time. The fasciitis is no better. This stopped being fun long ago. Answer: fly back to Schefferville, leaving an unfinished trip. Merde!"

running west to the horizon, which I planned to follow. A number of small lakes dotted the low spots like pearls on a string, their deep blue surface streaked by gusts of wind and set off dramatically by the gleaming white of a mini-glacier immediately below my vantage point. For the next two days my downhill progress toward Lac Audiepvre required a number of carries, including a couple around bodies of water that were shown as lakes on the map but were mere boulder fields.

Up to this point the weather had been uncharacteristically warm and sunny, and now it underwent a dramatic change. Within an hour the blue sky was obliterated by a wall of fog rolling in from the east. The temperature dropped from 20° C to just above the freezing point, and the lakes started to steam. The wind increased to at least 60 kph (it blew down the radio tower at Tuktu Lodge on Mistinibi Lake 50 kilometres to the northwest) and heavy rain began to fall. And at this least opportune time I made two mistakes—I portaged into the wrong lake and then passed up a safe campsite—just to get back on course. After two more portages, soaked and somewhat hypothermic, I spied a few scraggly tamaracks that provided enough wind shelter to put up the tent. Just then, by some miracle, the rain stopped for a few minutes, long enough to get set up without everything getting totally soaked. It didn't take me long to crawl into the sleeping bag and thank my guardian angel.

The storm raged on for two more days. On the second day my love affair with the sleeping bag was coming to an end and I started to collect firewood, which, in due course, became a wonderful source of heat. Gradually the monotony of the sky began to show some texture, the rain became intermittent drizzle and it was time to move on. Late in the day I portaged into the first large body of water in more than a week—Lake Bjarni. The southeast corner of this lake is bordered by high hills. That evening my mood was as dark as the surrounding scene. I was wet, cold and sore. The change of footwear had done nothing to relieve the fasciitis. The resulting discomfort had reduced my excursions in the countryside, a central element in my daily activities. Now I had to decide whether I should go on. I saw little reward in doing so.

At the start of this trip I had made arrangements with Alan Tardif, the manager of Tuktu Lodge in Schefferville, to ship one of my packs to their lodge on the shores of Mistinibi Lake. It contained food for two extra weeks of travel. By my original reckoning this would be enough to reach Nain on the Labrador coast, but as I approached the camp in pouring rain, I decided that the excitement and enthusiasm to continue was gone. The staff at the lodge—in particular, Alan Tardif, who flew me back to Schefferville and housed me for five days (for a total cost of $150)—were absolutely first class. Under the circumstances, it was the right decision, I think, but it still rankles a bit that I left this route unfinished.

·————————·

FOURTEEN

No Agenda on the Eastmain, 1997

When choosing northern wilderness trips, one of the most enjoyable quandaries is the almost limitless number of options from which to choose. As I get older though, the sand in the hourglass of life seems to run ever faster, and realistically, some of my potential choices can only be satisfied through reincarnation. In 1997, my plan was to return to the Eastmain shore of Hudson Bay make my way back up to the headwaters of the Clearwater River, portage into Clearwater Lake, from there go south towards the Little Whale River and follow the latter back to the coast. At least, that was the plan.

It is a 1,500 kilometre drive from southern Ontario to La Grande airport, my usual jumping-off place for trips in the Richmond Gulf area. The last 600 kilometres of this route was built by Hydro Québec to support the James Bay Hydro facilities. The forest industry was quick to take advantage of the new access road, and for other users of the route, one of the lessons this drive provides is the meaning of the word "clear-cutting" as practised here—it's utter devastation. The modest black spruce forest, hundreds of years in the making, has been obliterated along either side of the highway in less than a decade.[1]

Because of the mothballing of Hydro Québec's planned expansion projects, this year there was a pronounced reduction of economic activity in the region since my last visit in 1993. This was particularly noticeable at La Grande Airport, which this year was nearly deserted. The only airline servicing the communities along the eastern shore of Hudson Bay with regular passenger service is Inuit Air. However, because of the notoriously unpredictable weather of the region and changing priorities, the word "regularly" should be taken with a grain of salt.

Upon my arrival at the airport, as in previous years, I immediately went to the freight office to send my boat and one of my food packs ahead to Umiujaq on the afternoon flight. The good news was that Pierre, the man in charge, didn't use the volume formula for the boat to arrive at the cost. Instead, he assessed the boat and pack at 25 kilograms (together they weighed nearly three times as much). The bad news was that there was no flight, direct or otherwise, to Umiujaq. A few hours later I was told that there would be an unscheduled flight, mainly to fly a group of stranded passengers from the previous day's cancelled trip to Kuujjuarapik. That section would then continue on to Umiujaq with a load of freight, including my boat and me. There was more good news. When I obtained my ticket, the agent informed me that I was only entitled to a 20-kilogram baggage allowance, and then checked my two packs with a combined weight of at least 60 kilogram through without weighing them. She also advised me to take the third (and heaviest) pack with me as hand luggage.

When we arrived in Kuujjuarapik, everyone was ordered off the plane. It is standard procedure at any stop because a great amount of freight invariably has to be moved on and off the plane. What I didn't expect was that among the goods unloaded was my gear as well.

"A slight mistake!" I remonstrated.

"Not so!" was the reply.

"But I am going to Umiujaq!"

"The plane is going the Belchers. Umiujaq is completely fogged in."

All the freight for the Umiujaq was taken off, a load for the Belcher Islands taken on, and the plane disappeared into the evening sunshine, only to reappear a half hour later. The Belcher Islands were also fogged in. So now the plane was unloaded once again and returned to La Grande empty. I was told that I'd just have to wait for the next scheduled flight, two days hence.

And so, reluctantly, I set up my canvas cottage among the sand dunes near the runway and watched the locals roar about the countryside with their ATVs until well into the night. Morning dawned wet and dreary. Against all expectation a plane emerged from the low clouds and taxied to a top. I quickly rushed to the terminal to investigate.

"Yes, the plane is going to Umiujaq. You have about fifteen minutes if you want to get on."

An hour later we landed on the new runway, two kilometres south of the village. A light rain was falling and the place looked dismal beyond words. Fortunately, somebody took pity on me and gave me a ride to my old friend Eddie Weetaltuk's place. Eddie, who had put me up in 1990, was his hospitable self and soon all my wet gear, hastily thrown into a pack in Great Whale, was spread out to dry in his living room. The time passed pleasantly in reminiscence and conversation with several locals who dropped in during the day. I was more

This was to be another tidewater-to-tidewater extravaganza, but once Herb got on the water he decided to let go of his vertical agenda and concentrate on exploring things at sea level, including splendid beach campsites like this.

aware this time, of the casual way in which people come and go—enter without knocking or comment and leave the same way, often never saying a word, having had a look and a listen at the out-of-towner.

Overnight, a fresh nortwesterly breeze had blown away the clouds. I said my goodbyes and pushed off down the coast towards Le Goulet and Richmond Gulf in high spirits. The exuberance of starting on another adventure was soon tempered by the early onset of fatigue. The wind that had driven away the clouds had also raised waves of nervous proportions, and my heavily loaded boat wallowed about as if with a mind of its own. So, when a lovely little cove appeared along the way, I decided to stop for a quick cup of tea and to stretch my legs.

As so often happens, it became immediately obvious that the place had found favour with previous generations of travellers. The sparse remains of their encampments were bordered by a tiny stream that percolated through a gravelly substratum. I was totally captivated by the warm human aura that permeated the place. Despite awareness of the waves, which dissipated their energy on the bedrock at the entrance to the bay, a feeling of sublime tranquillity reigned. Beyond the cove the deep blue water of Hudson Bay merged seamlessly with the pale blue sky in the mist of the distant horizon. The velvety smooth bedrock radiated the warmth of the sun's rays. All of this—the look and feel of the place—sapped my motivation to continue. I felt invited to linger and enjoy the moment.

There is probably no rational explanation for what happened next. I was so seduced by the setting, that right then and then I decided to abandon my carefully planned trip itinerary.[2] To hell with ambitious schedules, this time I was going to do short excursions along the way and poke around the little Shangri-Las like this cove. Barely half a day into the trip, I had a new plan.

The striking topography of the Richmond Gulf region is the consequence of two gigantic geological faults running parallel to the coast. The resulting dislocation has given rise to the cliffs that dominate the western shore of the gulf. The first goal on my new agenda was to hike to the top of this escarpment. The ascent from the shore of Hudson Bay is an easy, albeit long, walk over the ice-scoured basalt covering the older bedrock in these parts. A smattering of well-travelled erratics dot the gentle rise to the top. In small grooves and hollows, sand and gravel have taken up residence. Here, trees and shrubs are engaged in a largely futile struggle for survival against the cold and frequently boisterous winds off Hudson Bay. As I approached the top of the escarpment keeping my balance became increasingly difficult. The breeze, which had made for challenging paddling at sea level, was a roaring gale here, so much so that photographs of Richmond Gulf taken at the top of the escarpment were taken in a prone position.

Overnight, the wind shifted. As the day progressed, the clouds descended lower and lower until they swallowed the ramparts. Finally, fog covered everything and a decided chill crept into the bones. An Inuk in a freighter canoe passed me on his way to the gulf and seemed quite concerned about my safety. I waved to assure the driver that I was alright. Some time later the fog thickened. The noise from breaking waves seemed to come from everywhere; all I could see were foaming wave fronts, moving rapidly and in various directions. It was a bit unsettling and so I decided to run to shore with the breakers—not my favourite manoeuvre, since you almost always get soaked—but this time I stayed dry.

When I arose the next day after ten hours of luxurious comfort in the sack, the scene was as dreary as ever. A light rain soon blossomed into a downpour, and the agitated sea and headwind combined to ensure that even under the spray cover everything was soaked. After four hours of hard paddling, I put to shore at the first sheltered cove and, having made little headway, decided to wait for an improvement in conditions. With no change by the next morning I set out again and was soon in the midst of the worst turbulence I've ever faced.

Point Pamiallualuk is a narrow spur of rock that juts out some two kilometres into Hudson Bay, just north of the entrance to Richmond Gulf. Here, the north-flowing tidal current of Hudson Bay collides with a weaker counter current to produce a lot of agitation, which is further enhanced by the strong wind. This collision of opposing waves creates not only total chaos but adds significantly to the sound effects. Against all expectation I emerged from this cauldron after a few minutes of frantic activity, still right side up, and paddled into a tiny cove immediately south of the Point. It is here that the old Indian portage trail into Richmond Gulf begins.

There are several Inuit campsites of considerable antiquity near the start of the trail. The latter follows a glacier-carved trough in the escarpment and is still recognizable in numerous places. It had obviously not been used in many years, and in spite of my inclination to follow the ancient trails, I took the lazy man's option and paddled into Richmond Gulf through Le Goulet. The local people called this narrow connection between Richmond Gulf and Hudson Bay the "Gulf Hazard" due to the sometimes violent tidal currents and whirlpools. It is certainly a place that demands attention. The plan was to time my passage into the gulf to coincide with the rising tide, but much to my surprise, I faced instead a strong outgoing current. It would appear that the warmer and brackish waters of the gulf continued to flow seaward over the top of the more saline and colder waters simultaneously entering from Hudson Bay on a rising tide.

The clash of these currents was also mirrored in the air above. The cold, moisture-laden westerlies, which shrouded the entrance to the gulf in dense fog, continually swept eastward into the sun-drenched interior. Here, the army of grey collided with the warm and dry air from the Gulf in a constantly shifting battle. It was easy to see why the Natives of the region thought that the passage was inhabited by malevolent spirits. My own priority, once past the narrowest part of the passes, was to dry out and quell the rumblings of the stomach, and so I headed for the north shore and set up camp.

As the day progressed, the low stratus clouds retreated westward and the uncertain outline of the landscape came into focus. The north shore of the passage is dominated by Presqu'ile Castle, which rises steeply nearly 400 metres from the gulf. The exposed bands of sedimentary rock between the cap of basalt at the top of the Castle and the basement complex at sea level reveal the geological history of the place, spanning nearly two billion years. The much more recent work of the glacier, which created the opening to Hudson Bay, is revealed in the wonderfully sculpted rocks near the present water level. Words fail to adequately convey the impact the scenery had on me, but I was humbled, filled with awe and happiness.

I spent the next two days excitedly exploring this enchanting place, looking over the remnants of human occupancy—several late-Dorset subterranean dwellings, as well as summer encampments—and just revelling at the beauty of the setting. Less well appreciated was the constant gale.

Moving day was windy and wet and highlighted by a bear who happened into camp. I was just preparing dinner when I first noticed him, doing his best to pretend that he was just passing through. For my part, getting more nervous by the minute, I was determined not to have to share my dinner. Finally, when he was within 20 metres, I fired a shell from my flare gun at his feet, and he ambled off but in no great panic. But it made for a nervous night.[3]

Two hours of paddling the next day brought me into the southeast corner of Richmond Gulf. Just beyond a sandy shoreline and scattered across a large meadow are the buildings of the Hudson's Bay Company post and the Pente-costal Church, abandoned in the early 1950s. The latter is a spacious two-story building, its roof and walls still in good condition. Upstairs were several beds with mattresses. I quickly decided to move in for the night, rather than put up the tent, because of the presence of well-used bear trails.

Immediately behind the old post, the land rises in a series of raised beaches of sand and shingles, the oldest of which is well over 100 metres above sea level. A small stream has carved its way through these deposits to the present shore. In the process it has created a tiny harbour, a welcome refuge, for once again I had to run to shore before a strong tailwind.

A short distance north of the old post buildings and near the water's edge I came across another indication of geological history of the region—the boulders of an ancient stream bed that had been cemented together by an outflow of lava and subsequently ground smooth by glacial abrasion. It was the start to an excit-ing afternoon of roaming the hills above the post, including making a rapid retreat from a rather massive black bruin. He was browsing in a little ravine upwind from me and had no idea he had company, which was fine with me. I am sure it was the same fellow who tried to join me in the church building later on. He gave the well-secured door a couple of solid if ineffectual thumps. This should have reassured me, but did not—he could easily have climbed through one of the broken windows. So, once again I spent an uneasy night.

Just a few kilometres northeast of the trading post, Rivière de Troyes enters Richmond Gulf in a foaming cascade from a height of nearly 100 metres. It had

The rocks and ramparts of Richmond Gulf were a big part of the draw to this area for Herb. This was a different sort of trip, with less emphasis on movement and more on seeing the universe in the minutiae of rocks found along the coast.

been my intention to revisit the place, but columns of breakers, urged on by the continuing strong westerlies, were marching into the shallow bay. Instead, I headed west toward Cairn Island. In 1753, the Hudson's Bay Company established a post here, which became the focus of violent confrontations with the local Inuit. It was here, while continuing on towards Presqu'île Castle, that I met two Inuit in a freighter canoe. Ostensibly, they were out looking for belugas and had the artillery to pursue the hunt. But belugas rarely venture into the Gulf and they would know that. My read of the situation was that the owner of the freighter canoe, a resident of Umiujaq, was taking his visitor from Povungituk on a sightseeing tour. By claiming to go on the hunt, he was entitled to get gas for his outboard motor at a subsidized price.

We had a long and friendly chat; my only complaint was that during our conversation we were constantly carried eastward by the brisk wind. It meant an extra hour of hard paddling for me. It also threw my timing off—I had planned to pass back through Le Goulet during slack tide, a period of relative calm between waxing and waning waters. But, having had this conversation, by the time I came abreast the Castle, the tidal current was racing along at surprising speed. The sound of breaking waves seemed to come from everywhere, but the waves responsible for the noise seemed rather ordinary. It was an aural illusion created by the amplification and reflection of sound waves from the surrounding walls of rock. Nevertheless, I was quite happy to leave this region of mischievous spirits behind.

Home that evening was on an exposed point just a few kilometres south of Le Goulet. After 12 hours of hard paddling, the camp chores seemed to take forever and it was dark when I finally crawled into the sack. During the night it rained; the wind shifted and grew in intensity. It provided a welcome excuse the next morning to call this a layover day. I had to find a more sheltered area farther inland for the fireplace, and after a very late breakfast, decided once again to journey to the edge of the escarpment for a last look at Richmond Gulf. Before noon, the sun came out and made the four-hour round trip a visual delight. This time, the wind blew even harder and I didn't dare to go near the precipice, lest I be blown down by a sudden gust. By late afternoon I was back at the sheltered fireplace, pleasantly fatigued. Here the swish and slap of the breakers running up the shore were barely audible. The low sun radiated warmth and colour, the little stream nearby murmured, and I had the most intense feeling of contentment and happiness imaginable.

Sometime during the night I woke. A faint aurora flickered in the starry sky and all was quiet. For the first time since I started out, the wind had died down and, encouraged by the prospect of easier paddling, I went back to sleep. I was up in the predawn dusk with the intention to make this a serious travelling day, but already the wind had reappeared and was getting stronger by the minute. In the first two hours I barely covered three kilometres. At the end of the next hour, I was making no progress at all, except in the worry department. The vista was glorious, the sea ruffled silver, the sky deep blue, the terraced land various shades of green—and the rocky shoreline a white band of froth. The white band was the rub.

After a long search for a place to land through the surf, I noticed a small opening among the rocks near the shore and, just beyond, a sheltered lagoon. Just in time, too, because the weather was starting to deteriorate. I set up camp in the lee of a two-metre-high wall of rock and within a few hours a tremendous rainstorm roared in from the west. The wind was buffeting the tent so fiercely that I feared for its survival. Throughout the night, a parade of "what-if" questions marched by my subconscious. Invariably, when this happens, and without very many reassuring answers, sleep tends to be fitful.

The wind shifted from SSW to NW during the night and, thankfully, moderated somewhat. The morning dawned clear and bitterly cold, but the wind was stronger than ever. With the greatest reluctance I put on my wet clothes, cooked breakfast on an equally reluctant fire and retreated back into the tent to escape the bracing wind. During the day, showers came back and alternated with brief periods of sunshine. At one point the sky cleared completely and a cold sun illuminated a wild scene of waves crashing onto the inhospitable shore. But before long the world was again reduced to a small sphere of grey. Such is life on the Eastmain.

Back on the water the following day, after several hours of wallowing about in irregular slop, I was approaching the mouth of the Little Whale River. As I rounded the last spur of rock, which defines the north shore of the river, a sudden squall swept down the valley and out to sea. Almost instantly the water became totally agitated and full of disorienting froth. I was only about 100 metres from shore, but it took half an hour of concentrated effort to get there. Once ashore, I noticed two *tupeks* a little farther inland and one of the occupants came over to greet me. He was a short, powerful-looking man with a deeply lined, weather-beaten face and taciturn demeanour. At one point in our walk towards the tents, and anxious to break the silence, I pointed to an indistinct footprint in the sand and said, "Bear!"

"Inuk!" answered my companion, without a hint to condescension or reproach. It was the imprint of his own sealskin boot made on his outward journey. I am sure they all had a good laugh about it later.

Once inside the *tupek* I was offered tea and *muktuk* and a place at the stove. The latter was particularly appreciated because once again I was soaking wet. The two families had come here to hunt belugas and had intended to leave some time ago. Now they were only waiting for an improvement in conditions to return to Kuujjuarapik. With typical Inuit hospitality they also offered to take me along, an invitation I declined as politely as I could.

Progress, for the remainder of the journey, was as slow as ever. Strong westerlies and periodic offshore squalls provided all the paddling excitement I could handle. There are many places along the coast that are attractive even in sober moods, but when the sun makes an appearance and illuminates the landscape, the scenery here is irresistible. My impulse under these conditions is to roam far and wide, to drink in as much of it as possible.

Returning from a hike and still a long way from the campsite, I drank in a scene that gave me a start. I looked down from a vantage point and saw that my boat, which I had left in a well-sheltered place next to the tent, had been picked up by the wind and cartwheeled to a place on the foreshore flats not far from the shore. I scurried down with all the haste I could muster to retrieve my means of easy transportation, before the rising tide added a long walk to Kuujjuarapik to my *laissez-faire* revised travel agenda.

The journey, such as it was, ended in Kuujjuarapik as it began, in pouring rain. And, just as three weeks earlier, the people at Inuit Air kept my expenditures at a very acceptable level; total return costs were just a bit over $500. This was the first time that I travelled without an agenda, no time restrictions and an excess of food. With more than enough excitement on water and a surfeit of interesting side trips I should have been very satisfied, but something was missing. Somehow it just didn't seem right not to have an ambitious linear objective—that one could decide willy-nilly to spend an extra day here and there.

FIFTEEN

East Natashquan—A Relaxing Alternative
to Pondhopping, 1999[1]

The plan for the last summer of the second millennium had actually been to finish a trip that I started along the height of land in northern Labrador in 1996, but after a sober assessment of the condition of the old carcass, I was not confident that I could cope with the wear and tear of cross-country travel. The search for an alternative led me back to a watershed that I had seriously considered 25 years ago—the Natashquan River on Quebec's North Shore, which enters the Gulf of St. Lawrence just north of Anticosti Island. What made the river more attractive was the fact that Quebec Highway 138 had been completed all the way to the village of Natashquan, and there was an air charter operator who was more than willing to take you to any point in the neighbourhood. Several weeks before I was planning to leave, a party of WCA members had started on a trip down the main branch of the river. Knowing this, and being the curmudgeon that I am, I opted for the East Branch as a starting point.

Leonard Deraps, the owner of the charter company, briefly tried to convince me that the East Natashquan was not suitable for canoeing because of impassable falls and a canyon on the upper river "so deep that you can't see the bottom from the plane," which, he said, the Indians avoided by following a portage route through a number of small lakes. When I persisted with my plan, Leonard obviously recognized he was dealing with an individual who was both stupid and incompetent because he told his wife, "I don't think we'll ever see this fellow again." I found that out afterwards.

All the North Shore rivers were very low due to the nice weather the region had experienced. True to form on most of my canoe trips in the area, this changed the moment I arrived on the scene. At the end of a long drizzly day sitting around, the ceiling lifted enough to take off from the south end of Lac Fonteneau. A later supper, prepared in a steady rain that continued all night, quickly reacquainted me with the joys of tripping in this part of the country.

Lac Fonteneau lies in a long narrow glacial groove. At the south end, tree-covered hills rise steeply more than 150 metres from the shore. In its sinuous progress towards the outflow at the northern extremity, some 40 kilometres away, the lake is seldom more than two kilometres wide. The high hills become attenuated until, near its northern terminus, the lake's shoreline is defined by low eskers. At several places the remnants of eskers, which at one time traversed the lake, provide attractive campsites.

The gloom of morning was not assuaged by the discovery that my heretofore trusty tent leaked. An optimist no doubt would see it as evidence that the floor of the tent is still waterproof. There was more bad news at breakfast when my non-stick frying pan (after a mere eleven years of service) refused to live up to its promise, forcing me to pry the day's pancakes from its crusted bottom. Despite this inauspicious beginning, I was whistling and singing as I proceeded northward into a stiff headwind. Paradoxically perhaps, I find that being alone in the wilderness calms the soul and excites the senses. Soon, clouds gave way to blue skies, the water sparkled, and as so often in the past, I was overcome by a feeling of undeserved privilege.

Evening was celebrated on a sandy spit about halfway up the lake. A steady procession of ominous dark clouds hurried eastward, but periodically the rays of a low sun performed their magic and warmed what was otherwise a sombre landscape. It turned cool during the night. In the grey of early morning scattered fog banks began to coalesce until they obscured the landscape altogether. By 6:00 a.m. I packed up and slipped into this mystical grey world that gradually dissolved into a brilliant morning with the urging of the rising sun.

The north end of Lac Fonteneau has all the physical features of Labrador—rolling hills covered with a thick carpet of caribou moss, a smattering of black spruce and tamarack and, of course, plenty of blackflies. In the few hours it had taken me to get here, the weather had changed once again to a dark wall of clouds, softened by streamers of rain. I hadn't bothered to get the map covering the north end of the lake and it cost me an extra hour of paddling to find the well-disguised outlet. Just a short distance downstream a waterfall, followed by several rapids, barred the way. Finding the start of the old Montagnais portage trail was not easy; long disused, it was partly overgrown and finally completely obliterated in a tangle of dead falls and willows. It made the decision to carry around the falls and run the rapids a lot more palatable, even though the sound effects and wave action made me nervous enough to scout the whole thing.

By the time I reached the East Natashquan, some three kilometres downstream from Lac Fonteneau, heavy rain raised its sodden hand and made the motion to stop for the day, but the vote was to carry on. I had been told that there was an old log cabin on Lac Le Marquand, some 20 kilometres downstream. After what must surely rank as the most tedious paddle ever, I was relieved to discover this refuge in the grey of evening. It had a solid roof and floor, but plenty of openings in the walls and so I put up the tent inside the cabin as a bug-free retreat, had a cold meal and escaped into the sleeping bag to warm up. It wasn't long before I recognized that I had invaded the home of a large number of bats who kept whirring about in the dark, trying to get out through the doorway and crashing into the now closed door. Obviously their sonar wasn't working too well. In time, they all found a way out through one of the cracks in the wall, and I nodded off to sleep.

The next morning, the water level had risen noticeably and it was still raining as hard as ever. I decided to stay put for the time being. All that was needed to make my shelter more homey was a supply of wood to feed the stove. Within an hour I had located a nice dry stand of spruce, which, when neatly cut and split, produced a batch of impeccable pancakes. Alas, the feeling of satisfaction quickly gave way to boredom. There was nothing to do once all the gear was dried. Late in the evening, the wind changed from northeast to northwest and ever so briefly a bit of blue sky emerged, raising hopes for a better morning.

The Native travel route from here to the coast leaves the river at Lac Le Marquand and, so I'd heard, followed a southerly course overland through several small bodies of water in order to bypass more than 25 kilometres of continuous fast water. Even a cursory look at the map convinced me that following the river was by far the easier option and so, with showers still trailing across the lake, I pushed off the next morning into a much swollen stream. The beginning of the first canyon was still ten kilometres away and the map promised flat water for most of the intervening distance, but within a short period of time, I was in the midst of class II rapids that continued to the brink of the first two falls. Here, the river cascades more than 50 metres into a deeply recessed valley in little more than 100 metres. From the base of the falls, the river continues a boisterous course for the next four kilometres as it drops another 40 metres. Beyond this section, the gradient becomes less pronounced, the walls of the canyon recede and the river continues to rush along in an ever widening stream bed.

I had planned to portage the five or so kilometres around this section, because a gradient of ten metres per kilometre in a bouldery stream bed demands respect from a solo traveller. During an extended ramble along the north rim of the canyon in an attempt to find the easiest carrying route, I cast the occasional

A view back towards the waterfall at first canyon.

glance into the depths below and, as the going on top became more onerous, the water route, albeit incompletely visible, appeared more doable. There seemed to be more than enough shoreline at the edge of the river to somehow make it past the worst turbulence. Right there and then, I committed to the "low road."

The portage to the river below the falls was very steep but easier than expected, and I pushed off into the turbulence with more than usual nervousness. All went well for the first few hundred metres—that part of the river which I had observed from above—but beyond that I was looking at a scene that was downright unsettling as the flood-swollen turbulence became compressed between vertical walls of bedrock. By now, however, there was no way I could go backwards or climb the walls, so there was no means of ducking this ride. Load 'em up!

Second canyon, portage or perish. Or maybe there is another way?

Somehow I managed to stay right side up through the canyon, and less than half an hour later, I emerged into a gentler landscape. The sun, finally, reappeared and transformed the ever widening river into a ribbon of silver. My own transformation from fear to exuberance was equally startling. For the rest of the day I was content to float along at the pace of this very purposeful stream. Camp that evening was at the edge of a gravelly cutbank covered with an invitingly thick layer of moss and lichen. Unfortunately, the previous days of rain had so saturated the land, that just below the surface of this cover, there was an ankle deep layer of water. The necessary adjustments dampened the mood of an otherwise fine evening.

Near the end of the next day, I had reached the top of a second canyon on the East Natashquan. It is similar to the first one in that I had an impressive falls near

When the two branches of the Natashquan unite, the river valley widens, making campsites with better views and more daylight more readily available.

the beginning with a steep rapid below for a distance of some six kilometres. At this canyon, however, the river was not nearly as deeply recessed and the shore-line was much more suitable for landing or launching at a number of places. The realization that good fortune, just as much as skill, was responsible for my tra-verse of the first canyon, banished all thought of trying my luck again. Instead, I went looking for the Montagnais portage trail, which reputedly bypassed the obstruction. After an hour's trudging through sodden vegetation, I discovered an old trail parallelling the river near the left shore and started to portage along it. Before long, however, the trail vanished, as *game* trails often do, and progress through the dense forest became very slow. The main problem was that there simply wasn't enough space to advance the boat between the closely spaced trees in a straight line. By the end of the day I had covered a little over one kilometre, managed to find a level space large enough for the tent, and retreated to its safety—exhausted—after a quick supper in pouring rain.

There was no doubt by now, that the portage trail had to be on the other side of the river. The next morning I continued a short distance parallel to the river, loaded the gear into the boat and began to lower it by rope down the steep embankment. At first, this proved to be an excellent idea, but within a scant 50 metres down the slope, my conveyance was firmly wedged between trees and I ended up having to yank my load the rest of the way down the hill. I came out on the river at a spot exactly the same as the figure-eight rapids on the Nahanni, albeit smaller. With some difficulty, I made it across.

Most of the land beyond the right shoreline had been recently burned leaving only the skeletons of trees standing. It made looking for and finding the old portage trail very easy. This time, to make sure it was the right one, I followed it downstream for some distance. Along the way I also took the odd peek at the roaring river, and against all common sense, decided, since I was already soaking wet, I may as well run it—just shorten the carry a little—and, in the process, almost made Leonard Deraps' prediction come true.

Everything went well until I approached a spot where the river narrows and the water is further compressed by several huge boulders. By the time I realized there wasn't a hope in hell of making it through there in one piece, it was nearly too late. I just barely managed to reach the last tiny eddy with the strength that only panic can provide and had no quarrel with being a beast of burden the rest of the way. The portage trail ends, not at the river, but at a shallow pond, the outflow of which almost immediately joins a swift stream that takes the traveller back to the main river. I was quite happy to call it a day near the edge of the pond, and set up the tent on one of several terraces, remnants of an old stream bed, one of which was nearly a 100 metres above the present valley floor. Late in the afternoon the sun made a much longed-for appearance, everything dried out and by nightfall contentment once again reigned.

Below the second canyon, the river runs swiftly in a wide glacial valley with prominent and near vertical rock walls that rise more than 300 metres above the river. The valley floor is occupied by several parallel eskers through which the river has carved a winding course. The dense forest comes right to the edge of the stream and a number of sand bars invite the traveller to linger. The day's journey was a continuous visual delight of deep green forest, a few white clouds offset by the blue of the sky and a glimmering of the river, ever in a hurry to carry one along. By late afternoon I reached the confluence with the main arm of the Natashquan River with the distinct feeling that I was parting from a good friend.

At this junction, the main river runs in a wide, shallow stream bed composed of sand and shingle. Compared to the valley of the East Natashquan, the hills are lower and set back from the river, giving a feeling of wide open space. I only carried on for a few more kilometres before settling on a gravel bar to enjoy the evening. From here to the coast, the river alternately runs in a wide, lake-like setting with a gentle current and numerous sandbars, and regions where the flow is narrowly constricted by hills. Here, the huge volume of water repeatedly tumbles over exposed bedrock in spectacular falls.

With the exception of a few ancient trapper's cabins there is absolutely no evidence of human activity until one reaches the last three falls on the river. Surprisingly, there were also a few signs of wild life. On two successive nights early on, a marten had inspected my camp during the night and once, while I had lunch along the river, two moose walked past me. Other than a that, I saw a number of otters and a few ducks, but, beyond that, there were not even the tracks of wolf, fox or bear along the sandy shore.

I had glorious weather the rest of the way and, nearing the coast, the benefit of the falling tide to speed me through the wide, sand-clogged mouth of the river in a very circuitous course. Two hour's paddling on choppy salt water brought me back to the village of Natashquan. After an absence of 13 days and many kilometres of portaging, the old body was in surprisingly good condition. Perhaps enough to go back to northern Labrador next year, or so I thought.

SIXTEEN

Finishing the Albany River Trip, 2000

In July of 1978, Paula and Karl Schimeck and I paddled away from Longlac bound for Fort Albany. Four days into the trip I wrenched my back while portaging around a rapid on the Kenogami River. Luckily we were within sight of the CNR line, the last connection with the outside world; I flagged down the next train and returned home, and my companions carried on alone. As the years went by, the memory of that event was filed under the heading of "unfinished business," but it wasn't until the summer of 2000 that the Albany River watershed became the destination once again.

Joining me on this trip were Mike Jones and, once again, Karl Schimeck. We made arrangements with Hearst Air to leave our vehicles at their base at Carey Lake, just a few kilometres east of our starting point on the Kabinakagami River. The Ontario Ministry of Natural Resources route book chapter called "Limestone Rapids to Fort Albany," accurately describes the majority of the route we planned to follow. However, their recommended starting point at the end of Rogers Road, some 55 kilometres downstream from where the river crosses Highway 11, means bypassing some exciting rapids and beautiful scenery as the river traverses the transition from shield rock to limestone. I didn't want to miss this section and so we started at the bridge on Highway 11. To extend the duration of the trip to three weeks, and save some money in the process, our plan was to continue beyond Fort Albany to James Bay and paddle down the coast to Moosonee.

The first series of rapids on the Kabinakagami appeared just a few hundred metres downstream from the starting point. As we made our way slowly down the boulder gardens, we were soon joined by a small plane that continued to circle overhead, much to my consternation.

What was the problem?

We found out later, that the owner of Hearst Air, when informed of our starting point, became very concerned about our safety and decided to check on us. Apparently everyone avoids this part of the river. We thought it was absolutely perfect—nice scenery and some excitement. Carrying around several waterfalls was a bit awkward because of the absence of portage trails, numerous deadfalls and dense vegetation, but, for me, that was nothing new. There was also enough turbulence to testify to the usefulness of spray covers;[1] Mike, who didn't have one, once had to abandon his sinking ship. But, as far as I was concerned it was an excellent way to start this journey.

The exuberance associated with the beginning of a new adventure was somewhat tempered later on. The sultry day came to a sudden end with a terrific downpour just as we carried around an obstruction. Predictably, my rain suit was at the other end and so I sought shelter at the base of a very large tree. It worked well for a while, but this was no ordinary shower. Before long the trunk of the tree, meant to shield me from the deluge, became the conduit for streams of water that would have made spa owners jealous. What made the situation more unpalatable was the sight of Karl in his rain suit, comfortably relaxing nearby and trying hard not to look too smug.

A more serious misadventure overtook us a day's journey farther downstream. Limestone Rapids, several kilometres long, is not a difficult obstacle at the high water levels we encountered. Indeed, about halfway down, Karl confessed that he hadn't had as much fun running whitewater in years. Shortly thereafter, however, while trying to add a little extra excitement to the descent, I aimed my boat into the largest waves. Alas, one of them was really a rock camouflaged by a thin veneer of water. There was a loud crack as I unwittingly unmasked the impostor. The sudden change of momentum called for a high brace, which produced another crack as the shaft of my paddle broke. The boat repair delayed us half a day, plenty of time to decry my stupidity.

Below Limestone Rapids, the Kabinakagami loses its exuberance but continues at a purposeful pace as it meanders endlessly toward the Kenogami River. As we paddled on downstream, flood-swollen tributaries transformed the water to a red-brown soup full of flotsam. It made potable water a priority, for a ferocious sun had assumed supremacy. Good campsites were scarce and, after a long day, we settled for a marginal place within sight of the Kenogami confluence. The Kenogami River in many ways is an enlarged carbon copy of the Kabinakagami, its upper section punctuated by turbulence as it drops off the shield. By the time it reaches the point where we joined it, it is a substantial stream, flowing along swiftly and unobstructed between low slumping cutbanks.

Two days later, at the end of a long and thoroughly miserable day, we reached the Albany River. It had rained incessantly and a cold wind added to the discomfort. After a long search, the gods relented and provided a campsite beneath the sheltering limbs of several huge white spruce. Here, despite the continuous downpour and strong wind, a dry haven awaited us, with a plentiful supply of firewood. Soon fire warmed body and soul, a divine gift to the weary traveller.

The next morning the scene beyond our shelter was as dismal as

A cross-cultural camp—every bit helps when the sky is about to fall.

ever. Wind-driven rain danced across the surface of the river. The already high water level had risen another ten centimetres, an incredible amount of water, since the river is well over half a kilometre wide at this point. I lit an early fire and tended it for hours beneath our now somewhat leaky canopy. My companions remained in seclusion, a silent vote that this was not a travelling day. While they read and I poked the fire outside, conditions slowly improved and, by evening, the rain ceased. During the night, a cold front went through and morning dawned cloudless and cold. Next day the sun gradually took form above the treetops on the far shore and spurred us on to a speedy departure. As if to make amends, the weather gods provided sunshine the rest of the way to Fort Albany.

The lower Albany River offers little white water and even less visual variety as it rushes along. The unstable banks of the river are composed of sediments, which are built up above the level of the waterlogged land beyond. They gradually increase in height as one proceeds downstream and are populated by spruce, poplar and birch of modest size. Despite the sameness of the scenery, there is never a sense of monotony; the river, ever more voluminous and impatient, is simply too majestic. Karl reminisced of nice campsites on gravel bars associated with many of the islands along the way, but this year these were hidden well below the waves, and we had to settle for the sloping and usually weeping banks along the shore. About 40 kilometres from James Bay, the river splits into several channels and continues through a maze of islands. We had been warned about rapids in this region, but high water left them quite harmless.

For me, one of the least favoured events while on a northern trip is meeting other people. I would have been quite happy to paddle past Fort Albany without stopping, but Karl, who always travels with the conviction of the minimalist, needed to augment his food supply and so we went in search of the Northern Store. Along the way, we met a number of friendly locals, who invariably asked the same question:

"Did you see any moose?"

Our own priorities were to learn about conditions along the coast, particularly the weather and tides, and so we dropped in on the local constabulary looking for answers based on Native insight. What we got instead was a printout of the weather forecast from the internet, which promised zero wind speed for the next day. It seemed a highly improbable prediction in the face of the blustery day and threatening storm clouds.

James Bay is not recommended for canoeists. Extensive tidal flats and sudden storms slow progress; dense fog and a low coastline devoid of prominent landmarks can make orientation difficult. Even potable water is not readily available. Probably the most intimidating element for someone to paddle along the coast are the many disaster stories dispensed by the local populace. Another one was added—just as we were on our way to Moosonee, two people in a freighter canoe perished.

I felt just a little extra tension when we continued downstream, trying to find a campsite among the willows, before the dark clouds gave up some of their promise. When we came abreast of Clark Island, we spied a small opening in the vegetative cover. A prospector tent and some nets testified that it belonged to a local fisherman, but there was no one around and, with little chance of finding a better place, we set up our own shelters just as the first of many showers struck. Throughout the night the wind rattled the tents and I was rather apprehensive about the prospects ahead. Without revealing my own reservations, I asked my companions whether they wanted to set off under these conditions and somewhat to my surprise they were for moving on and quickly, because the tide was running out.

All went well until we left the protection of the shore and moved out into the mud flats. The gusty north wind made paddling an adventurous activity for Karl and myself, and an impossible task for Mike. His Mad River Flashback canoe, great for whitewater, was utterly unmanageable in these conditions. He was constantly twirled about in the gale and couldn't keep the boat on course. After an hour, he wisely decided to stop, with the intention to return to Fort Albany and fly out to Moosonee. We said a hurried goodbye. Karl and I continued in an ever diminishing channel of water, surrounded by the emerging foreshore flats that stretched to the horizon. Inevitably, the tow rope replaced the paddle, and for several hours we slogged through the puddles, the sound of the wind augmented by expletives whenever I floundered into a knee-deep soft spot in the quagmire.

Eventually, the incoming tide restored us to a more agreeable mode of advance and, at the end of a long and tedious day of fighting the breeze, we reached Nomansland Point, the first of a number of landmarks that project into James Bay. Most of these have been used for generations during the fall goose hunt, and our stopping place showed much usage. Perhaps it was just a sense of relief to be on dry land, but I thought the place looked and felt wonderful. Even Karl, who was an absolute stoic in adversity, went about the chores with a cautious smile on his face.

Wind and tides are the determinants of travel on the western shore of James Bay. With the foreshore flats anywhere from two to eight kilometres wide, one quickly learns that movement is restricted to a few hours on either side of high tide, because one does not want to be caught in one of the frequent squalls too far offshore, nor to sit for hours in the intertidal muck. The next day we advanced a bare ten kilometres, starting near low tide with a portage and gave up fighting wind and waves when we reached Cockispenny Point. At this rate of progress we were going to run out of food long before reaching Moosonee, and so we decided to ship out at the next high tide around 2:00 a.m.

Prior to this, I had never tried paddling at night and found it a strange unsettling experience to push off into darkness. Keeping a parallel course to the shore, which was visible as a black mass against the slightly brighter sky, we advanced cautiously. Periodically, a full moon emerged, all too briefly. When it disappeared again behind the clouds it seemed to leave a dark world even darker. At some point there was the sound and feel of rushing water; the tide was running out. Shortly thereafter, with the first greying of dawn, we were sitting on a sandbar some distance from the shore. What might have been a very boring wait, was transformed by a show produced by Mother Nature.

Ever since we started out from Cockispenny Point, we had seen flashes of lightning associated with two storm centres far to the west. As they gradually converged with our location, the sound and light effects became more and more threatening. Wave after wave of black clouds, each trailing a sinuous curtain, hurried past us. Bolts of lightening streaked across the sky and once, for just a few seconds, a little seam opened in the clouds on the eastern horizon and the rising sun illuminated this macabre scene. Through all this elemental battle two thoughts were uppermost in my mind: The first was "what a pity I can't record this on film;" the second was simply an acute awareness that we constituted the highest elevation for some distance around and might get more of a charge out of this event than desirable. Meanwhile, my travelling companion had stretched out in his boat and was motionless under the groundsheet. I think he slept through most of it.

Once again afloat, we continued to Halfway Point and were all set for another early start, but during the night another violent storm began, changing the agenda. Fortunately, we were set up in a sheltered place next to a two-metre-high cutbank. Had we not been, the wind would have shredded my tent. Early in the morning, the gale was as strong as ever. To emphasize that point, one of our boats came tumbling by on its way out to sea. It came to rest against a large rock in the foreshore flats long enough for me to retrieve it. Ironically, one of the last

Karl Shimeck's identical canoe to Herb's sits atop another boulder rapid early in the trip. The Kabinakagami was not as negotiable as they had hoped.

comments I made during the previous evening was "Let's make sure the boats are secure. I wouldn't want to be marooned in this place."

Even though the rain stopped around noon, the day remained cheerless and cold, and the two of us rooted by the fire. During the next night, the wind died down completely. Recognizing a small window of escape, we broke camp in darkness, ready ship out on the incoming tide. Inexplicably, the tide never came in. And so, on the first perfect day for travelling—glorious sunshine, no wind or waves—we had to wait another twelve hours. It was not really a hardship, since the neighbourhood, as so much of the coastline, was visually quite attractive with a backdrop of fantastic cloud formations and an abundance of fresh gooseberries and strawberries for the picking.

The next day, the second last of our journey, was another memorable one. Starting from Long Point we bumped along in the shallows between rocks and ridges some distance offshore amid hundreds of ducks and shorebirds. The tidal flats in this region were the most extensive we had experienced and inevitably we were marooned for a while. Another nasty blow came in from the north, just as the tide began to liberate us from confinement, and pushed us along with great authority. Our course of advance was a compromise between the force of the wind, the degree of obstruction by rocks and our own directional desire. Concentrating on all of that, a dense fog rolled in several hours later and we had absolutely no idea of our position. Eventually, an uncertain outline of land appeared on our right. Determined not to lose sight of it again, we stayed close to shore even though we had to cope with quartering waves in very shallow water.

The shoreline of James Bay near the mouth of the Moose River is ideal habitat for geese and ducks. Large numbers of them seemed to enjoy themselves in the wide belt of marsh beyond the shore, in spite of the miserable day. Our own mood was somewhat less jubilant, because there wasn't a dry spot to put a tent on for as far as the eye could see. After a long search, our campsite that evening was on a sandy ridge some distance from the shore. With uncharacteristic largesse I offered to provide and cook supper on the stove, while Karl did the impossible and got a fire started. A little external heat and a full belly rarely fail to induce a feeling of contentment and did so again that evening, but retiring with sodden clothes to a cold and damp sleeping bag is the more vividly remembered event.

Upon reaching Moosonee, we spent two nights at Tidewater Provincial Park. Mike Jones had stayed there after flying in from Fort Albany and, weary of waiting for us, had departed. We made arrangements to have our boats shipped out and, in little more than nine hours after leaving Moosonee, we were back at our vehicles at Carey Lake. Total cost for the trip (apart from food) was $355, plus one paddle ($140); the excitement, as the commercial says, was priceless.[2]

SEVENTEEN

Still Finishing the Pondhopping Caper
—Mistastin Lake, 2001

When I returned home from my trip in '96, it was with a sense of regret and resignation that niggled away in the back of my mind for years, thinking that my wanderings in Labrador had reached their inevitable end. The fasciitis, which had caused me to terminate that trip at the halfway point, seemed to take forever to subside, and I interpreted it as a sign that I had to limit myself to journeys of a less demanding nature, at least in terms of portaging. And so, for several years I tried to put Labrador out of my mind. But there remained one unfulfilled ambition that would not go away—to see Mistastin Lake.

The lake occupies the side of a huge impact crater, created some 36 million years ago. A number of small streams enter it from various directions, but on the maps they appeared much too small to offer reasonable access for the canoeist. It was perhaps for this reason that I could find no reference in the literature of recreational travellers ever having visited the region, with the exception of William Brooks Cabot who made a short detour on foot to the northwestern shore of the lake in 1910, while on his way back from Indian House Lake to the coast.

I was also intrigued by the fact that the earliest maps of the region showed Mistastin Lake and its outflow to the coast without showing the Kogaluk River above its junction with the Mistastin River. That would imply a source older than Cabot, because he clearly showed the Assiwaban (Cabot's name for the Kogaluk) above the juncture of the two streams. I was puzzled. From what experience had this information originated? When? Such speculations were all the excuse I

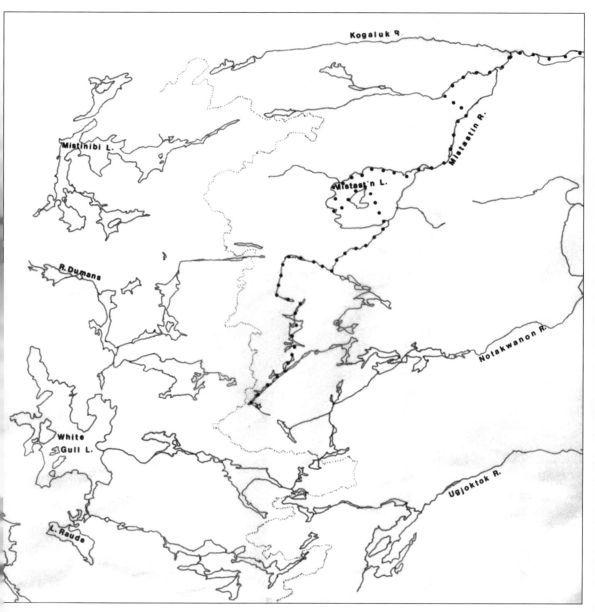

Herb's trip map for Mistastin Lake.

needed to want to visit the area, but years of staring at the maps convinced me that no matter what route I might chose, getting there would require an *inordinate* amount of portaging, even for me. And so the issue was put on the back burner time and again. By the time the year 2001 rolled around, I realized that there wasn't a back burner left in this man's stove, and so getting to Mistastin Lake was a *now or never* enterprise.

For many years Pat Lewtas and I had traded stories about our various experiences and made tentative plans to go on a trip together, but somehow it never worked out.

I suspect that Pat, who has done a number of remarkable solo trips, probably didn't want to compromise his independence. In truth, neither did I. So it came as a bit of a surprise for both of us when our annual discussions ended in his joining me on this occasion—with the understanding that we would be completely self-sufficient and could go out separate ways at any time, not unlike modern marriages. I suppose the glue that cemented the arrangement was sharing the high cost of getting to the proposed starting point, the headwaters of the Notakwanon.

It's a long drive from southern Ontario to Goose Bay and I thought I did well to cover the 2,800 kilometres in two-and-a-half days. Patrick managed the considerably longer journey from Michigan in a scant 36 hours. These travel times highlighted significant differences in our capabilities and I could only hope this difference wouldn't continue beyond the end of the road. I had made prior arrangements with Tamarlink Air to fly us into a small lake not far from where I crossed the height of land from Quebec into Labrador in '84. When I pointed out the unnamed lake on the large wall map to the agent, I was informed that Torngat Wilderness Adventures (TWA) had a hunting camp there.

"They are flying in supplies right now, because the hunting season is not far away," said the good man. Then he added with a knowing smile, "They can probably fly you in for less money than I can."

Apparently, it pays to travel with a slightly threadbare look and old well-used equipment; people take pity on you.

Jim Hudson, the owner of the TWA and pilot of a turbo Beaver, agreed to fly us into the camp from Churchill Falls for less than half the quote from Tamarlink, one boat and passenger at a time. This was a very much appreciated development, particularly since it promised a quick departure. Time was an important element because Patrick had some teaching commitments that meant we had to be in Nain on August 11th to catch the weekly trip of the *Northern Ranger* for the return journey to Goose Bay. This gave us three weeks, normally ample time for the distance we had to cover, but, as mentioned above, the expectation of much portaging was going to make this a slow trip.

Bad weather delayed our departure, and by the end of the second day, only I had made it to the hunting camp. It was situated on the shore of Crystal Lake, not an official name, but quite appropriate. Jim Hudson had had the good sense not to clear the area of trees but tried to fit the buildings into the existing vegetation. I instantly liked the place and so apparently did the caribou, as they moved through in large numbers on their southward migration without taking offence at our presence. Hunting season was still two weeks away and so I was the only man "from away" in the camp.

The staff members were old Labrador stock, Martin, MacLean and Blake, members of an almost extinct race, self-sufficient and hard-working, with keen senses of humour. They were wonderful samples of storytellers who use hyperbole with great panache. At times their delivery was so straight-faced that I had no real idea if they were joshing me or not. In the course of the evening, I told a few stories too and, while doing so, mentioned that my old acquaintance Horace Goudie claimed he was the best man in Labrador when it came to poling a canoe. That brought a wealth of stories of strength and endurance at competitions amongst the trappers of many years ago, with Horace as the central hero who once carried eight hundred pounds up a steep hillside. Horace himself told me later it was eight sacks of flour, fifty pounds each, still a staggering weight.

Pat didn't join me until the evening of the third day because of continuing bad weather in Churchill Falls. This allowed me to explore the region about the camp at leisure, but I was keenly aware that this delay was eating into our travelling time, and so as soon as possible after his arrival, we said our goodbyes and pushed off. By mid-afternoon we had covered about 15 kilometres and climbed a prominent dome of bedrock. It was the highest point around and allowed us to see the Labrador landscape at its very best, hills of glacier-carved corrugated bedrock covered with a thin veneer of lichen and moss and decorated with innumerable erratics, deep blue bodies of water surrounded by a green border of willows and scraggly trees. Fifteen years earlier on my way down the Notakwanon, I had experienced the nasty side of Labrador while camped at the base of this very hill, and so this was a homecoming of sorts and a deeply moving one because I never expected to have the privilege of seeing it again.

We stopped early at the start of the next portage because Pat had wrenched a knee on his way up to the top of our lookout and it seemed best to give it a rest. It gave me a chance to roam around the barren high ground, ostensibly to scout the next carry and get a glimpse of what lay ahead, but mostly to absorb the aura that permeated the place. The wind had picked up and hurried a succession of wispy clouds across the sky, which created alternating showers and evanescent rainbows. All the while, a distant dome of bedrock glowed in the orange light of the late sun. The silence was deafening. It was a scene that elevated the spirit and nurtured the soul more than I can describe.

An indifferent morning quickly deteriorated. A strong headwind, at first only bothersome, steadily increased in force and carried with it a deluge of cold rain. Just about the time when progress became impossible we reached a two-story building, another outpost camp of Torngat Wilderness Adventures. There was nobody there and the place was all boarded up, but an unlocked door on the second floor gave us access and we quickly moved in. It was an extraordinary stroke of good luck because it's doubtful our tents would have survived the coming blast in this exposed and barren neighbourhood. All day and throughout the night the wind roared around the building like a 747 on a takeoff, and soon I crawled into the sleeping bag to stay warm. By morning the cold front had moved through, the rain had stopped, and I went for a hike to high ground.

Shortly before noon the next day we were back on the water. The wind had subsided somewhat but remained bothersome, particularly for Patrick whose canoe had a lot of freeboard and was thus more susceptible to wind.

Before long, we were standing on a little rise of land at the head of a rocky groove of a valley, home to a string of small lakes; originally, these were hollowed out by an eastwardly moving glacier, but now they drained west. This was the beginning of a stream we planned to follow to Mistastin Lake. Camp that evening was on a bench of gravel that separated two lakes. The tents were tucked into a small opening where they were well defended on all sides by a thicket of willows and misshapen spruce. A cold wind once again carried along the odd brief shower, but before the day ended, the sun broke through and softened the harsh surroundings.

By the end of the next day, we had reached the confluence with the stream that I had followed northwards in '96. At that time, I had rejected it as an unsuitable approach to Mistastin Lake for three reasons: too steep, too rocky, too little water. A brief reconnaissance confirmed the assessment and added a fourth *too* to the list—too many blackflies. Wind and cold had confined them so far, but on this sultry evening, they were trying to make up for lost time. From an aesthetic point of view our little stream was rather pretty, in a wild sort of way. Our descent started with a portage past waterfalls to a bouldery stream bed. Occasionally, we'd paddle 50–100 metres and, because it was not suitable for lining or walking the boats downstream, we became quite experienced in the final alternative. At the end of the scorching day we had advanced four-and-a-half kilometres—excellent progress, all things considered.

But the day's exertions must have made an impression on my companion, because that evening he decided to lighten his load by pouring out a litre of fine brandy, half a litre of vegetable oil and a small mountain of jujubes, seemingly oblivious to a steady stream of reminders to him from me about Leonidas Hubbard (who discarded food early on his trip in 1903 and later starved to death). By now, though, I had recognized that his diet had no similarities whatsoever to mind, and I was glad of our separate meal arrangement. For me, unless the sky is about to fall, it's bacon, pancakes, maple syrup and tea for breakfast. Pat starts with a handful of cereal to which he adds cold water; that's breakfast. In fact, the only hot food he had each day was the freeze-dried contents of a package, again mixed with cold water, which he cooked over a stove. Now these packages had mouth-watering titles, but from the short distance from my fireplace to his stove each night, these gourmet dishes always looked and smelled about the same. Nevertheless, he never showed the slightest interest in the superior foods of his travelling companion. I recognized, of course, that his approach had certain advantages. While I was collecting stones for the fireplace and cutting wood, Patrick could ponder evolution or the compass bearing of the next portage.

On a fine cool morning we were immediately faced with a nasty stretch of river that I would have looked over carefully, had I been alone. Pat forged ahead without a moment's hesitation, and, because he seemed to know what he was doing, I followed. My companion had negotiated a boulder garden the previous day with an empty canoe and exhibited infinite patience and considerable skill in the process. He clearly was what the fellows at the hunting camp would call "a good canoe man." On this and later occasions he proved himself equal to every challenge and I watched his movements with some envy, particularly his agility in getting in and out of his boat at critical junctures. Me, I was not nearly so agile, and my boat paid the price.

On a short and unexpected stretch of flat water we stopped and climbed a conical hill, the only prominent elevation around, and had our first glimpse of Mistastin Lake in the distance. All around our observation post deeply recessed game trails indicated that large numbers of caribou had at one time inhabited the region, but that was decades ago as they were all overgrown. Now not a single footprint disturbed the ground. It was a clear indication of the unpredictability of caribou migration. Many years earlier these changes in the caribou migration had forced the Innu, whom Cabot had visited at Indian House Lake in 1910, to move to the more predictable sea-based food sources at the coast.

After many more steep and shallow rapids, some of them run very inelegantly and some portaged, we decided to head overland on a direct route to Mistastin Lake in order to avoid yet another long stretch of very difficult river. In a situation like this, my companion was a model of precision. Starting with the magnetic deviation adjusted to annual change and the co-ordinates of the starting and finishing points and who knows what else, he calculated the bearing and followed it come hell or high water. I don't know how to do any of that; in fact I don't always trust the compass. I just look at the map (which can't be trusted either), look at the land and then follow my nose. In more than three-quarters of a century that nose has always served me well. On this occasion we set off on our separate routes to the lake. Not surprisingly, the nose won because of some obstruction on the compass route delayed Patrick. It gave me a few minutes of solitary reflection at the end of the portage, a thanksgiving of sorts, because I had looked forward to this moment for years.

The view from the top of the gravelly shore some ten metres above the lake was captivating. The light blue lake was smooth as glass, reflecting white clouds in a pale sky, the water so clear that you could see legions of massive round boulders staring back at you from a great depth. Far to the northeast a range of barren rock gleamed in the sunshine. We spent the night on the large island in the centre of the lake and set off in the morning toward the base of the usual elevation on the western shore, which we called Table Mountain. A long and tiring hike to the top on another excessively hot day afforded a wonderful view in all directions. Table

Mountain is a remnant of the impact melt sheet of the meteorite collision that created the crater now occupied by the lake, a massive sentinel and awesome testimony to the enormous energy release of that event.

In the winter of 2001, Lynne Fitzhugh gave a talk at the annual Wilderness Canoeing Symposium in Toronto in which she mentioned that the Innu of Davis Inlet had established a retreat or healing centre on Mistastin Lake. One of our objectives on this trip was to visit the place, which was reportedly somewhere on the north shore of the lake. In our examination of the shoreline we came across signs of hunting camps and, finally, near the outlet of the lake, the foundations of a building and building materials as well as several snowmobiles and *komatiqs*; but that was all—no sign of recent human activity. As far as I was concerned, the most interesting elements at the site were two ancient teepee sites, one marked off with yellow tape, no doubt the work of my old acquaintance Stephen Loring, the archaeologist whom I had met in 1982 at Voisey's Bay.

This area has a most intimidating flavour. High walls of bedrock ring the outlet of the lake. They clearly show the effect of the direction of the movement of the ice during the last period of glaciation, which here was east-northeast. That evidence is accentuated by similarly oriented high eskers. The Mistastin River begins its journey with some exuberance and, for us, the worry about getting down the river was no longer about rocks, but about the size of waves and the sharpness of eddy lines.

Table Mountain, on Mistastin Lake, is a remnant of the impact melt sheet of the meteorite collision that created the crater now occupied by the lake, a massive sentinel and awesome testimony to the enormous energy release of that event.

We stopped for lunch not far below Mistastin Lake on the south shore of a small lake expansion and here came across a number of very old teepee sites, as well as signs of more recent occupation. Shortly thereafter, our progress came to an early halt at a place that had puzzled me from the first moment I saw it on the map—a place where the contour lines didn't quite match up. There was some-thing odd about it. The oddity, it turned out, was a large crack in the shield rock into which the river disappeared in a magnificent waterfall. The river continued in this fault, which was less that ten metres wide, with vertical rock walls rising a minimum of 20 metres on either side. It was a spectacularly wild place, around which we roamed for some time.

Since there was no obvious way to get down to the river, we set up camp and agreed that Pat would look downstream and I would investigate portage possibil-ities upstream. Within an hour, I discovered a way down and returned to our campsite and the usual chores. When it started to drizzle and there was still no sign of Pat, I became worried and started to look for him. He was in shirt sleeves, as I recalled. The blackflies were out in force and I knew he had no repellent with him. I was quite sure he wouldn't stay out under these conditions, which brought me to the unavoidable conclusion that something must have happened to him.

An hour's frantic rambles brought no answer to my calls. Back at the tent there was still no sign of the man. By now, it's dusk, the time of day when all sorts of thoughts surface: "If he's out there unconscious the whole night the blackflies will drain him." And so off I went again, praying and hollering and, finally, there came a faint answer. It turned out that he had been sitting near the brink of the waterfall the whole time, soaking in the scene, and never heard a thing. Hearing that, after all the calling and running around, I was too exhausted and relieved to do more than fill the air with profanity, but there was definitely murder in my heart that evening.

The Mistastin River, below "Pat's" fault, continues a turbulent course over falls and ledges. It was wildly beautiful to look at, and considerably less appreciated as a carrying place. The whole valley is composed of rock that has been fluted and ground into knolls and furrows by thousands of years of flow of an immense vol-ume of water. Where there weren't geological obstacles, there were trees, scores of huge trees to negotiate, some of which rivalled those of the British Columbia rain-forest in size. When all was said and done, at the end of a hard day we had advanced no more than three kilometres and settled for the best we could find—a truly miserable campsite made worse by relentless rain. Patrick crawled into his abode without supper, but I had discovered a dry *chico,*[1] which provided the fuel to cook my meal and I remained at the fire until the last morsel of food was gone.

Shortly before noon of the following day we reached a point where the river drops more than a 100 metres in a series of cascades before continuing in the narrow gorge of the fault on a steep descent. We had agreed before the start of our trip that a lengthy portage was required to bypass this part of the river, and

The Mistastin River drops into the fault in a magnificent waterfall. The river, a tributary of the Kogaluk, returned Herb to familiar territory and eventually to the last falls on the Kogaluk, the last portage before paddling north to Nain.

before long, we were on our way with the first load, up a long incline toward a small body of water shown on the map. From there, our route on the second day continued uphill to another small lake, over the crest of a high hill and thence down into a large glacier-carved valley. Our expectation was that the small meandering stream occupying the valley floor was deep enough to float our boats and carry us back to the Mistastin River, which it joins a short distance above the confluence with the Kogaluk River.

I am always surprised at how unreliable or selective memory is. Time modifies, amplifies and even occasionally erases the original experience.[2] Not long after our return home, Pat mentioned in conversation how excessively hot many days on this trip had been, something I couldn't recall at all; yet, when I checked my journal entries I complained about the same thing. There seems to be a general tendency to remember events in a more positive light. A good example are my recollections about the physical demands of this adventure—a good trip, some hard days, but no problem just a standard canoe trip. A typical comment in my journal paints a slightly different picture: "Had a good long night in the sack, but it seemed to make little difference, when I got up I was sore, tired and 103 years old."

What *is* recorded in the journal, consistent with my latter day recollections, was the incredible density of blackflies. On our journey away from the river, we camped at the first body of water. I got up with the first light of day to retrieve my boat, which was still at the river's edge, to try to get it done before the flies came out in full force. It was a failed strategy at best. When Pat, who had started out a little later, returned with his boat, I inexplicably missed out on taking a prize-winning photograph. My companion had obviously applied a liberal amount of repellant to his face. This, combined with sweat had become the final resting place for thousands of blackflies. You'd swear the man had a full beard. The next day's journey, high above the river valley, involved a surprising amount of boggy terrain and it was the high point of the portage, both literally and emotionally, when we could finally look down and see the river we were heading for, some 300 metres below.

For the descent, we loaded up the boats and took them down, one at a time with ropes attached to bow and stern. At the top, the going over barren ground was easy, but further down a jungle of alders, willows and spruce thickets and a near vertical slope caused some excitement, and was bloody hard work—bloody because the blackflies took full advantage of their opportunities. The worst part of the exercise for me was the scramble back up to the top. I had to stop a number of times to catch my breath, while Patrick seemed merely baffled by the slow progress. By mid-afternoon all our gear was at a nice open campsite above the river and we were dead tired. Pat put up his tent and disappeared in it. I felt duty bound to take some pictures, especially of our route down the mountain; it had seemed so adventurous in action but in the viewfinder was quite unremarkable, and I quickly gave up photography in favour of reclining against a tree for a much needed rest.

Out little stream, confined to a bed of sand and shingle, rushed along a sinuous and braided course and had just enough water to carry us without interruption to our reunion with the Mistastin River, which in turn joins the Kogaluk River just a few kilometres further on. At the confluence of the two rivers I tried unsuccessfully to find Cabot's campsite, but it was gone; the river had claimed it. It was a sombre day with frequent showers, and the rock walls of the Kogaluk River valley looked even more imposing than I remembered them. By evening we had covered more distance than in the preceding week and set up camp some distance below Cabot Lake, a site with a magical backdrop of swirling mists and red sunset.

Having finally made up some time and distance, we were now quite confident we could make it to Nain in time for the *Northern Ranger's* departure, provided that we did not meet an unruly sea along the way (an ever-present worry when travelling along the coast). When we reached saltwater, Voisey's Bay was tranquil and we stopped for an early camp a short time later in a little bay identified on Cabot's map as *E. Winters* place. Nobody lives there now, but it offers a safe landing spot, fresh water and a wide panoramic view of the offshore islands. Early the next morning a cold east wind freshened and made paddling not only hard work but in Patrick's case also worrisome, because he had no spray cover and the waves were getting playful. At one point Pat suggested I should carry on alone in an attempt to reach Nain before the arrival of the storm he thought was imminent. I didn't agree with his assessment and we spent the last night together on a barren island ten kilometres south of Nain. Looking back, I realize now that Pat just wanted to get rid of me to spend the last night alone. Solo trippers are funny that way—we like our solitude. Of course, the predicted storm didn't materialize, but the *Northern Ranger* did, and within a few hours after our arrival in Nain we were on our way south.

The journey to Goose Bay was blessed with exceptional weather. A slight breeze ruffled the sea and raised a few whitecaps, the sun performed its usual magic and softened even the austere grey of the barren outer island of Jacques Cartier's "Land God Gave to Cain."[3] We passed massive icebergs, blue-green islands in a deep blue sea, and the ship circled several of them to give the passengers a chance to take pictures. It was a nice final farewell to a remarkable part of the world.

EIGHTEEN

A Last Northern Hurrah—Clearwater River, 2003

At the annual Wilderness Canoeing Symposium in Toronto in January of 2003, I gave a slide presentation that focused on Richmond Gulf and its immediate neighbourhood. The images shown seemingly provided the stimulus for six people in the audience to want to visit the region. More specifically, they planned to fly into Clearwater Lake, follow the Clearwater River to Richmond Gulf and spend some time there before flying out from Umiujaq. One of the participants in this endeavour was John Schultz, a man I had met for the first time in Labrador in '82. He knew that I had a continuing interest in the region and invited me to join their charter flight from La Grande into Clearwater Lake.[1]

As I had done many times before, on the long drive north to La Grande, I stopped for the night at a small campground on the shore of the Waswanipi River, a couple of hours north of Val d'Or. There wasn't a soul around and the wildlife was limited to a few timid blackflies. After a tiring day of driving, the modest supper cooked on the stove together with the effects of some beer I had picked up along the way, made for a mellow mood. The river beyond my transient home, brown as all the rivers in the clay belt, moved along lazily. The shoreline, densely covered with shrubs and grasses, was rather unattractive; the land beyond more liquid than solid. And yet, from a vantage point somewhat above the water level, it was pleasing to the eye—the reflection of banks of clouds on the tranquil surface of the water and the slight orange tinge imparted on the scene by the late sun made it a picture of serenity. There was not a breath of wind and the silence was overpowering. Before long, the strains of Bach and Beethoven serenaded the emerging galaxies and brought a long day at the wheel to a reverent close.

The following evening in many ways mirrored events described above. The setting was a grove of jack pine on the sandy plain near the La Grande Airport. A lush carpet of reindeer moss provided comfort, and Mozart from the open window of the nearby car provided orchestral balm, but there was a bit more tension in the air. There was as yet no sign of my fellow travellers due to arrive from various parts of North America. What worried me was the carrying capacity of the Twin Otter that was to take us north. John had been assured that the aircraft could accommodate all seven of us, four boats and a mountain of other gear, but it was clear that I would be odd man out if it proved otherwise. Fortunately, when the others straggled in and the charter confirmed, the ingenuity of the pilots proved equal to the task of getting all seven of us and our small mountain of gear into the plane.

Mid-afternoon of the following day, we took wing in a wheeled aircraft and I looked forward with considerable interest once again, and probably for the last time, to seeing Clearwater Lake, that beautiful jewel set in an such an inspiringly raw land. But what I couldn't get clear in my head, was the landing spot the pilots had shown us on the map before departure. We were supposed to put down on a tiny island near the western shore of the lake, but my recollection from previous visits was that all the islands on this ancient crater lake were undulating piles of detritus and outcroppings of bedrock. Nervousness peaked as we circled, slowed and dropped down toward a mere hint of an esker on the island. After a hard touchdown the plane came to a stop well short of the hundred metre mark, to a collective sigh of relief. Just a routine landing, said the young captain.

A quick survey of the island revealed no attractive campsites and so, despite an invitation to supper by my companions, I pushed off and into a fresh breeze on an easterly course toward the next island. It's not that I'm anti-social, I just prefer solitude to companionship and silence to conversation. The first item on my agenda was to visit the northernmost of the ring islands. Arthur C. Twomey, in his book *Needle to the North*, mentions visiting a Cree encampment on his way back from the Seal Lakes in 1938, and I thought I knew just where it was. On an earlier trip I had climbed to the highest point on a nearby island and looked over into a nicely treed and sheltered valley where I thought the old encampment might be, but on that occasion I hadn't had time to explore. This time, I thought it might be one of my early rambles.

A southwesterly wind the next day made for an interesting and tiring paddle and it was mid-afternoon before I approached my target. The bouldery shoreline was steep, the following waves large, and despite my best efforts, I could not escape entirely dry on my run to shore. As soon as I reached shore, however, it was almost immediately obvious that the little valley, which had looked to inviting from a distance, had never been home to anyone. After roaming far and wide without finding a decent place to put my tent, I shipped out to a small adjacent island that offered a sheltered beach, and here I remained for two days to wait for the agitated lake to calm.

Being windbound is a fairly common part of northern canoe trips. Most paddlers welcome it as a rest period, a chance to read or to check equipment. For me, it is always a time of restlessness and exasperation, particularly when spatially confined. The first evening on the island passed well enough. Clearing a little space for the tent and another some distance away for a sheltered fireplace, the gathering of widely scattered firewood amongst the scrawny trees, kept me more or less occupied. During the night a thunderstorm played out its noisy symphony. Hours later, I awoke to the strong smell of woodsmoke and hurried outside. All was peace and quiet, the fireplace was cold and wet. It must have been a dream, I concluded, but wasn't totally convinced. The next day was spent scouring the island. Soaked by intermittent mists I returned several times to the sheltered fire to dry out and set out again, the only gain the discovery of the scarce remains of a hunting camp.

A dense fog had settled on the still restless waters on the morning of the third day, but it seemed manageable. I set out on a westerly course without breakfast hoping to reach the western shore of the lake before it became too unruly. Most people would have used a compass under the circumstances, but a steady northwesterly breeze seemed to me an adequate directional guide toward the next island two kilometres due west of my starting point. And so I pushed off at forty-five degrees to the direction of wind and waves. Some time thereafter the ghostly form of land appeared to the left, albeit a bit off course, which I interpreted as a sign that the wind had shifted to a more northerly direction. Convinced that the shadowy form had to be the island toward which I was aiming, I kept a parallel course. Visibility was limited, but after a while, the high red cliffs of this island looked disconcertingly familiar. By degrees, it dawned on me that I was heading east along the shore of the large island I had visited three days earlier. The wind had indeed shifted and was now coming from the southwest and I altered course accordingly. The breeze gradually scattered the grey void and distant landscapes emerged like miniature dioramas and, at last, the sun drew away the final curtain of fog and revealed a dazzling scene. I was in the very centre of the lake, surrounded by the ring of islands that define the impact crater, which gave birth to this body of water. With me that far off course, breakfast was going to be late.

The earliest European travellers in this region were employees of the Hudson's Bay Company. Their route from Hudson Bay to Clearwater Lake followed the Deer River (today's Caribou River) to its source, continued overland and reached the big lake at the western extremity of the channel we had followed eastward on our winter trip in '87. It had been my intention for some years to try to follow this route. My information was limited to the daily entries contained in the journals of 19th century HBC traders, William Hendry and Nicol Finlayson.[2] The accounts of their journeys, for the area in question, are remarkably similar, but no matter how hard I tried, I could not reconcile either of them with the modern map.

It was left to a contact in Ottawa to solve the puzzle. Prior to this final trip to Richmond Gulf, I had corresponded for some time with Jim Stone who was working on a biography of A.P. Low.[3] Over a span of many months, Jim had sent me copies of old maps, among them one ascribed to George Atkinson II, the son of a Hudson's Bay factor who had made a journey to the Upper Seal Lakes in 1818 and who was also a member of Hendry's party ten years later. It is clear from his map that the Deer River of old was now the nameless tributary that we had followed westward on our winter trip in '87. It was now my intention to follow this route for a short distance to see if I could find some of the old portage trails and campsites along the way.

After breakfast on one of the islands near the western shore of Clearwater Lake, I slowly proceeded into the narrow bay that had been the start of our winter trip. It was a bright and breezy day and I stopped frequently to examine potential camping spots. Everywhere, the products of glacial abrasion were piled in wild confusion between furrows of bedrock, the epitome of Craig Macdonald's "barbaric" landscape. After 40 kilometres of paddling and hours of roaming, I stopped for the day at a small and well-treed indentation in the bedrock. It contained the outline of what might have been a fireplace many generations ago; as well, it was the only potential campsite I had come across in some time.

It rained generously during the night, but the morning looked interesting. Transient patches of blue sky, rising fog and scudding rags of low clouds pushed along by a brisk west wind made for a constantly changing backdrop. It was time to pick up the camera and head for high ground. In order to avoid the moisture-laden vegetation on the most direct route, I decided to skip along the boulders at the shore to a patch of barren ground and thus reach my target with dry feet.

I didn't get very far before I slipped on one of the lichen-covered rocks and landed with a disturbing "crack" sound as my torso bore the weight of the fall on a protruding rock. Momentarily unable to inhale, I was instantly transformed into a worried man. At first I decided to lie down to catch my breath and quickly found out that just assuming a prone position and getting up again was unbelievably unpleasant. My assessment was that the third and fourth ribs on the right side were either cracked or broken. Healing was going to take some time, and progress from here on was going to be slow with this handicap. And so I decided to head for Richmond Gulf by the easiest and fastest route, to hell with the old trails and campsites.

It is amazing how quickly one adapts to new constraints, particularly when pain is the teacher. One learns to slow down and to avoid certain movements, how to lift a pack and to drop a canoe (without damaging it). I was fortunate in

South of the mouth of the Rivière à l'Eau Claire, on a broad curving beach, is the old Hudson's Bay Company post at Richmond Gulf.

that I could use my left arm with little discomfort and once a load was on my shoulders I felt no pain.

Paddling at first was very awkward. All I could do was hold my right arm in a fixed position. Fortunately, I didn't have to run any rapids for the next three days. Two days after my fall, I started on the traverse toward Clearwater River in a southeasterly direction along what looked on the map like an obvious route, and so it was. I remember it was an extraordinary day. Once I managed to get the boat on my shoulders and finally finished the first portage, the day seemed much brighter. The sun was shining on high barren hills and deep blue bodies of water and I advanced at a leisurely pace. The land looked, in turn, raw and pastoral; there was no sign of man or beast ever having passed through here and the only sound was the cawing of ravens who cruised updrafts along the hillsides. The best campsite of the trip awaited me on the shore of a gently curved beach of coarse sand. A thin line of spruce trees near the water's edge provided shelter from the bracing wind, the beach a generous supply of driftwood and I gratefully accepted nature's generosity.

Two days later, and with the lake section of the upper Clearwater River behind me, I was fighting the usual strong westerlies blowing right up the river. In the face of an ever more threatening sky, I continued to push toward a spot on the river where the contour lines on the map promised visual excitement. I made it there barely in time to set up the tent on a lush carpet of lichen at the base of an imposing rock face. My venerable shelter had not been equal to the task of keeping out moisture with annoying regularity on this trip. And so I quickly secured the ground sheet over the top because the coming deluge was sure to compromise the comfort I deserve. Right next to the tent was a large white spruce tree, its core encased in a multitude of branches reaching to the floor, a natural umbrella to which access was gained by the removal of a few bottom branches on the lee side. For once, it all worked out as planned. While a heavy shower soaked the neighbourhood I concluded dinner, cooked on the stove, with a nice cup of Tang tea, while propped up against the trunk of the tree, perfectly dry and rather pleased with myself.

Fog, drizzle and an ever increasing cold headwind defined the next day. Portages, while not overly strenuous, were nervous interludes because I didn't want to fall again on the slippery rocks. As the day progressed the weather took a turn for the worse. I began to look for a campsite, but all I could see were grey fog-shrouded rock walls on either side. Finally, at yet another portage, I managed to get to high ground and cleared out a tent site away from the wind. By five in the morning the wet tent was frozen stiff, an encouraging sign that good weather was on the way. Nevertheless, I crawled out of the cozy sleeping bag with some reluctance, put on my wet clothes and lit a fire in the predawn darkness.

Indeed, within an hour the pale orb of the sun began to make fleeting appearances and gradually an awesome landscape emerged. Before me lay a deeply recessed river, which hurried on in a series of cascades within the confines of a narrow rock-walled valley, and everywhere there was evidence of the enormous forces that shaped the land. It was a day of portaging and mad scrambles to high ground, of emotional highs and physical exhaustion. Along the way, I passed two magnificent waterfalls and one majestic rock wall that glistened in the evening sun like polished marble. Even the turbulent river seemed to pay homage to this particular cliff's authority because it passed by timidly and silent. In a vain attempt to capture its aura I put to shore to take a picture and was startled by the sound of human voices. I had caught up with John Schultz and company.

Only once before, and that was 25 years ago, had I camped on a northern trip with so many people. In this case, my fellow paddlers were all very experienced backcountry travellers. Friendly and hospitable, they invited me to share their dinner and were in every way solicitous of my well-being. They didn't realize, of course, that their kind attention disrupted my cherished routine and strained the solitary ear.

At this point in the journey, there were now only two portages left before the river ends its spirited run to Richmond Gulf. These, however, were by far the most substantial of the whole route. Not far below our campsite the river narrowed at the start of a turbulent descent, plunged 25 metres into a deep cleft in the rocks and disappeared from view on a steep and frothy course. Some time

One of the many spectacular falls on the Rivière à l'Eau Claire (and one of the many reasons why the Cree ascended the Wiachewan River).

was spent to capture the grand spectacle on film, but eventually, and with somewhat less enthusiasm, my companions joined me on the portage trail. Of course there was no trail and it was interesting to observe that each of my companions set out on a different pathway before eventually converging on a common track. It mirrored their approach to collective decision making, which was painfully democratic. It made me realize how lucky I had been all these years travelling alone. Consensus is never a problem when all you have to argue with is yourself.

Our campsite that evening was high above the river, at a place barely halfway across the portage. A rare east wind hurried along amorphous clouds and with it came sporadic showers. The corrugated ground beneath the tent made for an uncomfortable bed and I spent a shifty night. In part, the restlessness was due to my dissatisfaction with the slow pace of travel by my companions. In fairness to them, there was no need for hurry, but I was attuned to a travelling schedule that did not include dawdling and before the night was done, had decided to go ahead alone.

Beyond this penultimate portage on the Clearwater, the river flows swiftly between unstable clay banks, depositions on the old sea floor through which the water has carved an even deep course. Campsites are scarce in this region and I stopped at the first suitable place. The start of the next portage, another lengthy exercise, was just a short distance downstream at the head of a long and violent rapid that spills into Richmond Gulf. I hadn't expected to have company, but my companions must have picked up their pace because late in the evening they joined me at the fire.

Another storm blew in overnight, which morphed the clear river water into grey soup, and detained us for another day. The extra day's rest seemed to energize us all and we set out early into a cold and sunny morning to complete the final carry. The view from the start of the portage was rather intimidating—near vertical walls of rock and clay, a dense covering of alders, willows and small trees and no evidence that anyone had ever started a portage here before. Because I had reached the place a little ahead of the rest, I climbed to high ground for a quick reconnaissance and a first look at the Richmond Gulf. By the time I returned to the river, the fellows had already started to cut a passage through the dense vegetation, a process that advanced with surprising speed up the steep slope.

Evening found us comfortably encamped near the shore of a small pond high above the Gulf. Our course from there involved some more trail cutting, which eventually brought us to salt water, and thence a paddle southward to the old mission house that had been my refuge in '97. In the six years since then, the building had noticeably deteriorated, but the roof was still watertight and, after a bit of cleanup, it became home for the next several days. Of course, we had to share the place with a number of other creatures, among them a squirrel, a weasel and an adorable little grey rabbit.

During our residence at the place, the various members of the party pursued their own agendas. My own priority was to revisit the falls of Rivière de Troyes. On my way upstream to Clearwater Lake in '90, I had portaged past the 100-metre drop and never paused to take a picture. Now, on a wonderfully calm and sunny day, I set out to remedy the omission. Along the way, I passed several places with interesting geological formations and a nameless stream that entered the gulf in a spectacular cascade. Examining each of these features required time and energy, and it was after noon before I reached the mouth of Rivière de Troyes. An hour's hard paddling and tracking brought me close to my objective, but my efforts to get a good vantage point of the falls were thwarted by the dense vegetation, and I retreated back down the river toward evening light on the shimmering waters of the Richmond Gulf.

As I slowly made my way toward an island en route back to our campsite, a curious cloud emerged above the headland of the southern shore and rose rapidly into the clear sky. A storm, brief and violent, was not long in coming and I gleefully photographed the spectacle from the safety of the island. When I thought it was over, I set off for home in a happy frame of mind. But it wasn't over. Within minutes after I was back on the water, wind and rain returned and life aboard ship became uncomfortably bumpy. When I finally came ashore an hour later I was knackered and *very* happy to be back on solid ground.

The end of the trip was rather anticlimactic. From our comfy camp, John made arrangements by satellite phone for boats from Umiujaq to pick us up. Because of bad weather, we had to wait two days before two large motorboats arrived and ferried us to town. I just had time to visit Eddy Weetaltuk and Noah Inukpuk and say what were probably my last goodbyes to them and to the magnificent landscape they call home.[4]

Afterword
The Journey Ends

Herb Pohl's nature was such that when he started something it was his duty, his responsibility to himself, to finish. We see this repeatedly in his writing: the aborted Albany trip in 1978 that he finished a full 22 years later; and, with particular intensity of regret, he lamented the 1996 "pondhopping" trip in Labrador, which he never really finished to his satisfaction. He did paddle the East Natashquan as an alternative—no small accomplishment—and he did make the trip to Mistastin Lake with Pat Lewtas, but he never considered these jaunts in any way the completion of the ambitious journey of '96 that he had to abandon because of fasciitis. In fact, Herb's displeasure with incomplete trips and his intense desire to enact his plans fully had a role in creating the circumstances in which he lost his life.

After his group trip on the Clearwater River in 2003, Herb, now in his 70s, knew that his days of tripping in Labrador and the far Northwest were done. The psyche was as willing and as nimble—well, almost—as ever, but the soma was not. His joints were wearing out, his stamina wasn't what it once was, and his drive to push and to compete were exercised as much as he'd dare at the bridge table, during the occasional game of ping-pong, or maybe on walks or short paddles with his friend Rob Butler, rather than on any far-flung wilderness river. He had a bicycle accident that left him with injuries that seemed to take forever to heal. And, said Maura, he made the world's most cantankerous patient. Forbearance was not something Herb Pohl had in spades. But still, closer to eighty than seventy, he longed to get out on the water in his canoe.

After sharing a campsite on Lake Superior, Herb said goodbye and paddled away. Larry Ricker's photograph of that moment records the last time anyone saw Herb Pohl before he died less than 48 hours later on the same lake, in a very different frame of mind. *Courtesy of Larry Ricker.*

In 2004, having already paddled a number of the rivers flowing into Superior and having read much about the history and character Gitchi-Gumi, he decided to follow Eric Morse and Bill Mason and any number of other paddlers on a solo journey from Hattie Cove, in Pukaskwa National Park, south and around the horn of Superior to the Michipicoten Mission at the mouth of the Michipicoten River. It was a trip that, to his great frustration, never really got started. It was a trip that in its finishing two years later set in place the circumstances of his death.

His last journal, like so many others, was a cheap little dime store *Selectum* brand, spiral-bound, three-holed school notebook entitled simply "Lake Superior 2004/2006." Because the writing so starkly captures Herb's frame of mind on the aborted 2004 trip and again on his final trip in 2006, and because it is only fitting that his voice, as purely rendered as possible, be included in this final chapter of his book, here then are Herb's trail jottings on where he was in his life, where he was in his paddling career, what was going through his mind during his last days and hours on the water:

August 21, Saturday 2004

As always, slept very poorly when faced with an early start. Decided to get up at four, away by 4:45, filled up at the first Service Centre + kept at it thereafter with only a coffee at Blind River. Turned off the highway at Michipicoten to look for the outfitter located at the mouth of the river. They offered to drive me back to my starting point at Hattie Cove whenever I'll get to their place (for $260). Less welcome was the news that one of their trips (from Hattie's Cove to Michipicoten) had been held ashore for the past four days by strong winds. It added a lot of tension to the enterprise because it brought to the surface the knowledge that fall is the season of prolonged storms hereabouts. When I looked at the lake at Hattie Cove things did not look inviting + the forecast was for more bad weather. The stranded party, I was told, had been ashore at Willow River, a half-day's paddle from here. Two had walked back out on the Pukaskwa Trail, the rest rescued by large motorboat.

All of a sudden I felt very old + unsure of myself. Should I go at all? The thought of being stranded ashore endlessly, of taking weeks to get to my destination, of miserable wet + cold weather, was black indeed. In fact, any of the alternatives—short trips of a day or two which I had contemplated—all of a sudden seemed unattractive + pointless. Maybe it was time to throw in the towel. Take a seat on the couch, read the paper + take little walks.

After nearly 1300 km of driving, I arrived at Hattie Cove around 6:00 p.m.—13 hrs of driving, got a campsite ($21.75, I nearly fell over) cooked supper + had a beer. Then I went to look at the lake; not nice.

Sunday Aug. 22 [2004]

Slept in the car, quite comfortably. It rained, starting about 4:00 a.m. The person at the gate said the forecast was for 60 km/hr wind + rain all day. Obviously no point in thinking paddling. Mind you, the wind didn't seem all that strong.

I decided to hike along the Pukaskwa Trail to the suspension bridge, a 15 km round trip, in the rain. Found it both tedious + tiring. The rain stopped after about two hours + the wind diminished.

Didn't get back until after 2:00 p.m. Too late to start now, particularly after a Red River Cereal breakfast. Registered my paddling trip with the authorities ($18.00) + am set to start with the first light, but with little enthusiasm. Now I'm just killing time after a baked potatoe/bacon/onion dinner which was meant to cheer me up. A fine mist has driven me into the car. It's the sort of weather forecast for the next day or two. I may still change my mind + just go home.

The next entry in the same log is dated two years later. Obviously what happened was that Herb never did extract himself from the funk or the weather he was in at Hattie Cove; he aborted the trip and headed home. However, as with his other "incomplete" trips, this one niggled obsessively in the back of his mind. He discussed options for going back with various friends and paddling cronies, but, when all was said and done, he ended up going back alone in July 2006. Here, then, are the poignant final journal entries of his life, that pose at least as many questions as they answer:

The cover of Herb's last journal.

Tuesday, July 11, 2006

Two years, more or less, and I am back at Hattie Cove. It's sunny and calm this time, the mood is equally bright. Two years ago, unsure of myself and faced with an angry lake, I turned back. On the way home I spent a few days here + there paddling + hiking but the flavour was one of disappointment in myself— an old man who lost his motivation. It stayed with me; a creeping sense that I'm giving up too soon when there was sill the capacity to keep going.

And so here I am again trying to finish what I never started. The journey up was much as last time, an early start (3:30 a.m.) but this time I got someone to drive my car back to Michipicoten immediately ($190).

So now, even if I wanted to change my mind, I can't. I hope to get away early—after bacon + pancakes of course—the lake is calm, the forecast good and I hope to finish the 200 km in six days.

I have noticed that I'm quite out of practice doing the trip routine. No system—one has forgotten some very basic things—like how to light the stove or prepare for supper. It will fall into place, no doubt. Now, after 13 hours of driving + a lot of fidgeting at the campsite (this time $28.75!) I'm ready for bed.

Wednesday, July 12 [2006]
An exceptional day, bright sun, little wind and the lake is asleep.
Got up with the first hint of grey. Despite the lack of routine I was on the water by seven after a very satisfying bacon and pancakes.

For some inexplicable reason paddling seemed hard work. The boat was front-heavy + got easily off track. Tried to find a gentle stroke but just couldn't make it work. Still, the miles went by as I went on. The coastline along here is corrugated but with only a few larger bays and many a prominent headland. The land is all wildly up and down but of modest elevation, not like the coastline south(east) of Michipicoten.

Reached Fisherman's Cove before noon + stopped for a leisurely lunch— met a couple from Ottawa there who had been out for two weeks or more. Fisherman's Cove is a lovely place of nice campsites. Went on to Oiseau Bay, my intended stopping place when I set out. Got there at 1:30 p.m. + should have gone on, but noticed that fatigue was setting in; paddling got even harder + so I stopped at a nice sandy site. The only trouble—no shade.

It's now nearly six and I have puttered around in the nude. The usual camp chores two hours. Build a fireplace, cut wood, set up the tent, have a good wash. Now it's time to get the dinner started.

Tried to take some pictures but can't figure out how the bloody camera works! Did about 28–30 km + hope to do forty tomorrow. The weather is expected to be nice!

Thursday, July 13 [2006]
Hardly able to write, I'm so tired.
Had a terrible, almost sleepless night. Mainly because I ran around in the nude for too long + now parts of the anatomy which never see the sun are rather badly burned. Today started well enough. No clouds + a southern breeze which make for more work than yesterday. Got up at five (predawn in these parts) + had a very disorganized start, mainly due to fatigue. Got away by 7:30 a.m.

Trimmed the load a little better + so the paddling was more positive. Stopped several times to rest, then to look for campsite. Not an easy task because this is very difficult, wild + irregular country. Ended on Otter Island after more than forty km badly dehydrated + overheated—a scorching day

Friday, July 14 [2006]

As mentioned yesterday, I really was in bad shape when I arrived at the old residence of the lighthouse keeper of Otter Island, long disused of course. The grounds offered a decent place for the tent + all in all was much better than a site elsewhere. Went for a hike to the lighthouse some distance away. The facility is still working, by remote control. Spent a half decent night; the sunburn still makes contact with the ground unpleasant + so a good part of the night was spent changing positions.

After a leisurely bacon + pancakes (on the stove) I got away by 8:00 under a partly overcast day + somewhat bothersome wave action—still a headwind but one knew a change in the weather was coming. Made good speed for the first 12 km but from then on the advance slowed inexplicably. Part of the reason was that the waves were getting bigger. Lost track of where I was on the map + started to worry about rain—the first wave of dark clouds went by noisily (thunder) but no precip. So when a suitable place appeared I went to shore to put up the tent before it got wet. Lo + behold there were two fellows from the states (One from Rochester, the other from Illinois) who had gone ashore not long before me. They started from Hattie Cove on Sunday; in other words they took twice as long to get here than I. We are camped a short distance apart. Not a great place, I might add.

It rained a bit + a heavy fog now blankets everything. A pleasant change in temp. I ended up just one bay short of my intended stopping place. Made 22–24 km today. Tomorrow's target is Floating Heart Bay~28 km away.

Saturday, July 15 [2006]

Spent a very good night, no aches or discomforts + the bed seemed wonderful. Tucked in a nine + got up shortly after five. I fully expected a cold overcast day or worse + dressed accordingly without even looking out. Actually it looked like the sky was blue when the dense fog parted, which wasn't often for the first few hours.

Paddling was quite a different experience with only vague outlines, hints even, of where land was, even from a hundred feet away. At one time a strange crescent or dome shape apparition followed me—a fog bow, with only the faintest hint of colour. If I could only have taken a picture of it.

In time the fog cleared, transiently at first but now, five p.m., it's totally clear + an excitingly colourful scene. For a while the wind came up + made paddling hard work. All along here the coast is low, rock + forest, almost no hint of sand or gravel to the point I got worried my target—Floating Heart Bay—was going to be the same unfriendly place.

Not so; it's beautiful, coarse sand, lots of places to put your tent, but no firewood. Had to go some distance before I found a small dead standing spruce + brought it "home." No fireplace either + very few rocks.

Now the tent is up, the fireplace ready, wood cut + split. Everything is spread out to dry (packed everything wet from dew), the wind had died down + the lake is calm. It's very peaceful, the only sound the lapping of wavelets on the shore + birdsong in the air. It feels good to be here now, but the getting here seemed a chore at times.

Saw fairly recent caribou tracks which surprised me—at a place I stopped for a snack—amongst the rocks, there was a campsite, a big concrete chimney + the remains of a log cabin. One never knows where people have lived. I'll have my second potatoe/onion/bacon dinner tonight + then one more stop at the mouth of the University River~30 km away. From there it's another day's paddle back to the car. Of course the weather may not hold.

Right now, I'm just a bit tired, perhaps a few minutes on the thermarest are in order.

Sunday, July 16 [2006]

Woke about 2:00 a.m. to the most elemental display of lightning all over the sky, just awesome flickers and flashes with only a few rumblings of thunder + little rain.

Of course it was enough to wet everything + the gear had to be packed away wet. The bacon and pancakes didn't taste as well as usual, I was a bit disorganized + tired. Away at 8:00 + almost immediately paddling seemed hard work + I seemed to be very slow for the first five km. I was all prepared for a cloudy day + possibly rain but within three hours the sun came out + it got almost instantly too hot.

Made it to the University River by 2:00 p.m.—thirty km in six hours with a couple of stops between, but it was hard going. The lake was actually quite nice, little wind, just a long powerful swell which made landing ashore a worrisome enterprise.

My campsite is fully exposed to the sun + even now (8:00 p.m.) the tent is like an oven. Felt dutibound to head upstream to the famous falls but turned back at the halfway mark. It seemed too much work for this tired old man.

If there is one thing that this trip has done for me, it is that my tripping days are over. Everything seems such an effort and even if you reach your objective it doesn't satisfy as it used to. Getting in + out of the boat when things are awkward is just ridiculous, no balance or agility, stumbling all over the place. I'm just grateful nobody is there to see the performance. Another 30 km tomorrow. If the weather holds I should be re-united with my car ~ 2:00 p.m.

And that's the end of Herb Pohl's last journal. The only other writing in the scribbler is a note from outfitter David Wells of Naturally Superior Adventures to say that he had found Herb's canoe on Monday, July 17, floating upside down

The lake was actually quite nice, little wind, just a long powerful swell which made landing ashore a worrisome enterprise. My campsite is fully exposed to the sun & even more (8:00 p.m.) the heat is like an oven. Felt duti bound to head upstream to the famous falls but turned back at the halfway mark. It seemed too much work for this tired old man.

If there is one thing this trip has done for me, it is that my tripping days are over. Everything seems such an effort and even if you reach your objective it doesn't satisfy as it used to. Getting in & out of the boat when things are awkward is just ridiculous, no balance or agility, stumbling all over the place. I'm just grateful nobody is there to see the performance. Another 30 km

[margin note:] Dénison Falls @ Dog River

Second to last page in Herb Pohl's final journal entry.

at the mouth of Michipicoten River. A couple of days later, Herb's body was found by police divers in six metres of water, not far from where his canoe had turned up. He was not wearing a PFD. Because it mattered to him so much, it should be noted that what ever transpired to take his life, he died within sight of the end of the journey, so by some measure he had *finished* the trip! About how and why he died, there has been much speculation ranging from accidental upset as a result of high winds on the lake, combined with unusually high water in the outflowing river, to falling on slippery rocks whilst trying to land in heavy seas, to darker and possibly far more mysterious causes, the truth of which can never be known. Perhaps we should heed Herb's example and be careful about that for which we wish.

What is clear is that less than 24 hours after a man who lived for the freedom of the wilderness, and who had just tried, unsuccessfully, to get to one of canoeing's most sacred places, Denison Falls, wrote: "If there is one thing that this trip has done for me, it is [to confirm] that my tripping days are over"—the day after writing that, he died.

Whatever there is to be said, whatever Herb Pohl's ultimate legacy, those of us who read his work might wish if we too must die on a Monday, that on the Saturday before, doing what we love, in a place of our choosing—having arrived there self-propelled—that we too might be in frame of mind to write: "The tent is up, the fireplace ready, wood cut and split. Everything is spread out to dry. The wind has died down and the lake is calm. It's very peaceful, the only sound the lapping of wavelets on the shore and birdsong in the air. It feels good to be here."[1]

Appendix I
Herb Pohl Chronology

1930   March 26—born in Austria
1950   20 years old—came to Canada
1957   Met Maura in Thunder Bay (Port Arthur)
1958   Goes back to high school?
1968   Graduates with a BSc from McMaster (Mac)
1969   Abitibi River—Iroquois Falls to Moosonee (solo)
1971   Begins working as an instructional assistant and lab demonstrator
        at McMaster University
1975   Graduates with an MSc from McMaster
1976   Missinaibi River—Peterbell to Moosonee (solo)
1978   Albany River—aborted when he hurt himself on day 4
        Moisie River—(solo, crossing paths with Luc Farmer & Dave Winch)
1979   Family holiday
1980   South Nahanni River (group trip)
        Barron River in Algonquin Park on Thanksgiving weekend
1981   Family holiday
        York River to Palmer Rapids (group trip in the fall)
1982   Kogaluk River—"Across Northern Labrador" (with Ken Ellison)
        Opeongo River with Wilderness Canoe Association (WCA)
1983   Algonquin winter trip on North Madawaska River with John Cross
        Family holiday in the Grand Canyon
        Petawawa River at Thanksgiving

1984	Big East River in Algonquin on Victoria Day weekend
	Notakwanon River—(solo)
1985	Ugjoktok River—(with Jim Greenacre).
1986	North Georgian Bay—French River (WCA group)
1987	Richmond Gulf winter (group trip with Craig Macdonald)
	Fraser River—(solo)
1988	Coppermine River—via Snare from Rae (solo)
1989	Local trips, travel with Maura
1990	Baffin Island winter (with George Luste)
	Nastapoca River circle (solo)
1991	White River (solo)
1992	Kanairiktok River (solo)
1993	North River semi-circle (with Rob Butler and Mike Jones)
1994	Marian-Snare River circle (solo)
1995	Auyuittuq Hike (WCA group trip)
1996	Pondhopping on Quebec/Labrador Border (solo)
1997	Hudson Bay—Richmond Gulf (solo)
1998	Bloodvein River (group trip)
1999	East Natashquan River (solo)
	Algonquin—York River (with Rob Butler)
2000	Albany River (small WCA group trip)
2001	Mistastin River (solo with Pat Lewtas)
2002	Michipicoten/Sand rivers (solo)
2003	Clearwater River—(solo with group)
2004	Aborted Lake Superior trip (solo)
2005	Local trips only
2006	Lake Superior—Last run (solo)

Appendix II
Herb Pohl Bibliography

Published Writing by Herb Pohl
"Wanpitei River" in *The Wilderness Canoeist,* December 1978
"Moisie River" in *The Wilderness Canoeist,* Spring 1980
"Bancroft to Griffith" in *The Wilderness Canoeist,* Winter 1981
"Barron River" in *The Wilderness Canoeist,* Spring 1981
"The Great Escape" in *Nastawgan,* Autumn 1982
"Labrador" in *Nastawgan,* 9(3), Autumn 1982
"Grand Canyon" in *Nastawgan,* Winter 1983 (photos taken on family holiday)
"Thanksgiving on the Petawawa" in *Nastawgan,* Winter 1983
"In Search of the Phantom Road" in *Nastawgan,* Winter 1983
"Hiking in the Alps" in *Nastawgan,* Summer 1984
"Big East River" in *Nastawgan,* Spring 1985
"Journey to the Notakwanon" in *Nastawgan,* 12(2) Summer 1985 (Part 1)
"On the Notakwanon" in *Nastawgan,* 12(3) Autumn 1985 (Part 2)
"North Georgian Bay" in *Nastawgan,* Winter 1986
"Ugjoktok River" in *Nastawgan,* 14(3) Autumn 1987
"Journey to the Fraser River" in *Nastawgan,* 16(4) Winter 1989
"Following Ancient Trails" in *Nastawgan,* 16(3) Autumn 1989 (Coppermine R.)
"Richmond Gulf Revisited" in *Nastawgan,* 18(3) Autumn 1991.
"The Kanairiktok River" in *Nastawgan,* Winter 1993
"North of Great Slave Lake: Part 1—Going Up" in *Nastawgan,* 22(1) Spring
    1995

"North of Great Slave Lake: Part 2—Coming Back" *Nastawgan,* 22(2) Summer 1995

"In Northern Quebec" in *Nastawgan,* Summer 1996.

"Pondhopping: Exploring the Que/Lab Height of Land" in *Nastawgan,* Autumn 1998

"Panhandling in Alqonquin" in *Nastawgan,* Autumn 1999

"East Natashquan River" in *Nastawgan,* Spring 2000

"Rob's Quest for Fitness" in *Nastawgan,* Winter 2001

"Cooking with Herb" in *Nastawgan,* Spring 2001

"Richmond Gulf Revisited" in *Nastawgan,* 29(2) Summer 2002

"From Rapids to Tidal Flats: Paddling the Albany Watershed & James Bay" in *Nastawgan,* Autumn 2003

"The Lure of Mistastin" in *Nastawgan,* 33(2) Summer 2006

Writing About Herb

"Herb Pohl Memorial Edition" of *Nastawgan,* Fall 2006 Issue.

"Meeting Herb Pohl" by Larry Ricker

"Herb Pohl and the WCA" by Bill King

"Herb Pohl: A Wild and Glorious Land," reprint of an interview in Autumn 2002 issue of *Nastawgan* by Rod MacIver. This piece was first published in *Heron Dance,* Issue 32, October 2001.

"Open Waters" by George Haeh

"The Last Trail" by Damir Kusec (2003)

"Into the Barrens" by Greg Went

"Herb Pohl Accident Analysis" by George Haeh

"Herb Pohl" upcoming in *Canoeroots* Magazine.

Appendix III
Cooking with Herb
(from *Nastawgan*, Spring 2001, 21)

Herb Pohl is one of the Wilderness Canoe Association's much revered members. He has travelled solo in many remote areas of Canada. His wonderfully written articles in *Nastawgan* are always looked forward to, and his slide presentations are very slick and highly entertaining. But, you may ask...can he cook? Well, he certainly can, in his own way.

Breakfast Favourites: bacon and pancakes
Lunch Favourites: bacon and cheese
Supper Favourites: bacon, potatoes and onions (see recipe below)

As this menu suggests, Herb likes bacon. According to Herb (and those who know), fat is the best source of energy. Fat packs nine calories of energy per gram compared to four calories per gram for protein and carbohydrate. So, if you expend energy like Herb does on a canoe trip, bring lots of bacon. Herb is a definite carnivore and eats meat at most meals. Herb buys a heavily smoked and salted bacon that is partially cooked and he packs about 1.5 pounds per week. It can be eaten without cooking if fires are scarce. He also enjoys salami and sausages, which he has vacuum-packed for the trip. Dehydrated extra-lean ground beef and dehydrated chicken (1/4 pound per serving) rounds out his meat allowance. Herb favours cheeses from Holland with a wax coating such as

Edam, which will keep well. Along with potatoes, he enjoys pasta and rice. To spice up his meals, he packs some currry sauce. Herb doesn't have much of a sweet tooth—his only desserts are granola bars or fruit bars (those whose wrappers are easily burned).

To counter his bacon diet, Herb drinks lots of tea and Tang. He consumes 7–8 cups of tea per day. He prepares two flasks per day, mixing orange pekoe and orange zinger tea bags along with black currant and mint. He premixes Tang with sugar (two parts Tang to one part sugar) and spices (cinnamon and ground cloves) and packs this in milk bags. For each 10-oz cup he adds three heaping teaspoons and drinks this either hot or cold.

Herb's receipe for bacon, potatoes, and onions:
Cut bacon into snippets and fry this along with chopped onion. Boil one large baking potato, chop this, and add to the frying pan Voilà…a feast fit for a King!

Notes

FOREWORD: THE REMARKABLE LIFE AND LEGACY OF HERB POHL

1 Raffan, James, "Enchanted River: Canadian Odyssey on Waters Clear and Wild," in *America's Hidden Wilderness: Lands of Seclusion*, published by the Special Publications Division, National Geographic Society, Washington, DC, (1988) 164–195.

2 Twomey, Arthur C., *Needle to the North: The Story of an Expedition to Ungava and the Belcher Islands*. London: Herbert Jenkins, 1942. Note: The first half of this book (the part pertaining to the Richmond Gulf area) was republished in paperback in 1982 by Oberon Press in Ottawa.

3 This town, at the mouth of the Great Whale River has the unusual distinction of having four names that mirror the cultural makeup of the place: in English—Great Whale River; in Cree—Whapma-goostui; in Inuktitut—Kuujjuarapik; and in French—Poste-de-la-baleine.

4 Herb's friend Rob Butler explained that in later life Herb did not sleep well. He would rise very early in the morning and drive toward Toronto, sometime calling Butler to meet him at one high-way rest stop or another for coffee. Butler would show up at the arranged place, often just in time to see Herb flailing his arms to music blasting out of the car sound system. On some occasions, Herb would not get out of the car for coffee until the conducting was done.

5 This achievement was written up in one of the Lakehead papers under the headline, "Father Becomes Ontario Scholar." The article went on to say that "the Port Arthur man" won the $400 scholarship by obtaining an average of over 80 per cent in his top eight exams, and that two of these had to be in senior level English.

6 www.nebula.on.ca/hamiltonassoc/

7 www.wildernesscanoe.ca

8 King, Bill, "Herb Pohl and the WCA" in *Nastawgan*, 33(3) (2006) 4.

9 This sentence is paraphrased from Alfred Lord Tennyson's famous poem, "Ulysses."

CHAPTER 1: THE LURE OF FARAWAY PLACES

1 It is on the basis of this statement that we can position the farm on which Herb grew up, quite accurately as being 25 kilometres south of the City of Graz in the Mür River valley.

Chapter 2: Moisie River, 1978

1   Rugge, J. and J.W. Davidson, *The Complete Wilderness Paddler*. New York: Knopf, 1975, distributed by Random House. This is one of the first and still one of the best books on how to plan a wilderness canoe trip. The pencil illustrations are excellent and the narrative style, complete with creative suggestions (and diagrams!) about how to foist your cloud of bugs onto your paddling mates, is quite charming.

2   On the original manuscript, Herb had pencilled this note under the heading "General Comments": the trip was taken at the beginning of September 1978 and took nine days; the usual time taken by travellers is 14–16 days. Even now (2005), with many more trips behind me, I still consider this to have been one of the most physically demanding. The weather had a lot to do with that, but also at that time there were no well defined portage trails. And yes, "upset rapids" is still the scariest ride I've ever taken on purpose.

Chapter 3: To Labrador—From Schefferville to Nain—Kogaluk River, 1982

1   It is a four-year jump from the trip described in Chapter 1 to this multi-watershed extravaganza. In the middle, in 1980, Herb and a WCA group paddled the Nahanni River—a story he chose not to write up in *The Wilderness Canoeist*. But he was busy paddling short trips and on weekends at this time in his paddling career and was also cutting his writing teeth on quite a number of shorter reports of his adventures in the WCA newsletter: "Wanapitei River," December 1978; "Barron River," Spring 1981; "Bancroft to Griffith," Winter 1981; and "The Great Escape," Autumn 1982, which features an adventure with *The Lure of Faraway Places* cover model, Dave Berthelet.

2   A friend he made through the WCA.

3   Wallace, Dillon, *The Lure of the Labrador Wild: The Story of the Exploring Expedition by Leonidas Hubbard, Jr.*, New York: Revell, 1905. Note: This book has since been republished and is available in paperback, published by Breakwater Books in 1983 and 1997.

4   Cabot, W.B., *In Northern Labrador*. Boston: R.G. Badger, 1912.

5   Prichard, H.V.H., *Through Trackless Labrador*. London: W. Heinemann, 1911.

6   Built between 1951 and 1954, the Quebec North Shore and Labrador Railway was an engineering marvel in its day, much celebrated at the time. It was originally built to bring iron out from Schefferville. As the fortunes of the mining industry have waxed and waned, so too have the fortunes of the railway, but it remains one of the last reasonably priced and romantic providers of access to wilderness in Canada.

7   One reason why this trip is not for the faint of heart.

8   Cabot, W.B., 106.

Chapter 4: Notakwanon River, 1984

1   Again, Herb has skipped a year in his choice of trips on which to report since the big Kogaluk trip with Ken Ellison. In the meantime, however, he was far from idle. He travelled to the Grand Canyon with Maura in 1983 and wrote this up in *Nastawgan* (Winter 1983) and, as well, he continued his shorter trips and his journalistic efforts, with both writing and photos, to bring the stories of these to the WCA audience. In the Winter 1983 issue of *Nastawgan*, he had articles entitled "Thanksgiving on the Petawawa," in which his photo of Dave Berthelet was first published in black and white, and "In Search of the Phantom Road," which is a tale of hammering around in Algonquin Park in the winter with his friend and long-time WCA member, John Cross. It also appears, based on another story called "Hiking in the Alps" (*Nastawgan,* Summer 1984), published while he was on the Notakwanon, that during his "off" year, he also took a quick trip home to visit with his brother Oskar and his mother in Austria. However, by the summer of 1984, having not been on a long trip for two years, he was on his own again and headed back to The Land God Gave to Cain—for what Herb always considered to be the most memorable trip of his life.

2   There were three people who paddled identical Femat-designed canoes with the distinctive double-bladed paddle: Herb Pohl, Karl Schimeck and Dave Berthelet. Sadly, with Herb's death, all
three have passed away. Among them, Herb was the most vociferous defender of the fact that these
decked craft, in which the paddler sat with a double-bladed paddle—in spite of all these signs that
led people to believe that these fibreglass craft were kayaks—were canoes. Herb always maintained that he paddled a *canoe.*

3   In addition to being an accomplished wilderness canoeist, Stewart Coffin is perhaps best known
as the world's best designer of polyhedral interlocking puzzles. His book, *The Puzzling World of
Polyhedral Dissections* is, apparently, the definitive work on interlocking puzzles that have a geo-
metrical theme.

4   Having sold his last tired specimen to Bill Ritchie at the end of the Kogaluk trip two years before.

5   The recipe for this meal is contained in the appendices of this book.

6   This passage, written in celebration of landscape, is all the more remarkable when one considers
that on this trip his canoe has caught fire and he had nearly been killed in a dumping incident. Any
other paddler, travelling alone, might well be too busy focusing on staying alive and getting out as
soon as possible, having had these brushes with danger. Not Herb Pohl.

7   Two big trips, two big boats—it all seemed part of the game to Herb. In his original manuscript,
he had this note appended below the last paragraph: Trip started June 29, 1984 at Iron Arm just
east of Schefferville and finished July 27 in Davis Inlet on the Labrador coast. The distance is
approximately 550 km.

CHAPTER 5: UGJOKTOK RIVER, 1985

1   Jim Greenacre was another friendship Herb made through the WCA. Greenacre, an Englishman,
though he looked similar in age to Herb, was nine years older, making the two of them 55 and 64
years old, respectively, on this trip.

2   Hubbard, Mina, *A Woman's Way Through Unknown Labrador: An Account of the Exploration of the
Nascaupee and George Rivers/by Mrs. Leonidas Hubbard.* New York: McClure, 1908. Note: This
is one of the most fabled stories of 20th century exploration in Labrador, which had been written
about by many historians and other writers. One of the most engaging contemporary accounts of
the tale is another book by Rugge and Davidson called *Great Heart: The History of a Labrador
Adventure.* New York: Viking Press, 1988.

3   Jim Greenacre wrote about this experience in an earlier issue of *Nastawgan.*

4   In fact, in Labrador, the "Border Beacon," to which Herb refers in this instance, could not be a
Distant Early Warning installation because this line of defence, built during the early days of the
cold war, was much farther north. There were three interconnected lines of early warning radar and
radio listening stations across North America. The northernmost of these, largely located in the
Arctic Archipelago, was the DEW Line. The southernmost was the Pinetree Line, which ran closer
to the Canada/USA border. And between these two early warning systems was the Mid-Canada
Line, which ended at its easternmost extent at Hopedale, Labrador. Border Beacon may well have
been an installation associated with this family of radar stations.

5   Parks Canada, *Wild Rivers: Newfoundland and Labrador.* Ottawa: Parks Canada ARC Branch
Planning Division Wild Rivers Survey, 1974. This was part of an extensive survey, done in the
1970s that involved teams of paddlers, during Pierre Trudeau's tenure as prime minister, criss-
crossing the country to write detailed planners for trips on Canada's wild rivers. In many cases,
they are still excellent sources of information for planning remote river trips.

6   On the bottom of his original manuscript Herb made the following codicil: Jim recovered in a surprisingly short time and we have been out a number of times since. On one occasion, not long after
our return, I developed a sore back, and it was Jim who offered to carry my canoe over a portage.
My response was, "If I can't carry my own boat then I'll quit," to which Jim replied, "Now you
know how I felt on the Ugjoktok!"

CHAPTER 6: CLEARWATER WINTER, 1987

1   Craig Macdonald, who for years has been a recreational trails specialist for the Ontario Ministry of Natural Resources in Algonquin Park, has spent most of his life researching and learning about winter and summer trails used by the Anishinabi people across Northern Ontario, Quebec and parts of Manitoba. In addition to producing a detailed map (published by the MNR—a description of this map and notes on how to order can be found at www.ottertooth.com), Craig has done much empirical research into travel methods and technologies. In 1982, he tested the limits of these "hot" camping techniques on the west side of James Bay with a trip from Fort Albany to Moosonee ("Tumpline Trek on James Bay Shores," in *Canadian Geographic* 102 (6), 54–59). This trip in the Richmond Gulf area was an effort to test the limits of the method in taiga country a little farther north and on the east side of Hudson Bay.

2   Radisson is an unincorporated area that was created to house the workers who built the La Grande power project. It is located just downstream from the LG-4 power dam.

3   *Tupek* is the term for a traditional Inuit summer dwelling and, in modern parlance, still refers to a simple canvas tent structure, of particular design—usually with one wooden pole and a door flap on the angled canvas surface, that can accommodate one or two people.

4   On his original manuscript, Herb added the following note: "A comprehensive treatment of the subject can be found in *A Snow Walker's Companion* by Garrett and Alexandra Conover, and Craig's account of the trip can be found in *Nastawgan* vol. 14, no. 4." For anyone interested in tracking down this second account of the trip, Craig's story of striking out with Tony to find Umi-ujaq with only minimal equipment is very different than Herb's story of a leisurely wait during the last couple of days of the trip. For Craig and Tony, it was a very different part of the journey—during which they very nearly were mistaken by hunters as caribou—and had a couple of other hair-raising moments as well.

CHAPTER 7: LABRADOR'S FRASER RIVER, 1987

1   This was an unusual year for wilderness trips insofar as Herb was able to manage two in one season. He only had so much vacation time from the university, but there was also the matter of funds and negotiating time away with Maura. Maura said that she would always know that Herb was planning a trip, or an extra trip, weeks before he would actually broach the subject with her. But almost without exception she knew that once Herb had made up his mind that the best way to proceed was to agree that this was the absolutely the thing that must be done. Still, Maura's participation and support of his travelling was important to Herb.

2   Like so many ships, the *Taverner* was an institution on the Labrador coast, with a history through her name that went back to the days of the *Caribou*, one of the most famous ferries that ran between Newfoundland and Canada before the Second World War. The *Caribou* was torpedoed by a U-boat on October 14, 1942, and all hands, including Captain Ben Taverner and his two sons, went down with the ship. The coastal supply vessel *Taverner* was named in his honour.

3   It is noteworthy that Herb did not carry this incomplete trip like an anvil on his record as he did other trips that were changed or cut short. In this case, he was disappointed not to have had a chance to look for Prichard's canoe but it appears that he accepted, based on on-the-ground proofing of his original plan, that what he had thought he might do was impossible, even for a man of his drive and tenacity. Another factor in this acquiescence to the situation might have been the fact that on this whole journey, since stopping on the island to video the other WCA group, that he had been travelling without a map. The tone of his prose in this instance also seems to indicate that he was well pleased that he had done something, in going up the Fraser from the sea as far as he did, that this was new ground for modern day adventurers.

CHAPTER 8: ANCIENT TRAILS TO THE COPPERMINE RIVER, 1988

1   Franklin, John, *Journey to the Shores of the Polar Sea, in 1819–20–21–22: with a brief account of the Second Journey in 1825–26–27*. London: J. Murray, 1829. This classic of northern exploration literature, which is of special interest to canoeists because it involves detailed descriptions of winter travel by snowshoe and summer travel by canoe from York Factory (at the mouth of the Hayes River on Hudson Bay) to the Arctic coast and back, is a must read for anyone travelling between Yellowknife and Kugluktuk, or in the Bathurst Inlet area, and is available as an e-book at no charge from www.gutenberg.org.

2   Shawn Hodgins, son of veteran canoeists Bruce and Carol Hodgins, is the co-owner (with his partner, Liz McCarney) of Wanapitei Canoe, an outfitter and northern expedition operator that grew out of Camp Wanapitei on Lake Temagami.

3   Information about Dogrib canoe-building activities and much more of a cultural nature pertaining to the area through which Herb travelled this year on his way to the Coppermine River, arises from fascinating research done by Tom Andrews, Subarctic Archaeologist at the Prince of Wales Natural Heritage Centre in Yellowknife, in association with Dogrib researcher and land negotiator, John B. Zoe, and elder Harry Simpson. A good portion of this work is available on a highly interactive website at www.lessonsfromtheland.ca. This work is also published as "The Îdaà Trail: Archaeology and the Dogrib Cultural Landscape, Northwest Territories, Canada," in G.P. Nichols and T.D. Andrews (eds.), *At a Crossroads: Archaeology and First Peoples in Canada* (Vancouver: Simon Fraser University Press, 1997) and "On Yamözhah's Trail: Dogrib sacred sites and the anthropology of travel" in J. Oakes, R. Riewe, K. Kinew, and E. Maloney (eds.), *Sacred Lands: Aboriginal World Views, Claims, and Conflicts.* (Edmonton: Canadian Circumpolar Institute, 1998).

4   Herb, ever the iconoclast, chose a canoe at the beginning of his wilderness paddling career and stuck to it. It was a CDR-C2 made on a mould that was owned by Emile Maschek, proprietor of Femat Boat Company in Shelburne, Ontario. After Maschek went out of business, Herb was still able to get boats from him and, when that was no longer possible, he went in with his friends Dave Berthelet and Karl Schimeck, and commissioned Niagara area builder, Russell Miller, to make craft for them using the Femat mould. The CDR-C2 was 15′8″ long, 34″ on the beam and, when constructed from polyester resin and fibreglass cloth, weighed about 55 pounds. It had a load rating of 650 pounds. Femat put different tops on this hall and called them different models. The one Herb paddled had a moulded yoke and one seat inside a large cockpit, for which he had made separately detachable splash covers. Having used and abused this same canoe on all of his backcountry trips, Pohl was intimately familiar with its handling and also with how to fix it when it was fatigued or damaged, having had fires and all manner of other physical insults that compromised the integrity of his craft. It is his coolness in responding to serious boat damage that boggles the mind. Ever the pragmatist—he was anything but sentimental about his boats, or anything for that matter—this was yet another craft that he would sell *as is* at the end of his trip to a willing buyer, knowing that by the time he got it home and fixed it up again, he was probably ahead saving freight charges, getting what he could for the boat in the north, and having another made to strike out fresh the following year.

CHAPTER 9: UMIUJAQ CIRCLE—WIACHEWAN AND NASTAPOCA RIVERS, 1990

1   Having had a year off to travel with Maura (and lots of smaller trips with WCA cronies), and having had a new canoe made and outfitted, Herb was looking at 1990 as another two-major-trip year, one that marked his 60th birthday. In the spring, he travelled to North Baffin with his long-time friend and organizer of the Wilderness Canoeing Symposium in Toronto, George Luste; interestingly, although he kept a detailed journal of this trip and took some superb photographs, he never wrote about this trip for readers of *Nastawgan*. And, in the summer, with a new canoe, he was back in his second favourite area, around Richmond Gulf. The drive to return here may have been part of his "completion" ethic—having experienced the land in winter with Craig Macdonald, he felt

compelled to make the effort to see it in summer as well, drawing on research and intelligence that included Matthew George's line that Herb had transcribed onto his maps of the area.

2   Low, A.P., *Report on Explorations in James' Bay and Country East of Hudson Bay: Drained by Big, Great Whale and Clearwater Rivers*. Montreal: W. Foster Brown, 1888 (CIHM/ICMH Micro-fiche series No. 59199).

3   Low, A.P., *Report on Exploration in the Labrador Peninsula: Along the East Main, Koksoak, Hamilton, Manicuagan and portions of other rivers in 1892–93–94–95*. Ottawa: S.E. Dawson, 1896 (CIHM/ICMH Microfiche series No. 29438).

Chapter 10: Kanairiktok River—From Knox Lake to Hopedale, 1992

1   By now, any notion of alternating family vacations with canoeing has gone out the window. Although Herb has chosen to skip, in this collection from his trip in 1990 to his trip in 1992, from 1990 onward, with the exception of 2005 when he was injured from his bicycle accident, he mounted a major trip every year for the rest of his life. In 1991, he paddled in the Pukaskwa area, including the White River. In 1992, he was back for a month-long journey in Labrador.

2   Amongst the research available to Herb in preparation for this trip was a then recent paper in the journal *Arctic* that gave him some idea of what was going on with these planes, and how they might affect his experience on the Kanairiktok. See Harrington, F.H. and A.M. Veitch, "Short-Term Impacts of Low-level Jet Fighter Training on Caribou in Labrador," in *Arctic* 44(4) December 1991, 318–327.

3   Again, having examined conditions on the ground, Herb was able to agree with himself that the planning with maps and ephemera at home had been good in theory but unworkable in practice, allowing him to be satisfied with an alternate route rather than carrying with him the burden of another unfinished trip.

4   Registered for Newfoundland and Labrador ferry service in 1987, the *Northern Ranger*, at 2,261 tonnes is nearly four times bigger than the *Taverner*.

5   Herb added a note at the bottom of his original manuscript that read, "The journey, significantly reduced in scope from the original plan, had taken 20 days [he had food for 32] and covered approximately 540 km."

Chapter 11: First Descent of Rivière du Nord, 1993

1   K. G. Davies, (ed.), *Northern Quebec and Labrador Journal and Correspondence, 1835–35*. London: Hudson's Bay Record Society (No. 24), 1963.

2   G. Williams, "James Clouston's Journey Across the Labrador Peninsula in 1820." in *The Beaver*, Summer (1966) 10. A copy of this map is also held by the Hudson's Bay Company Archives in Winnipeg, 11M1, G.1/43.

3   Atkinson, George, *A Chart of the Survey of the Easternmost Branch of the Great Whale River, Eastmain Coast, Hudson Bay. 1816,* Hudson's Bay Company Archives, 11M1, G.1/40. See also, *Map of East Coast and Interior of Hudson Bay*, 11M1, G.1/42.

4   On his original manuscript, Herb added the following: "Duration of trip: 28 days. Distance ~ 600 km. Portages: 44.

5   Herb was particularly pleased and proud with this pioneering that he had done with Rob Butler and Mike Jones, and took the opportunity to mark and celebrate the achievement by writing to his Labrador explorer/author hero, Elliott Merrick. In a card by return post, handwritten in fountain pen ink, Merrick replied:

Nov. 18, 1993
Dear Herb,
    Such a fluent and vivid pictorial letter from you—such as few people nowadays could or would even think of writing! "Having a wonderful time, wish you were here."

I read your letter over and over again, and wonder how you could have managed to pick such congenial companions who would remain congenial on the bug-filled portages. Your trips never cease to amaze me.

I'm glad you can retire soon from teaching. A little place in the country is the answer.

Thanks for the kind words. I plan to come to Toronto one last time in January, and we'll have a good old gab fest then.

Elliott M.

Merrick, who was 87 years old when he wrote this letter, gained general popularity as a writer of books set in Labrador and northern Vermont. His best-selling book *Northern Nurse*, about his first wife whom he met while teaching in Labrador, is perhaps his best-known work but, in canoeing circles, it is his first book, *True North,* that is considered a classic. Merrick, who obviously had a genuine affection for Herb and his remarkable wilderness resumé, died on April 22, 1997, at 91 years of age.

CHAPTER 12: RETIREMENT ODYSSEY IN THE GREAT NORTHWEST, 1994

1   Edmonton-based John McInnes, an indefatigable explorer of routes between Great Slave Lake and the Barrens, was a regular correspondent of Herb's, comparing notes about possible routes and their historic significance. There is likely no one who knows this country better than McInnis.

2   There are examples of this type of canoe and the people who made and used them in the Prince of Wales Northern Heritage Centre in Yellowknife.

3   The construction of this sentence betrays Herb's knowledge of the literature of the north, insofar as it echoes the words of a Yellow Knife Indian, Saltatha, as quoted in Warburton Pike's 1892 book, *The Barren Ground of Northern Canada*. He said: "My father, you have spoken well; you have told me that heaven is very beautiful; tell me now one thing more. Is it more beautiful than the country of the muskox in summer, when sometimes mist blows over the lakes, and sometimes the water is blue, and the loons cry very often?"

4   Named after the famous pioneering bush pilot, Wop May.

5   Morse, E., *Freshwater Saga: Memoirs of a Lifetime of Wilderness Canoeing in Canada.* Toronto: University of Toronto Press, 1987.

CHAPTER 13: UNFINISHED BUSINESS ON THE QUEBEC-LABRADOR BORDER, 1996

1   Another gap here in Herb's selection of stories to include in this collection. In the summer of 1995, and Herb and several others hiked the Pangnirtung Pass in Auyuittuq National Park on Baffin Island, but he chose not to write about this journey. In 1996, he is back in to his first love, his "mistress," the wilds of Labrador for a journey that, to his great regret, was beyond his physical capabilities that year, at 66 years old. What is remarkable about this journey, besides the physical and mental stamina it took to get as far as he did, was Herb's route-finding ability. He was adept with map and compass, but, in this part of the world, where at time there was nothing more than bog as far as the eye could see in every direction, he also used his innate sense of direction to find his way where others have died trying.

2   A popular starting point for bow-hunting caribou in the fall but also a popular outfitter for canoeists as well (www.airsaguenay.com).

CHAPTER 14: NO AGENDA ON THE EASTMAIN, 1997

1   Although Herb makes the odd snide reference to low-flying fighter jets and environmental devastation here and there, the paucity of comments in his writing about this did not mean he was not a staunch protector of the natural world. When he spoke he would talk about the importance of wilderness, he was a member and supporter of a number of national environmental organizations, but mostly he lived richly and simply, consuming as little as possible and living a conserving lifestyle as

much as he could. This comment about clear-cutting is one of the few times in his writing where his utter distaste for those who do not respect the value of the natural world is front and centre.

2   Looking back retrospectively on the grand scheme of Herb's life, this is a pivotal moment in his coming to terms with ageing. He is still not back to 100%, after spending the winter trying to recover from the foreshortened "pondhopping" escapade the year before, and in this instance he is trying to find another way to interact with the land that doesn't involve a driving linear agenda. As he finds out, having given the *laissez faire* approach to travel a good try, this way of operating is just not in his genes.

3   There is a pan-North American aboriginal teaching that says that each of the four directions contain lodges or dwelling places from which people come. Each of these has its own characteristics and dispositions, each has a colour and an animal associated with it. In the north, the animal is often the buffalo, the colour is white and the teaching is that this is the place of integrated knowing, of wisdom. In the east, the animal is the eagle, the colour is yellow, for the rising sun, and this is the place of the big vision, the synoptic overview—people born in the lodge of the east see the big picture. In the south, the animal is often the mouse, the colour is yellow, and this is the place for people who see and appreciate the fine detail, sometimes without full comprehension of the big picture. And, in the west is the lodge of the bear, the colour is often black, and this is the place of introspection. There are many, many versions of the so-called medicine wheel teaching, and an equally large number of interpretations but one common message, across traditions, is that everyone tends toward the qualities and characteristics of a particular direction and that to live a full life, one must visit the other three lodges—one must dance around the fire, as it were—to appreciate how other people see the world. A related teaching is that each of us has a totem, a special animal, with whom we share certain characteristics. Herb, with his solitary, introspective ways, demonstrates the qualities of the bear. He loved to watch the setting sun, in the west. And, whether one subscribes to these teachings or not, of all the animals Herb encountered along the way, it is the black bears who seem most often to cross his path, enriching and occasionally confounding his life, but never really doing him any harm, perhaps drawn to a kindred spirit?

Chapter 15: East Natashquan—A Relaxing Alternative to Pondhopping, 1999

1   Again, Herb has skipped a year in his collected trip reporting. In the summer of 1998, he made a departure from his usual haunts and paddled the Bloodvein River from Artery Lake, on the Manitoba/Ontario border down to the eastern shore of Lake Winnipeg. It was a group trip—six paddlers in all, including his good friend, Karl Schimeck—but from the outset the whole experience was far too crowded. On the very first day of the trip, having flown in on four flights from Matheson Island, he wrote: "All along the to me strange interplay among the disparate participants was a source of some dissatisfaction. Annoying delays, the constant search for consensus, it baffles the solo traveller. Now we have agreed to stay at the same site tomorrow so that the Spence's (Glenn and his wife Gerry) can get their arses in gear—get their gear sorted out before we head downstream. From the air the river looks pretty + harmless in spite of reports that there are some one hundred rapids + falls. We'll see." It was not a great trip for Herb and, perhaps for that reason, he chose not to write about it, perhaps driven by the axiom, *if you can't say something nice then say nothing at all*. But, in 1999, he was back on the finishing agenda. If he didn't have the oomph to go back to the Labrador height of land, then he would do something a little more relaxing like the East Natashquan. Right, Herb!

Chapter 16: Finishing the Albany River Trip, 2000

1   By now, having outfitted several versions of the same canoe, Herb had the cover design down to a fine art. These were made by a custom powerboat cover and sail maker in the Burlington area, and included a front combing protection that was on all of the time and a larger piece of cover that would be rolled back or forward, depending on the need for protection, and, when closed all the

way, would allow access to the load through flaps secured with Velcro closures. The whole cover assembly was affixed to the side of the fibreglass combing with turn-toggles and metal grommets affixed to the waterproofed cordura material.

2 On his original manuscript, Herb wrote the following note: "We travelled in separate boats, slept in separate tents, drove up in separate vehicles. Karl also had his own food while Mike and I shared meals but not lunches. I think Mike spent an extra $500 to get out from Fort Albany. Starting date: Aug. 1; Finish: Aug. 19. Distance ~ 630 km. The people at Hearst Air were very accommodating, charged us $40 for parking and shuttle."

CHAPTER 17: STILL FINISHING THE PONDHOPPING CAPER—MISTASTIN LAKE, 2001

1 A standing dead tree, usually weathered and without bark, that can be cut to provide a night's firewood for campers. Possibly the term derived from an original Ojibwa term.

2 Herb's comment about selective memory brings to mind the fact that when he came home from this trip, all he would talk about (when he started to talk, which was sometimes several days after his return) was a third member of the trip, who drove him nearly crazy. This was Pat's dog, an undersized Nova Scotia Duck Tolling Retriever named "Cabot." Fortunately, for the curious, Pat wrote an account of the same trip that was published in the same Summer 2006 issue of *Nastawgan*, where the whole sad tale of his efforts to see his much beloved dog through what was a very trying trip is presented in beautifully crafted counterpoint to Herb's view and memory of what went down as they travelled together that summer. To provide a small taste of this other view, Pat had some very interesting things to say about two dyed-in-the-wool hermits teaming up. He wrote:

> Most solo travellers I suspect, present an odd blend of romantic and realist, conqueror and flake. Romantic, because only deep passion pushes one so completely into the wilderness. Realist, because one needs hard-headed judgement to flourish in tough country without other voices to correct mistakes. Conqueror, because a long, solo journey calls for tremendous, perhaps misdirected, drive. And flake, because the solitary muse brings with it a tendency to hold aloof where others throw themselves in.
>
> Unsure whether we'd get along and jealous each of his own experience, Herb and I planned two solo trips to the same place at the same time. Each of us took our own food, tent and boat. Of course we stayed together, paddled together and camped together. But we didn't have to. Strangely enough, the very looseness of our ties bound us more strongly. Our little group had a contingency that kept both of us attentive to its well-being. And our independence undercut the politics that so often complicate and mar wilderness journeys. We remained together and companions by choice.
>
> Everything worked well. Herb and I maintained an amiable distance during the trip—often the wisest policy when two people isolate themselves in the wilds. But we became fast friends afterwards, a result of having done the trip. *Nastawgan* 33(2), 8.

3 When Jacques Cartier first sighted the north shore of the Gulf of St. Lawrence in 1534, alluding to Genesis 4 and the story of Cain, having killed his brother Abel, was condemned to till barren land, he called it "the land God gave to Cain." This term has been used in various contexts since then to refer to tundra landscapes across the north, especially in Labrador and northern Quebec.

CHAPTER 18: A LAST NORTHERN HURRAH—CLEARWATER RIVER, 2003

1 By now, Herb had reluctantly accepted the creeping limitations of being a septuagenarian, at least to the extent that he was no longer contemplating totally self-contained trips in remote northern locales. The previous year, he had done a solo circle route in northern Ontario, but he knew that without help, it would be taking unnecessary risks to go much beyond that without companionship of some kind. Over the years, with the possible exception of his Bloodvein trip, he had more

or less perfected the fine art of choosing like-minded companions and travelling solo together. This final return to Richmond Gulf was a variant of those strategies and, with only minor issues of control from time to time, worked out quite well for all concerned. But even with this safety net beneath him, Herb still managed to find a solo experience that allowed him to soldier through paddling and portaging with two cracked or broken ribs he never happened to mention to the others when he might have asked for help!

2   Parts of Nicol Finlayson's and William Hendry's story can be found in Hudson's Bay Record Society Volumes III (Fleming, ed.), XIX (Rich and Johnson eds.), XXIV (Davies and Johnson eds.) and in R.M. Ballantyne's 1857 book *Ungava: A Tale of Esquimaux-land*. Enacting Sir George Simpson's plan to expand trade into Inuit territory along Hudson Strait, Hendry went first to Ungava, followed by Finlayson in 1828. It is likely that Herb found their accounts of travel in the HBRS volumes, which he regularly mined for route information.

3   Max Finkelstein, and James Stone, *Paddling the Boreal Forest: Rediscovering A.P. Low*. Toronto: Natural Heritage, 2004.

4   An alternate account of this trip, written from the point of view of a member of the other part of the group, was published in the Herb Pohl Memorial Edition of *Nastawgan* in the Fall of 2006. See, D. Kusec, "The Last Trail," *Nastawgan* 33(3), 11–15.

AFTERWORD: THE JOURNEY ENDS

1   Immediately following Herb's death, there was an outpouring of comment and affection for him that totally surprised his wife, Maura. Donations were made in his honour to The Canadian Canoe Museum in Peterborough, Ontario, where, in due course, his canoe, slides and papers will be part of the research collection. As this book is going to press, plans are being drawn to create a suitable memorial project within the museum context. What that memorial will be and what it might look is yet to be finalized.

Bibliography

Atkinson, George, *A Chart of the Easternmost Branch of the Great Whale River, Eastmain Coast, Hudson Bay, 1816.* Hudson's Bay Company Archives, 11M1,G.1/42.

Cabot, William B., *In Northern Labrador.* Boston: R.G. Badger, 1912.

Davies, K.G. (ed.), *Northern Quebec and Labrador Journal and Correspondence, 1835–1838.* London: Hudson's Bay Record Society, No. 24 (1963).

Dillon, Wallace, *The Lure of the Labrador Wild: The Story of the Exploring Expedition Conducted by Leonidas Hubbard, Jr.* New York; Toronto: F.H. Revell, 1905.

Finkelstein, Max and James Stone, *Paddling the Boreal Forest: Rediscovering A.P. Low.* Toronto: Natural Heritage Books, 2004.

Franklin, John, *Journey to the Shores of the Polar Sea, in 1819–20–21–22: With a Brief Account of the Second Journey in 1825–26–27.* London: J. Murray, 1829.

Harrington, F.H. and A.M. Veitch, "Short-Term Impacts of Low-Level Jet Fighter Training on Caribou in Labrador" in *Arctic* 44 (4) December 1991, 318–27.

Hubbard, Mina, *A Woman's Way Through Unknown Labrador: An Account of the Exploration of the Nascaupee and George Rivers by Mrs. Leonidas Hubbard.* New York: McClure, 1908.

King, Bill, "Herb Pohl and the WCA" in *Nastawgan* 33, 3 (2006) 4.

Kusek, D., "The Last Trail" in *Nastawgan* 33, 3 (2006) 11–15.

Low, A.P., *Report on Explorations in James' Bay and Country East of Hudson Bay, Drained by the Big, Great Whale and Clearwater Rivers.* Montreal: W.F. Brown, 1888 (CIHM/ICMH Microfiche Series No. 59199).

_____, *Report on Exploration in the Labrador Peninsula: Along the East Main, Koksoak, Hamilton, Manicuagan and Portions of Other Rivers in 1892–93–94–95.* Ottawa: S.E. Dawson, 1896 (CIHM/ICMH Microfiche series No. 29438).

Macdonald, Craig, "Tumpline Trek on James Bay Shores" in *Canadian Geographic* 102 (6), 59.

Merrick, Elliot, *True North.* New York: Scribner, 1933.

Morse, Eric W., *Freshwater Saga: Memoirs of a Lifetime of Wilderness Canoeing in Canada.* Toronto: University of Toronto Press, 1987.

Parks Canada, *Wild Rivers: Newfoundland and Labrador.* Ottawa: Parks Canada, 1977.

Pike, Warburton, *The Barren Ground of Northern Canada.* London; New York: Macmillan, 1892.

Prichard, H.V.H., *Through Trackless Labrador*. London: W. Heinemann, 1911.

Raffan, James, "Enchanted River: Canadian Odyssey on Waters Clear and Wild" in *America's Hidden Wilderness: Lands of Seclusion*. Washington, DC: National Geographic Society, 1988.

Rugge, John and James West Davidson, *The Complete Wilderness Paddler*. New York: Knopf, 1975.

Twomey, Arthur C., *Needle to the North: The Story of an Expedition to Ungava and the Belcher Islands*. London: Herbert Jenkins, 1942.

Williams, G., "James Clouston's Journey Across the Labrador Peninsula in 1820" in *The Beaver*, Summer (1966) 10.

Maps:

The Atlas of Canada, http://atlas.nrcan.qc.ca/site/english/index.html, accessed March 10, 2007.

Index

About the Editor

PHOTO BY MOLLY C. RAFFIN

James Raffan is a writer and geographer and one of Canada's foremost authorities on canoeing and wilderness experience. He is author and editor of a dozen books including his best-selling biography of Bill Mason, *Fire in the Bones*, and *Deep Waters*, which became the basis of a film called *Acceptable Risk*, a radio documentary called "One Blue Canoe," and a powerful new exhibit called "Remembering Temiskaming," at The Canadian Canoe Museum in Peterborough. He has written for *National Geographic* and *Canadian Geographic*, as well as for radio, film and television. His work has been adapted for audio books, translated into French, German and Italian and, in 2006, inspired a musical suite called "Tumblehome," by Canadian composer David Reed.

A much experienced writer, paddler and northern traveller, Raffan has been recognized with many honours including the Queen's Golden Jubilee Medal. He is a Fellow and Past Governor of the Royal Canadian Geographical Society, Past Chair of the Arctic Institute of North America and a patron of the Canadian Parks and Wilderness Society's Boreal Program. James Raffan lives in the Rideau Lakes, north of Kingston, Ontario, where he combines writing and work as an independent scholar, editor and public speaker with new responsibilities as part-time curator of The Canadian Canoe Museum in Peterborough, Ontario.

The Notakwanon was Herb's most memorable trip. This is a shot of his canoe awaiting his return from a last look around before carrying on.

MEMBER OF SCABRINI GROUP

Québec, Canada
2007